HELMUT KOHL

HELMUT KOHL

Henrik Bering

Since 1947
**REGNERY
PUBLISHING, INC.**
An Eagle Publishing Company • Washington, DC

Library of Congress Cataloging-in-Publication Data

    Bering, Henrik.
        Helmut Kohl / Henrik Bering.
           p. cm.
        Includes bibliographical references and index.
        ISBN 0-89526-325-4 (alk. paper)
           1. Kohl, Helmut, 1930–   . 2. Heads of state—Germany—Biography. 3. Germany (West)—Politics and government. 4. Germany—Politics and government—1990–   I. Title.
        DD262.B47 1999
        943.087'8'092—dc21
        [b]   99-19324
                                                            CIP

Published in the United States by
Regnery Publishing, Inc.
An Eagle Publishing Company
One Massachusetts Avenue, NW
Washington, DC 20001

Distributed to the trade by
National Book Network
4720-A Boston Way
Lanham, MD 20706

Printed on acid-free paper.
Manufactured in the United States of America

10 9 8 7 6 5 4 3 2 1

Books are available in quantity for promotional or premium use. Write to Director of Special Sales, Regnery Publishing, Inc., One Massachusetts Avenue, NW, Washington, DC 20001, for information on discounts and terms or call (202) 216-0600.

To Helle, my wife

CONTENTS

ACKNOWLEDGMENTS

O N THE AMERICAN SIDE, I would like to thank the following for their kind help in the writing of this book: George Bush, Brent Scowcroft, James Baker, Richard Burt, Robert Kimmitt, Caspar Weinberger, Richard Perle, Vernon Walters, Philip Zelikow, and Robert Zoellick. Special thanks to Helmut Sonnenfelt, who gave his generous advice on key aspects of the book. Thanks also to David Dixon.

On the German side: Helmut Kohl, Wolfgang Schaeuble, Joachim Bitterlich, Horst Teltschik, Wolfgang Bergsdorf, Elizabeth Noelle-Neumann, Eduard Ackermann, Gerhard Stoltenberg, Rudolf Seiters, Juergen Aretz, Hans Terlinden, Friedhelm Ost, Juergen Ruettgers, Matthias Wissman, Alfred Dregger, Peter Hartmann, Michael Roik, Michael Mertes, Stefan Eisel, Oliver Schramm, Bernd Pfaffenbach, Peter

Hausman, Klaus Gotto, Ruediger von Voss, Horst Koehler, Michael Rutz, Christoph Stoelzl, Hermann Schaefer, Karl-Dietrich Bracher, Leo Wieland, and Katharina Jestaedt.

Also in Europe: Michael Gurfinkiel, David Gress, and Jan Bo Hansen.

1

TAKING CHARGE

FOR SIXTEEN YEARS, longer than any other political leader in postwar Germany, Chancellor Helmut Kohl dominated German and European politics. With Kohl's election defeat in the fall of 1998, the last of the great Cold War leaders of the West left the political stage.

Despite a persistent tendency to underestimate him, Kohl's record rivals that of the most remarkable postwar European statesmen. Before unification, he presided over eight years of unbroken economic growth with two tax cuts, which in most other European countries would make him a candidate for an equestrian statue in every city square.

On foreign policy, among his key achievements was to honor the German commitment to accept U.S. medium-range missiles in the early 1980s. The Kohl government faced massive public demonstrations, but Chancellor Kohl stood fast and in

1983, the missiles were deployed in Germany. Without Kohl's decision, Europe might have looked very different today.

Kohl's greatest achievement, the one that earns him a place in the history books, is, of course, unification. Almost alone among West German politicians, not only among opposition Social Democrats, but also within his own party, he believed in eventual unification though he could not have known it would come so soon. When the right moment presented itself, he seized the opportunity and ended the division of Germany that had lasted since the end of World War II.

But Kohl's mission did not end with unification. His last years in office he devoted to the cause of European unity and to introducing the common European currency, a measure designed to tie Germany economically and politically to its European neighbors.

Still, it is unfortunate that Europe's most important political figure remains largely unknown to most Americans. Unlike Margaret Thatcher, with her swinging handbag and her admonitions to George Bush not to go wobbly on this or that, Kohl has never captured the American imagination. Somehow, Kohl mainly seems to be the big guy in the official pictures, towering mutely over everybody else.

Admittedly, Mrs. Thatcher had some built-in advantages: She was Ronald Reagan's ideological soul mate. She tamed the unions, which for decades had made Britain ungovernable. She recaptured some of Britain's former glory by defeating the Argentineans over the Falkland islands. And most importantly she spoke English—very emphatic English, one might add.

Helmut Kohl does not speak any foreign languages and hence does not project in quite the same way on the international stage. This does not make him less significant; it just makes him less accessible. As has often been remarked, unlike Ronald Reagan in America and Mrs. Thatcher in Britain, there is no -ism or revolution named after Kohl, no set of readily identifiable catchwords associated with his name such as, in the cases of Reagan and Thatcher, getting the government off the people's back. There is no such thing as Kohlism, which, given Germany's past, perhaps is a good thing. This does not mean that there are not certain ideas he believes in strongly and will press hard to achieve.

Of course, Kohl could not have achieved unification without support from the United States. What made the crucial difference from the standpoint of the United States was Helmut Kohl's strongly pro-Western orientation and his commitment to NATO membership. Here Kohl's personality played a crucial role; reassuring and dependable, he was the ideal German chancellor. Attempts to cast him as Jabba the Hun failed, because they were patently untrue.

To this very day, there are those who peddle the argument that German Foreign Minister Hans-Dietrich Genscher was the real brains behind unification. These are mainly people who find it impossible to believe that one can be of great girth, happy, ruthless, conservative, and a statesman, all at the same time.

To bring Kohl to life for an American audience, the following account relies heavily on interviews with top Reagan and Bush administration officials, who have dealt with the German leader on a host of subjects, as well as interviews with Kohl's inner circle of advisers. And, of course, the book relies on the words of the chancellor himself, who kindly agreed to be interviewed by this author.

Like all great political leaders, Kohl embodies his country. A book about Helmut Kohl, therefore, is as much a book about the new Germany he has created.

To measure Helmut Kohl's achievements, you have to go back and see what Germany looked like when Kohl came to power in 1982. Though some may find it hard to believe, there actually was life in Germany before Kohl. Before Kohl, there was another Helmut, Helmut Schmidt, who for a long time was regarded as one of Europe's indispensable men, not least by himself.

FOR EIGHT YEARS, FROM 1974 TO 1982, Helmut Schmidt, a Social Democrat, had projected the image of a superefficient technocrat, the epitome of German managerial competence, a dapper dresser in his natty suits and elegant shoes. Schmidt was a big-city northerner from Protestant Hamburg, a man whose acid tongue had earned him the nickname "the Lip" and who felt free to dispense advice to foreign politicians in their own language. Schmidt was able to despise and at the same time fascinate the German press corps with his sarcasm and arrogance.

Having held posts as minister of defense and as minister of finance before succeeding Willy Brandt as chancellor, Schmidt steered Germany safely through the first oil crisis. A strict fiscal policy helped Germany avoid the raging inflation that beset most of the industrial West. Germany, moreover, did not experience the kind of ideological polarization that was seen in Britain. Schmidt bragged about being the first monetarist in office, years ahead of Margaret Thatcher and Ronald Reagan. His admirers bestowed on him the grand title of *Weltoekonom*—world economist.

Schmidt had also successfully battled the scourge of terrorism, which afflicted Germany in the mid-1970s, culminating in the shootout in the Mogadishu airport in Somalia in 1977, where West German special forces stormed a Lufthansa jet hijacked by Arab terrorists, freeing the passengers. The outcome caused key members of the Baader-Meinhof gang to commit suicide in their cells in despair and earned Schmidt the sobriquet "hero of Mogadishu." Highlighting these achievements, one of his biographers subtitled his book, *Helmsman of Germany*.[1]

But in the early 1980s, things started to go wrong for Schmidt and for Germany. Part of the problem was the German economy, long regarded as the locomotive of Europe. The year 1981 saw record unemployment, firms heading into the bankruptcy courts, falling investment, and a rise in inflation to 5 percent. Five percent inflation may sound enviable to some nations. But to Germans, whose strong Mark had become a symbol of the country's postwar success, inflation brought back memories of the interwar Weimar period, when runaway inflation made the currency so worthless, people would cart home their wages in a wheelbarrow.

Much of the economic mess of the early 1980s was caused by the dramatic expansion of the welfare state. This had begun in the early 1970s, when Chancellor Willy Brandt declared he would test the limits of Germany's economy by extending social services. By the beginning of the 1980s, German workers and public sector employees had become among the most pampered on earth, and German industry was staggering under the burden. In the period 1980–1982, Germany had a public sector deficit of more than 4 1/2 percent. The public sector share of the GNP was more than 51 percent in 1982. Even newspapers sympathetic to the Social Democrats, like *Die Zeit*, took a bleak look of the future. "Never has German industry been so gloomy," an editorial commented.

Given this downturn, Schmidt, who had made the fatal mistake of not insisting on being party chairman as well as chancellor, began to lose control of his own party, both on domestic and foreign policy issues. (In 1981 Schmidt had to have a pacemaker installed; he was clearly not in the best of shape physically.) Over the decades, the Social Democrats had gone from being a workingman's party to a party hijacked by hardliners, ideologized middle-class types, teachers, and social workers, with very different ideas of how Germany should be run. The atmosphere within party ranks was such that one of Schmidt's harshest critics, Oskar Lafontaine, a left-wing firebrand from the Saarland who later became an unsuccessful chancellor candidate, said of Schmidt that he was "fit to run a concentration camp."

Schmidt's famous July 1982 statement to the Social Democratic parliamentary group summed up his economic disagreement with his party: "You want to spend more and that cannot be done with me, and I want to cut and that cannot be done with you."

The other great challenge facing Schmidt was foreign policy. The early 1980s marked an extremely tense time between the superpowers. And nowhere was that tension felt more keenly than in Germany, which constituted the front line of the Cold War. Since 1975, wherever you looked in Africa and Latin America, the Soviets had been on the march. The West was in retreat, and it took the Soviet invasion of Afghanistan in December 1979 to force President Jimmy Carter to confess that, for the first time, he really understood what the Soviets stood for. As a consequence, Carter blocked U.S. participation in the Olympic Games in 1980.

Helmut Schmidt had never bothered to hide his contempt for the weak and moralistic Carter White House. Much of his ill-feeling stemmed from Carter's 1978 mishandling of the neutron bomb, a weapon that had been developed to offset the huge numerical advantage in tanks and artillery enjoyed by the Soviets over NATO in Europe and that Schmidt had accepted despite intense opposition from within his own party. After much heated debate, Jimmy Carter backed out of the plan, having been persuaded by peace movement propaganda, which painted the neutron bomb as a weapon too immoral to use: the ultimate capitalist bomb, it killed humans but let the buildings stand.

Still, Schmidt's complaints about the absence of leadership on Carter's part, while not unfounded, would have looked a little more convincing if his own actions had been more firm. One of the reasons Carter canceled the neutron bomb was Schmidt's own maneuvering to make it look as if the Americans were forcing the weapon on him. It was also Schmidt who suggested that Carter shut down Radio Free Europe "because it was contrary to the spirit of detente." And barely six weeks after the invasion of Afghanistan, Schmidt insisted on going to Moscow, where he prided himself on delivering the toughest speech ever by a foreign statesman in Moscow, but somehow managed to spoil the effect by signing a long-term trade agreement with the Soviets.

When Ronald Reagan beat Jimmy Carter in the U.S. election of 1980, Schmidt was anxious to be the first foreign leader to meet the new president-elect. The visit did not go well. Reagan clearly did not measure up to Schmidt's standards. Former Secretary of Defense Caspar Weinberger recalls, "I think Schmidt was contemptuous of Reagan. I think he felt Reagan did not have the qualifications necessary for the job. He measured everybody against himself, and he always came out ahead." Schmidt, it turned out, handed out unsolicited advice to the new administration on everything from inflation to unemployment to the budget.

But when the leadership for which Schmidt had been clamoring actually started emanating from Washington in the form of a tougher line toward the Soviets, Schmidt became concerned that this was too much of a good thing. Ronald Reagan did not believe in arms control agreements like the past SALT agreements, which provided for measured rates of increase in the number of nuclear weapons. He wanted real cuts, believing that no agreement was better than a bad agreement. And he wanted to resist Soviet expansionism around the globe. Where Carter had been too weak, Schmidt saw Reagan as too aggressive, prone to do something rash.

The main foreign policy issue facing Schmidt was the NATO deployment of medium-range missiles as a counterweight to the Soviet SS-20s, which were trained on Western Europe. The Soviets had started their deployment back in 1974, and it was Helmut Schmidt himself who originally argued that countermeasures were necessary. The Soviets described their SS-20 program as just a normal replacement of their older SS-4s and SS-5s, a routine modernization program, but of course it was much more than that.

Carrying three warheads instead of one, the SS-20s were far more powerful, and there were more of them. Whereas the old SS-4s and SS-5s took twenty-four hours to prepare for launching, the new SS-20s could be launched instantaneously. This made them a much more destabilizing weapon than the old

Soviet forces. They could hit any city in Europe with no response possible except an intercontinental ballistic missile, which would immediately escalate the situation into a full-scale nuclear war.

As the time drew closer for the deployment of the medium-range missiles, the Soviets cranked up the propaganda volume. Soviet leader Leonid Brezhnev had warned in the harshest terms that a European conflagration would be inevitable and that "walls of fire would be the result" if the European NATO partners went ahead with the deployment. Meanwhile in the German Democratic Republic (GDR), East German leader Erich Honecker spoke darkly of a coming "ice age" in East–West relations.

On the other hand, should the Germans decide not to deploy, so went the old Soviet siren song, a united Germany might still be possible. The Soviet game was to cut a wedge between America and its European partners, forcing the latter into a state of weak neutrality and *de facto* Soviet domination.

It was working. In Germany, arms negotiations had traditionally been accorded almost religious significance as the barometer of East–West relations, the end all and be all of international diplomacy that must never be endangered, regardless of Soviet actions. And on defense the consensus within the Social Democratic Party was breaking down. Many Social Democrats subscribed to the widespread German view of Ronald Reagan as some kind of B-movie cowboy, a dangerous man to have his hand on the nuclear trigger. The Soviet Union, on the other hand, was seen as a power of stability and the status quo. "Sophisticated" ideas about moral equivalence between the superpowers became fashionable within party ranks. Party leaders, like arms specialist Egon Bahr, took to referring to the United States as "the former occupation power." The new Social Democratic catchword became "in the German interest," implying that this was very different from American and NATO interests.

Old issues that had been thought long settled were suddenly raised again, among them whether the original mistake had not been committed by Konrad Adenauer in the early postwar years when he chose to tie the fate of Germany so closely to that of the United States. In the new Social Democratic view, Germany should act as a "mediator" or an "honest broker" between East and West. Needless to say, this idea was anathema to Washington; a mediator by definition is somebody who is no longer on your side.

By this time, Helmut Schmidt's cool facade was cracking. Schmidt worried publicly about the possibility of a third world war. In April 1980, in a speech in Essen, he compared the situation to that of Europe in 1914, after the murder of Austrian Archduke Ferdinand and his wife by the Serb nationalist Gavrilo Principe in Sarajevo. Schmidt also bitterly complained about the gullibility of the electorate and the evils of "TV democracy."[2]

Schmidt had been among the originators of the so-called two-track strategy, the idea that the Western side would deploy their missiles but would continue to negotiate their elimination with the Soviets at the same time. However, "as we pursued it," recalls Weinberger, "he seemed to forget he was the author of it and made all kinds of critical remarks that we were being too provocative and that we weren't doing enough negotiating while we insisted on deploying."

A clear sign of Schmidt's own faltering resolve, and his attempt to rationalize it, according to Richard Burt, who at the time was director of the Political-Military Affairs Bureau of the State Department, was when on one occasion Schmidt declared that he had been prepared to go ahead with deployment under a Democratic administration, but did not trust Ronald Reagan. He suggested that implementing the two-track decision would have meant something entirely different under Jimmy Carter. "This was clearly nonsense," says Burt. "Realistically, Ronald Reagan was the only one who could have implemented the two-track strategy."

In September 1982 things came to a head. Schmidt's cooperation both within his own party and with his coalition partners, the Free Democrats, was breaking down. He seized on the tough demands of his coalition partners for economic reform to trigger a crisis within the government. While privately not unsympathetic to the tough economic policies advocated by the Free Democrats, Schmidt was able to pin the entire blame for the coalition breakup on them. A vote of no confidence in parliament followed, which allowed Schmidt, who was thoroughly fed up, to resign on September 17, 1982.

Schmidt's resignation caused major domestic concern; some German commentators went so far as to predict imminent civil war. The leading German left-wing weekly magazine *Der Spiegel* carried an update of John Tenniel's famous nineteenth-century cartoon "Dropping the Pilot" with Otto von Bismarck disembarking from the ship of state, this time with Schmidt as the Iron Chancellor being forced from office. In the American press, too, there were dire warnings about the end of German stability, the crumbling of the national consensus. Former National Security Adviser Zbigniew Brzezinski noted, "Schmidt's departure means the end of postwar stability in Europe." In retrospect, Schmidt was clearly a case of a politician being overvalued in his own time by people rating style over substance.

IT WAS UNDER THESE RATHER inauspicious conditions that Helmut Kohl assumed responsibility for forming a new government, which was sworn in on October 1, 1982. He was cut from a very different cloth. As chairman of the conservative Christian Democratic Union (CDU) since 1973 and leader of the parliamentary opposition in Bonn since 1976, Kohl was well known in Germany but largely unknown outside the country. Alone in its prediction, *Time* magazine in 1974, in a rare moment of prescience, had named Kohl as one of five European politicians who could make a difference in the world.

Whereas the snuff-pinching Helmut Schmidt gave off the impression that he was born to the role of chancellor, Kohl had to grow into it. A southerner from the Palatinate, his whole life had been devoted to politics, starting with his joining Konrad Adenauer's newly founded CDU in 1946. As one of Adenauer's protégés, Kohl had risen steadily in the party ranks. However, much of his time had been consumed with internal fights for survival within the conservative group, which had left him little time to establish himself abroad as an alternative to Schmidt. The common assumption at the time was that Kohl was a machine politician, and most political observers believed he would not last long. Instead of the great "helmsman," Germany had seemingly acquired a barge skipper from the Rhine.

From the start, Kohl had certain image problems to overcome. "For the first three or four years the press described him as a big boob. They thought he was an idiot," recalls Richard Burt, who went on to become U.S. ambassador to Germany. Kohl's provincial background was immediately seized upon by his political enemies; he was described as the bumbling country bumpkin who somehow ended up as chancellor. "Avuncular," "jovial," and "down to earth" were about as positive as they could bring themselves to be about him. Nor did it help that Kohl spoke in a thick southern accent.

Recalls one close Kohl adviser, "This was an image that was heavily exploited by Helmut Schmidt's people, with Hamburg being portrayed as the big, outward-looking city as opposed to the landlocked and provincial Rhineland." To make him sound even more provincial, in Social Democratic parlance he became not Helmut Kohl from Ludwigshafen, where he grew up, a major industrial center in the region, but from Oggersheim, a suburb of Ludwigshafen, where he has his private residence. The American equivalent of Oggersheim would be some benighted suburb of Cleveland.

As opposition leader, Kohl had had to put up with Helmut Schmidt's sarcastic taunts in the Bundestag, the German parliament. Once, when introducing Kohl to visiting President Gerald Ford on a cruise down the Rhine, Schmidt airily dismissed him with the words, "This is the man who wants my job, but he will not get it." Some commentators trace Kohl's abiding contempt for intellectuals to these encounters with Schmidt. Kohl tends to see intellectuals as cynical sophisticates, products of big cities like Hamburg and Berlin who have lost touch with ordinary Germans.

Kohl's first order of business in September, when the Schmidt government fell, was to find a coalition partner for his government. At the time, the German Bundestag contained two major groupings, almost equal in strength, the Social Democrats on the one side, and a conservative grouping on the other, consisting of the CDU and its Bavarian sister party, the Christian Social Union (CSU). The balance of power was held by the party in the middle, the tiny Free Democratic Party, which normally hovers just above the 5 percent limit required for representation in parliament.

Accordingly, the Free Democrats have wielded influence far out of proportion to their actual numbers. They are known as the party of professionals, doctors and dentists, people who want lower taxes but also want to parade a strong social conscience; the party is conservative on economic issues and leaning toward the left on foreign policy and civil rights issues. To stay alive, the Free Democrats were forced to maintain their own profile, which meant continually taking positions that are slightly out of kilter with coalition partners—while, at the same time, of course, offering their services to the highest bidder. Thus in the 1970s, the Free Democrats sided with the Social Democrats; in the 1980s, they switched to Kohl's conservatives.

But the Free Democrats' general fuzziness infuriated both conservatives and Social Democrats alike. Helmut Schmidt once referred to the leader of the Free Democrats, Hans-Dietrich Genscher, as a tactician without a concept. Another prominent Social Democrat described the difficulties of working with Genscher in more blunt terms: "You can't nail a jelly to the wall."[3] And the late prime minister of Bavaria, Franz Josef Strauss, once described belonging to the Free Democrats as more indicative of a character flaw than real political conviction.

On this rather wobbly foundation, Helmut Kohl took office. He left no doubt that Germany needed a new direction.

Helmut Kohl recalls, "Domestically, the Federal Republic in 1982 found itself in a deep political and economic crisis. Chancellor Helmut Schmidt, my predecessor, no longer had the support of the majority of his own party. The Social Democratic–Liberal Alliance was totally split in fundamental questions: Social Democrats and Liberals could not agree how to fight the high national debt and the high unemployment."

In what has become known as "*Die Wende*" (the Change), Kohl launched a platform that broke with the Social Democratic emphasis on class differences and the idea that the government should take responsibility for all aspects of life. Instead, his policies were aimed at the middle class. Immediately, Kohl announced a program of government spending cuts and tax relief for entrepreneurs.[4]

Overall, Kohl called for a spiritual and moral change, and accused the Social Democrats of helping to undermine faith in the democratic state and its legal system by not standing up intellectually to the challenge of the radical left. On foreign policy, he called for a return to a solidly pro-Western stance.

WHEN KOHL ARRIVED IN WASHINGTON for his first meeting with the Reagan administration in November 1982, few people knew much about him. There was little of the fanfare that had usually accompanied a Schmidt visit. In fact, the visit was all but ignored by the press. "They didn't know him from Adam, or from Eve, for that matter," says Richard Allen, Ronald Reagan's first national security adviser, who had introduced Kohl to Reagan back when Reagan was governor of California and Kohl was opposition leader. (To help edify the public, Allen wrote an op-ed for the *Washington Post*, explaining who the large gentleman from Germany was and what he stood for.)

First on Kohl's agenda was a certain amount of repair work that had to be done on the state of U.S.–German relations. In the Bundestag, Kohl had declared that he "would dispel the doubts that have fallen on German–American relations" and work to "reaffirm and stabilize our relationship." In Washington, the administration was relieved by the change in tone. "I think the transfer of power to Kohl was a watershed event in safeguarding the strength of NATO," says Caspar Weinberger. "From the very beginning, we worked very well with Chancellor Kohl. Though initially not much was known about him, he was considered basically pro-American and not given to lecturing people."

Kohl was fundamentally a deep believer in the NATO alliance. As was common in his generation, Kohl believed that the Germans needed the Americans in Europe, in Germany to be more precise, as an important stabilizing factor for the German psyche. And the two-track decision on the missiles had become, for better or worse, a kind of test of whether the Americans should stay. What was at stake was Germany's position in the Western alliance.

Looking back on his first days in office, Helmut Kohl recalls:

In the area of foreign policy the situation was enormously complicated. In 1982–1983, the debate over the deployment of the American medium-range missiles on German soil was at its high point. It was one of the most dramatic situations in German postwar history. The majority of the Social Democrats fought the deployment of Pershing II and cruise missiles, which Helmut Schmidt had recommended.

If we had followed these voices then, in my firm opinion, it would have had devastating consequences. The Soviet leadership would have been successful in their attempt to decouple American and European security with their SS-20s. With that, an important pillar of the Atlantic Alliance would have been seen as fragile, and as a consequence, it could have resulted in the breakdown of NATO.

Today, the emotional intensity of the debate of those days seems far distant. But at the time, according to Richard Burt, the U.S. State Department perceived this as a European Vietnam-type issue, which had all the possibilities of polarizing public opinion in Germany, tearing the country apart.

Young Germans in particular seemed to be suffering from a collective case of Stockholm Syndrome, a kind of self-delusion caused by fear. The term was coined after an incident in the Swedish capital in 1973 when two armed robbers took four people hostage in a bank in the Swedish capital. In due course, the hostages began to identify with the people who threatened them rather than with the police outside who were trying to free them.

Suddenly, many Germans saw NATO, not the Warsaw Pact, as the aggressor. The title of a book written by Oskar Lafontaine sums it up: *Angst vor den Freunden,* "Fear of Our Friends"— meaning of course the United States.[5]

According to Kohl's then–national security adviser, Horst Teltschik, Kohl was up against a much tougher quality of opposition in Germany than in any other European country. The French, of course, had their own independent nuclear deterrent, the *force de frappe,* and never experienced much of a problem with nuclear protesters.

Mrs. Thatcher also had her own nuclear deterrent, and the antimissile movement in Britain, while loud enough, never reached German proportions. Her main headache was a group of singularly unattractive women camped outside the cruise missile base on Greenham Common. Furthermore, says Teltschik, "The difference between Britain and Germany was that Margaret Thatcher had a clear majority government, while Germany always had a coalition government, and within the big parties, even the Christian Democrats, you always have a left wing."

Kohl's opposition came from two quarters. On the official level, it included individuals who were widely respected as experts and who had held ministerial level positions in the

Schmidt government. Says then Assistant Secretary of Defense Richard Perle, "It contained people who had a claim to expertise on these matters, people like Egon Bahr, who had been the architect behind Willy Brandt's opening to the East back in the 1970s, and Horst Ehmke, a former chief of staff in the Chancellery who had been around the issues a long time and who mastered the vocabulary, never mind how real this claimed expertise was."

For instance, among the false notions spread by the Social Democratic defense intellectuals was the idea that the Pershing missiles could be used as first-strike weapons to decapitate the Soviet system. According to this view, which clearly parroted the Soviet line, a NATO preemptive strike would enable the West to destroy the Soviet military's capability to retaliate.

But the Pershing missiles never really had that capability. There were not enough of them, and they did not have sufficient range. They could barely reach the outskirts of Moscow, and therefore could not have hit the key command and control centers situated further east. Furthermore, the idea that a democracy would initiate a war on the Soviet Union was itself an absurd notion.

The other main source of opposition to Kohl's defense policies came from the environmentalist Green Party, which had been founded in 1979. Initially the party was dismissed in the words of one Bavarian conservative, quoted in the London *Sunday Times*, as "a bunch of Commies, nut cutlet freaks and poofs of no consequence." This turned out to be a grave underestimation.

With its shrill irrationality, apocalyptic visions, and self-induced hysteria, the Green movement was a puzzling phenomenon in West Germany, contrasting strangely with the country's well-fed prosperity. A product of the student movement of the 1960s and the peace movement of the 1970s, the Greens appealed to the young and the disaffected, to students, pacifists, ecologists, and Christian activists, tapping into deep and long-buried passions. Many of them were the sons and daughters of the well-heeled bourgeoisie.

The Greens gained their first Bundestag seats in the March 1983 election, and their entry into German national politics was spectacular, to say the least. Like ancient druids, they brandished pine branches withered by acid rain, and yammered about dying woods and broken ecosystems. "First the woods will die, then the people," went one of their slogans. A particularly revealing photograph shows a heavily hirsute young man on the podium in the Bundestag, wearing a huge woolen sweater like some pillaging Visigoth on the rampage. In the background, Helmut Kohl is looking on with obvious disapproval; he clearly does not consider this young man boardroom material.

It was easier to determine what the Greens were against than what they were for. They were against nuclear weapons, nuclear power, industrial growth. And they were masters of political theater, much of it classic 1960s American-style activism with more than a dash of German Expressionist seasoning. Their ultimate target was the United States and all it stood for—industrialism, the consumer society, the destruction of some mythic European way of life. Instead of nasty modern lawn mowers that would pollute the universe, they recommended that German homeowners raise flocks of geese to trim their lawns.

Commentators at the time such as Luigi Barzini[6] traced the Greens' roots back to pagan worship of trees and rivers and to a romantic German nineteenth-century enthusiasm for nature, with its *Wandervoegel*, who roamed the countryside in delirious search for roots and fruits and nuts, a strain in the German character the Nazis had certainly known how to appeal to.

One of the Greens' early leaders was Petra Kelly, who commanded global attention with her flaming Joan of Arc–like conviction, dark shadows under her eyes, always looking on the edge of a breakdown from sheer exhaustion. In fluent American English (acquired during a childhood in California where her stepfather was stationed as a U.S. marine), laced with a trace of an indignant German accent, she incessantly denounced world-wide American aggression. With customary hyperbole she once stated that the nuclear codes should be encased in the heart of a child, which President Reagan would have to rip open to begin a nuclear war.[7]

Another prominent founding member of the Greens was lawyer Otto Schily, who had defended terrorist Andreas Baader during his trial, and who later hinted that Baader and fellow terrorists Ulrike Meinhof and Gudrun Ensslin had not com-mitted suicide in their cells, but had been murdered by the state.

At the time, the Greens were split on whether to seek parliamentary influence and how to use it, or whether this influ-ence was really preferable to extra-parliamentary activities such as "citizen initiatives"—demonstrations, blockades, and human chains. Another uncharming feature of the Greens, nominally a pacifist party, was their aggressiveness, and their highly ambiva-lent attitude toward violence.

While some rejected violence as a means towards their political goals, others defended terrorist actions such as the murder in 1977 of industrial leader Hans Martin Schleyer by the Red Army Faction, arguing that the repressive traits of West German society were responsible for provoking the urban ter-rorism of the 1970s. As one Green leader put it, "This state needed and still needs almost nothing as much as terror and fear." To describe the Green phenomenon in all its militant pacifism, *The Economist* at the time very aptly coined the phrase "National pacifismus."

The main target of the Greens was the intermediate-range nuclear forces (INF), the cruise and the Pershing missiles. Huge demonstrations were arranged. The Soviet support for the peace movement was loudly denied at the time, but it is now clear that the Soviet Union exploited it and that large amounts of money were funneled into Germany and other countries. Official U.S. estimates set the cost of the 1978 cam-paign against the neutron bomb at about $200 million. Analysts believe that the campaign against the intermediate-range nuclear missiles cost three to four times that amount.

"We now know what we suspected in 1982–1983," says Horst Teltschik, "that these groups were subsidized by East German and Soviet so-called peace organizations. We know that special people were mobilized to run these demonstrations." One drunken KGB officer, who was picked up by Dutch counterintelligence at the time, boasted, "If Moscow decides that 50,000 demonstrators must take to the street in the Netherlands, then they take to the streets." The same applied to Germany.[8]

The importance of the German election of March 1983, which Kohl had called to consolidate his mandate in the Bundestag, was indicated by the international attention it attracted. Droves of foreign dignitaries descended on Bonn; in January, Soviet foreign minister Andrei Gromyko arrived, followed by then–Vice President George Bush.

A political master stroke on Kohl's part was to enlist the help of French President Francois Mitterrand, who delivered a powerful speech in the Bundestag on the importance of deployment, much to the discomfort of the German Social Democrats. Here was a French Socialist lecturing the Bundestag on the necessity of a strong Western defense. Prior to the speech, Mitterrand had summed up the problem succinctly: "The missiles are in the East, the pacifists in the West." Says Horst Teltschik, "President Mitterrand's support for Kohl was absolutely crucial."

The Kohl government handily won the election on March 6, with the CDU and the CSU together receiving 48.8 percent of the vote, compared to the Social Democrats' 38.3 percent.[9]

Nevertheless, huge demonstrations continued throughout Germany. In cities like Stuttgart and Frankfurt, there were demonstrations several times a day, snarling up traffic and forcing office workers to plan alternative routes home. Vice President Bush experienced the full fury of the peace movement in June 1983 when he visited the city of Krefeld to celebrate the 300th anniversary of German settlement in America. Bush and Kohl were in a motorcade when demonstrators dressed in black and wearing masks started stoning the cars. At one point the car carrying the vice president and the chancellor had to seek refuge in an underground garage as it was being followed by protesters. The protesters came so close that Bush remarked that if this had been America, "Our secret service guys would have shot them."[10]

In Bonn, in October, up to 400,000 protesters gathered for a "peace march." Hysterical demonstrators dressed up as skeletons, carrying coffins and other grisly props. Doctors in full surgical gear carried posters proclaiming that in case of nuclear war, they would refuse to treat the victims.[11] Schoolchildren were hauled out for the peace marches, encouraged by their teachers with the underlying threat that their grades might suffer if they did not attend.

Recalls Peter Hartmann, then a foreign policy adviser in the Chancellery, "Some of it was absolutely irrational. My daughter went to secondary school here, and on the day when the decision to deploy was taken, a lot of girls came to school wearing black dresses, saying, 'We are in mourning because the Third World War is imminent.' This sort of thing was widespread."

Kohl himself has described the events in Bonn in October. From his helicopter, he could look out over the great mass of people assembled in the Hofgarten Park at Bonn University. "When you sit alone in the helicopter and look down on that, you can't help but ask yourself: Are they all wrong? Or are you?" Fortunately, the question was rhetorical. Kohl never really had any doubts on the issue.[12]

Not only did Kohl have to deal with the Soviets, the Social Democrats, the Greens, and other assorted radicals, he also had the difficult task of keeping his own political team together. Says Horst Teltschik, "I remember members in the CDU party presidium who asked the chancellor if it was really necessary to deploy. They were afraid of public opinion."

Moreover, Kohl had the problem of dealing with his coalition partner, Hans-Dietrich Genscher, the German foreign minister. As is the case with all foreign ministries, including the U.S. State Department, the ability to empathize and get along with foreigners is highly valued in a diplomat, occasionally a little too highly valued. Genscher tended to take this to extremes and seemed incapable of uttering a sentence without words like "cooperation," "peace," "dialogue," "conciliation," "European security conference," or "detente" tumbling uncontrollably from his tongue. He invariably managed to undercut Kohl's firm stand on the missile issue, and gave the impression that the Kremlin would merely have to wait rather than negotiate. What Mel Tormé is to song, Genscher was to diplomacy: velvet fog.

Genscher's willingness to compromise on the missile issue was regarded with suspicion in Washington. The Americans saw him as a diplomat in the Bismarckian tradition, maneuvering between East and West and trying to set them off against one another. In fact, officials in the Reagan administration tended to see Genscher as a right royal pain in the neck.

In this, they formed a unanimous chorus. Secretary of Defense Caspar Weinberger has his own definition of Genscherism. "The first word that comes to mind is weakness. He believed in appeasement or accommodation or whatever you want to call it. He was an ambiguous figure. He sort of encouraged the Soviets to think they could win."

Richard Perle seconds this opinion: "We were constantly going back to Kohl to stiffen the German position, and Genscher was constantly maneuvering to prevent Kohl from implementing the policies he wanted. Fortunately, Kohl and Defense Minister Manfred Woerner understood what had to be done."

Richard Burt agrees: "I never was able to get a clear statement of Genscher's strategic views. You could only read the tea leaves. Genscher was a trend reader. If he saw an advance trend coming, he would position himself so he could jump on the train. In Genscher, Kohl had to deal with a guy who was very slippery, who could change anytime." In return, snooty Genscher aides would shoot back that their boss's thinking was far too complex for those unsophisticated Americans, who see things only in black and white.

ARMED WITH HIS POPULAR MANDATE to deploy the Pershing II and the cruise missiles, Kohl went ahead in December 1983. "Germany is not governed by the street, Germany is governed by the Bundestag," said Kohl. On November 22 the German Bundestag voted in favor of deployment, and the first Pershing IIs were rushed to Germany within twenty-four hours, as had been carefully planned. Washington was not going to have any more delays.

And lo and behold, the sky did not fall. There were no walls of fire, as Brezhnev had promised. What the Soviets did do was to walk out of the Geneva talks on intermediate-range missiles on November 23 and refuse to set a date for the resumption of long-range strategic missile talks. But after a prolonged period of sulking under Yuri Andropov and Constantine Chernenko, a time during which Foreign Minister Andrei Gromyko accused the Reagan administration of "churning out new missiles, bombers, and aircraft with pathological obsession," the Soviets finally agreed under Mikhail Gorbachev to reopen negotiations in Geneva.

Kohl's decision to deploy was justified when the treaty on intermediate-range missiles was concluded between Michael Gorbachev and Ronald Reagan on December 8, 1987. It eliminated medium-range missiles from Europe, the first time in history an entire category of weapons had been eliminated. Says Weinberger, "I was very pleased when in December of 1987, they signed the precise same agreement President Reagan offered them in October of 1981. That would never have come about without deployment."

Many, including Kohl himself, have seen the missile deployment as a precondition for unification. "It is my conviction that we would not have achieved German unification if we had not in 1983 started to deploy the middle-range missiles on German soil," says Kohl. "Mikhail Gorbachev himself once told me that the steadfastness of NATO in this decision substantially contributed to the new thinking in the Kremlin. The Soviet leadership had to acknowledge that they had no chance of driving a wedge between Europeans and Americans, between Germany and the United States."

2

KOHL THE POLITICIAN: BACKGROUND, STYLE, AND CONVICTIONS

AS CHANCELLOR, Helmut Kohl held court at the Chancellery at Adenauer Alle 141 in Bonn. It is a complex of low square black buildings that represent the worst of 1970s architecture. The front sports an uncharming Henry Moore bronze sculpture, which looks like a bunch of intertwined buttocks, something ordered by Helmut Schmidt to liven up the front lawn of the complex.

The chancellor's office is located on the second floor of the main building. In Helmut Schmidt's day, the office was all gleaming functionalism, but Kohl liked to surround himself with personal memorabilia—his collection of minerals, his coins, his famous aquarium of tropical fish, which were said to have a soothing effect on him in times of trouble.

Behind his massive desk and chair hung a painting of Johann Joseph Goerres, an early nineteenth-century democrat from the Rhineland, considered the father of German journalism.[1] There was a coal drawing of his friend Francois Mitterrand (who turned out to be not quite as good a friend as Kohl thought he was). A special touch was the German flag behind his desk. Helmut Schmidt did not have that.

How does Kohl see the role of the man who occupies the chancellor's desk? Those who have interviewed Kohl know that direct personal questions will not get you very far. But he is eager to discuss historical figures and topics, and in doing so he indirectly reveals a good deal about himself.

In the 1960s and 1970s, in Germany as elsewhere, recalls Kohl, it was fashionable to see history as the clash of impersonal forces and individuals as powerless to influence events, a legacy of Hegel, Marx, and Lenin. "This is nonsense," says Kohl. "It is men and women who create history."

"The Marxist-Leninist belief in historical necessity was and is a superstition. Human freedom, human thought, and human action, those are the real driving powers of history. That is also the great lesson of the shipwreck of the totalitarian ideologies of this century."

It is telling that one of Kohl's favorite pastimes has always been biographical reading. Despite his unassuming image, Kohl is probably the most well-read of Germany's postwar chancellors. The objective of biography is to precisely describe the contribution of the individual to his times. For instance, before going to Poland in 1989 on his mission of reconciliation, in addition to the standard briefing papers, Kohl read a biography of the Polish national hero Marshal Jozef Pilsudski to get a better feel for Polish fears and aspirations, something mere statistics cannot convey.

Accordingly, Kohl attached great importance to establishing personal relations with fellow world leaders. This is not a matter of being chummy for the sake of being chummy. What is involved is an ability to create a certain atmosphere, a chemistry conducive to mutually beneficial solutions, the ability to put oneself in the shoes of the other fellow and see how the world looks from his perspective in the search for common ground.

Of course, Kohl realized one cannot change the world in this way; the national interest remains the ultimate arbiter. But it can make it easier to work together. Above all, Kohl prized trust among statesmen; you need to know that when a statesman has promised something he will keep his word. Trust became an essential element in Kohl's dealings with George Bush and Mikhail Gorbachev during unification.

The outbreak of World War I shows what can happen in the absence of such trust and communication. Even though all the royal houses of Europe were related by blood—the German house of Saxe-Coburg Gotha, for example, had provided numerous sons and daughters to the European thrones, including the British royal family—war broke out, a war nobody really wanted, but one nobody could stop.

In Kohl's definition of the statesman, character and intelligence rank highest. "Of the two, character is the most important. Intelligence can always be bought," says Kohl. In other words, expertise is always available but character is something you have to bring along yourself. "The values that lead a politician are like a compass that helps him to hold the right course, even in unpredictable situations." The statesman must have clear goals, and he must know how to reach them. Under character comes staying power, courage, thoughtfulness, and common sense.

Add to this an instinct for spotting opportunities when they present themselves. "I deliberately use the word 'instinct,'" says Kohl, "because even the most extensive analyses from the most well-respected experts and 'think tanks' are no substitute for intuition." Intuition involves a sense of the spirit of the times, a sense of where things are moving. Kohl likes quoting Bismarck on grasping the mantle of history: "We can only wait until we hear God's footsteps echoing through events, and then leap forward and clutch at the corner of his mantle."

Finally, says Kohl, the statesman needs luck. This keeps him from becoming arrogant and too full of himself. "Pope John XXIII warned about this with a wonderful phrase. When he looked into the mirror, he would admonish himself: 'Giovanni, do not take yourself so seriously.'

"He who does not regard himself as the measure of all things, he is also capable of gratitude for everything good that is offered him," says Kohl.

HARRY S. TRUMAN IS KOHL'S FAVORITE American president. Once, when at a meeting with Ronald Reagan, Kohl and Reagan wrote down on separate pieces of paper who they thought was the greatest U.S. president of this century. When they compared notes, both had come up with the same name: Harry Truman.

Kohl's admiration for Harry Truman is partly explained by his gratitude for what Truman did for Europe out of humanitarianism and enlightened self-interest with the Marshall Plan and the creation of NATO. But it goes beyond that; there is clearly an element of personal affinity. In describing Truman, Kohl is partly describing himself: like Kohl, Truman came from a modest background, had a keen interest in history, was down-to-earth, direct, and full of common sense. He lacked pretense and looked at people living in ivory towers with a certain wry skepticism.

Also like Kohl, Truman entered office under difficult circumstances, following a celebrated figure. "Truman was treated as a joke," recalls Kohl. Franklin D. Roosevelt was indeed a hard act to follow, the patrician with his cigarette holder (shades of Helmut Schmidt), a leader who in his own lifetime was already considered the world's foremost statesman, the originator of the New Deal, and the victor of World War II.

Yet it was Truman, the hick from Missouri, the owner of a failed haberdashery store, not Roosevelt, the sophisticated man of the world, who recognized what Josef Stalin was up to in Europe and took the appropriate countermeasures, thereby saving Western Europe from falling under Soviet domination.

And typically, with the pride of the professional politician, Kohl adds that even though the Marshall Plan may have been the brainchild of Secretary of State George Marshall, whose name Truman graciously allowed it to bear, Truman had to give it the green light, overcoming considerable opposition in the process. In short, Truman was the Boss. Without the backing of a politician, even the most farsighted and revolutionary plans can be doomed to oblivion—mere paper schemes. The politician has to go out on a limb and spend his political capital making them into reality.

To begin to understand Helmut Kohl, one has to know where he comes from. He was born in 1930 in the industrial city of Ludwigshafen in the Palatinate, an area neighboring the Rhineland and dominated geographically by the winding Rhine River. To the west, the area is bordered by Belgium and Luxembourg and to the south by France. Where other parts of Germany, particularly Prussian-dominated parts, have a tradition for strong government by the emperor, the king, the church hierarchy, due to the influence of France and the political currents of the West, the Rhineland and the Palatinate saw the fermentation of democratic ideas that led to the failed uprisings on the Continent in 1848–1849.

Furthermore, like all great rivers, the Rhine itself has shaped the region into something of a European melting pot, as Kohl has often pointed out. He also likes to quote a passage from the playwright Carl Zuckmayer that describes the Rhine as the great mill of peoples, the wine press of Europe, where people from all over have intermingled, from the Roman centurion to the Jewish spice merchant, the Greek doctor, the Swiss mercenary, the Napoleonic foot soldier, Gutenberg, Goethe, Beethoven, and, incidentally, Kohl himself.[2] "The people were blended together there. Blended together, like the water from the springs and brooklets and streams so that they all flowed into one big, living river. To be from the Rhine means to be from the Occident."[3]

The city of Ludwigshafen, however, does not have quite this romantic sweep, nor does it fit the pastoral image of the surrounding wine country. A major industrial center, it is known primarily as the seat of the region's second major industry, chemicals. It is the home of BASF, the Badische Anilin-und Soda-Fabrik, founded in 1865, which today employs fifty thousand people, almost one-third of Ludwigshafen's population. As one travel brochure puts it rather bluntly, "Ludwigshafen has no points of interest."

But don't tell that to Helmut Kohl, who has always shown great attachment to his hometown. Like Margaret Thatcher, the grocer's daughter from Grantham, he is fiercely proud of his middle-class roots.

His father, Hans Kohl, was a local tax collector, and, as Kohl himself has described it, the household was strictly Catholic and very frugal—every phennig was counted; luxuries were out of the question. They were, writes Kohl in *My Parents' Home*, "always aware that money didn't grow on trees but had to be earned through hard work."[4] Hans Kohl was the kind of man who would bike to work in all types of weather, wearing bicycle clips so as not to get his trouser legs covered with oil or stuck in the chain.

"A typical minor civil servant's household," writes Kohl, "just like millions of others. What we had was—relatively— secure, but sacrifice and the law of moderation were ever present in our minds. They governed our daily routine from morning to evening. Mother went to the market when the vendors were already starting to take down their stands, for prices were always a little lower then. She had a guilty conscience if she treated herself to a cup of coffee while shopping in the city."

Hans Kohl served at the front in World War I, attaining the rank of first lieutenant. As Kohl likes to point out, his father was a so-called *Aufstiegsoffizier*, an officer who had risen from the rank of private.[5] When Hitler came to power in 1933, Kohl senior quit his membership in the Stahlhelm, the Steelhelmet, an organization of World War I veterans, a clear sign that he did not approve of Nazi policies. "He saw a second world war coming in the wake of Hitler's seizure of power, and he feared it," writes Kohl. "And he despised the crimes that were being committed in the name of Germany in the climate of racism and Teutomania."

But when Hitler started World War II, Kohl's father had to put on his uniform again, this time with the rank of captain in the Wehrmacht. Hans Kohl became city commandant of the Polish city of Zirals. He was appalled by what his country was doing. Writes Kohl, "I vividly recall one time during his vacation when he concluded a report on his experiences 'abroad' with the sentence, 'God have mercy on us if we ever have to atone for that....'" Later Kohl's father was transferred to France, where a heart condition sent him home in 1943. But the Kohl family was not spared death. Kohl's elder brother Walter was killed in 1944 when a low-flying allied bomber was shot down and hit a powermast, which came crashing down on him.[6]

Kohl was nine years old when the war broke out. When large parts of Ludwigshafen were destroyed by Allied air raids, Kohl was enlisted in the fire brigade; at the age of twelve, he saw firsthand the horrors of war. (About 25 percent of the city was destroyed.) At the end of 1944, when the German war effort was growing increasingly desperate, Kohl was sent to paramilitary camp to be trained as an aide to an anti-aircraft gunner. He also served as a messenger in Bavaria in the Volkssturm, Hitler's last frantic effort to save the Third Reich, enlisting boys and old men in the final fight. At the end of the war, Kohl made his way back to the Palatinate by foot, witnessing along the way the devastation of his homeland. On the journey, Kohl and his friends, still wearing their uniforms, were beaten up by Polish forced laborers. In June 1945 Kohl finally reached Ludwigshafen.

The first task of Kohl and his classmates on their return home was to rebuild their school so that they could resume their education. In a sense, Kohl literally belonged to the first generation of builders of the postwar German state. Following Kohl's *Abitur*, or high school diploma, he decided to go for a degree in agriculture, a smart move given that food was exceedingly scarce and that farms were, after all, where the food was. But he quit after his apprentice year, when it became clear that the agricultural sector would be overwhelmed by the great influx of German farmers who had been driven from the former German territories of East Prussia and Silesia, which now belonged to Poland, and from the Czech Sudetenland. To this day, however, Kohl tells with pride how he could plow a field with two oxen.

In 1947, at the age of seventeen, Kohl joined the Christian Democratic Union (CDU), a party dedicated to rebuilding Germany on a Christian foundation. But can you take a seventeen-year-old seriously, let alone a seventeen-year-old with political commitments? Most seventeen-year-old boys have other things on their minds. But these were not normal times. The boys had seen and experienced more than teenagers are supposed to.

In a situation in which your country has suffered total defeat, it is natural to think about what the future will look like, which means thinking politically. In Germany, the political parties had to be built from scratch. Under the emperor they had been without power; in the Weimar Republic they had been anarchic; and under the Nazis they had been banned.

Says Kohl:

> The thought of being able to shape and help build something fascinated me. The end of World War II has often been called the "Zero Hour" of German history. Materially and morally, Germany lay in ruins, and we Germans faced the task of making a new start in the name of freedom and democracy.
>
> Equally, the thought moved me of making a contribution so that the enemies of freedom and peace would never get a chance in Germany. The "Never Again" that we then swore to each other inspired many of my generation to become politically engaged. It has often been said that the first German democracy, the Weimar Republic, failed not so

*much because its opponents were so many in number, but
because there were too few democrats.*

    *And I am to this day very grateful that I had the luck to
meet political mentors who before Hitler's takeover had
been members of democratic parties—people who embodied
the values on which the second German democracy was
built.*

Perhaps a more pragmatic consideration also entered the
young Kohl's calculations: in times of chaos, it seems a good
idea to belong to an organization that will give a measure of
structure and support. At the time it was said that if you were
not dead, if you were not a Nazi, and if you were Catholic, the
CDU might have a future for you. Kohl fit all three criteria.

    Among his first assignments in 1947 was to put up political
posters in the first election to the Landtag (state legislature), a
job for which his height (6'4") was certainly an advantage.
Occasionally, postwar German politics could be muscular in
nature, and when Kohl tried to hang his posters, there were
sometimes scrapes with the rival Social Democrats. As a joke,
Kohl later taught his dog, a German shepherd, to growl at the
command of "soz," short for socialist.

    Kohl had started his studies at the University of Frankfurt in
1950, intending to study law, but transferred after one year to
the University of Heidelberg, where he majored in history, with
law and political science as his minors. To make ends meet as a
student, he worked at BASF as a stone polisher during his vaca-
tions. He would commute to class on an Italian Lambretta
scooter, which must have looked rather amusing, since the
scooter, as one of Kohl's contemporaries noted, had been
designed mainly with Audrey Hepburn and *Roman Holiday* in
mind. He finished his Ph.D. thesis in 1958, which can be read as
a piece of autobiography, given that the subject was the building
of democratic parties in the Palatinate after 1945. He landed a
job as a functionary in the Chemical Industry Association, but
this was clearly secondary to his political ambitions.

To call Kohl a career politician would be an understatement. Extremely ambitious and hardworking, he found before long that politics had circumscribed his entire life. Though this may come as somewhat of a surprise, Kohl was also seen as a rebel at the time. He wanted to look to the future and build a party with broad popular appeal, a party beyond its base of aging dignitaries from the Weimar period. Furthermore, he was convinced that the CDU could not forever rest on the achievements of the postwar period under Chancellor Konrad Adenauer.

Kohl and his generation, having seen where unquestioning obedience could lead, were not exactly overawed by authority—much to authority's dismay. He felt he must transform the Palatinate (which in 1946 had been combined with the Rhineland to form a federal state) into a model for the rest of Germany. And he stepped on plenty of toes to achieve this. Always the youngest in whatever post he occupied, Kohl bulldozed his way in 1966 from being a regular member of the state legislature to becoming state chairman of the CDU parliamentary group; in 1969 he became prime minister of the Rhineland-Palatinate; in 1973 he was federal chairman of the CDU; and finally, in 1982, he reached his ultimate goal of becoming chancellor.

KOHL BROUGHT A DISTINCTLY DIFFERENT style to the German Chancellery, characterized by familiar people, familiar objects, familiar routines. Kohl liked to surround himself with people he had known for a long time. Some had been with him as far back as Mainz and his days as state prime minister. Predictably, there was turnover over the years, but scattered in key posts throughout were people who had worked with him for decades.

Among the inner circle of Kohl's court, the following names stood out:

- Juliane Weber, Kohl's private secretary, served Kohl for thirty years. Weber was the gatekeeper to Kohl's office without whose approval nobody would get in to see the chancellor. With no formal role in policy-making, she was still among the most influential people in the Chancellery, overseeing every detail in the office, right down to what the chancellor had for lunch every day.[7]

- Wolfgang Schaeuble played a key role in hammering out a governing framework between the CDU, the Christian Social Union (CSU), and the Free Democrats in 1982; he was the big dealmaker in parliament. At first Schaeuble was Kohl's chief of staff, then became minister of the interior, where he played a central role during unification. Schaeuble was Kohl's designated successor for the chancellorship and today is the chairman of the CDU. He is paralyzed from the waist down as a result of a 1990 assassination attempt by a deranged person.

- Wolfgang Bergsdorf, an intense and cerebral workaholic who functioned as a sort of court intellectual, had a talent for skewering Kohl's opponents in print, which was invaluable over the years. Chief of the cultural section of the Department of the Interior under Kohl, Bergsdorf is the publisher of Bonn's *Rheinischer Merkur*, a newspaper that supported the chancellor, and he is also a contributor to *Die Politische Meinung*, a political magazine, which is essential for anyone who wants to know what really goes on in Germany.

- Elizabeth Noelle-Neumann is the founder of the Allensbach Institute, Germany's leading polling firm, located on the Bodensee, which borders Switzerland. Noelle-Neumann is famous for her uncanny ability to forecast opinion and played a central part as adviser in Kohl's early election campaigns.

- Horst Teltschik, one of Kohl's close associates for nineteen years, was his foreign policy adviser during unification and is now chairman of BMW in Munich.

■ Eduard Ackermann, before he retired, was Kohl's trusted press spokesman. Almost equally important, he was one of the chancellor's favorite dinner partners. Ackermann would join Kohl at one of his favorite Italian restaurants in Bonn, where his fondness for having his pasta cooked in a particular way led the chancellor to bestow on him the nickname "Dr. Carbonara." Today, Ackermann is the chief repository of Kohl lore.

While it is a common affectation among some politicians to pretend that public service is a tremendous sacrifice and that they would really rather be doing something else—reluctant Coriolanuses, so to speak—Helmut Kohl has always been unapologetic. As in the case of Charles de Gaulle or Mrs. Thatcher, in Kohl's mind, there always was a fortuitous coincidence between the interests of Germany and the interests of Helmut Kohl.

As chancellor, Kohl liked to exercise power and made no bones about it. As he himself once stated, "We have the curious habit in Germany of defaming power. Power in itself is neither good nor bad. The question is how you use power. You cannot perform a political job of any kind without exerting power. You cannot become a successful mayor in a village or a community if you do not use the competence and the area of responsibility that you have."[8]

Most people who have held power for a long time show the strain in their faces. Many politicians walk around as if they carry the weight of the world on their shoulders. Helmut Kohl has certainly been known to fret. But an optimistic nature and an ability to leave defeats behind helped him through times of trouble. As a young man, he was fond of quoting one of the less-well-known sayings of the father of the Reformation, Martin Luther: "Out of a timorous arse, no happy fart will fly." As chancellor, Kohl would probably have put it differently, but his underlying robustness was palpable.[9]

Political longevity demands great physical stamina as well as mental strength, a body that can absorb the punishment of daily public life. Being 6'4", weighing some 320 pounds (the actual figure was a state secret, Kohl would joke), and wearing a size 11 1/2 shoe, Kohl had what it takes. In fact, he relished his sheer physical stamina, his reputation for being "invincible as an ox," as he once put it.

All of this was closely connected to personal qualities; Kohl is gregarious—he loves company. To borrow a word from James Boswell, he is clubbable. "Kohl is a very sociable being," says Ackermann. "He likes to relate to people. In contrast to Helmut Schmidt, who gave an impression of being rather ascetic, a very disciplined kind of person, Helmut Kohl is quite the opposite. He likes to enjoy himself, he likes to live and likes good food and drink."

Indeed, Kohl's appetite is legendary and has been compared to that of Bismarck, another great trencherman of German history, who when ordered to eat less by his doctor bitterly lamented that he was being starved: All he was allowed to eat was a steak in the morning and a mutton chop in the afternoon, and the next day the same routine, just the other way around.[10]

Before a state banquet, Kohl was known to eat a real dinner, just to make certain that he would be properly fed. When entertaining foreign dignitaries, Kohl often invited them to his modest bungalow in Marbacher Strasse 11 in Oggersheim, a suburb of Ludwigshafen, where he would treat them to Eisbein, giant pigs knuckles, or Saumagen, stuffed pig stomach, a manly German delicacy which, for some reason, only Germans seem to appreciate.

One photograph shows George Bush engaging in this ritual: The photograph is inscribed, "Dear Helmut, Here I am eating some of the best food I have ever had. Warm Regards and many thanks, George Bush." Bush's guarded facial expression somehow contradicts his words. (For those interested in the Kohl cuisine, in 1996 he and his wife, Hannelore, published a book of his favorite dishes—pigs knuckles, pigs stomach, and all—entitled *Kulinarische Reise durch deutsche Lande*. Though some of the recipes are indeed hearty fare, the satire it has evoked has been somewhat exaggerated; not all recipes start with the instruction to break twenty eggs and kill a large farm animal.)

Stern magazine once produced a memorable front page, tracing the girth of the chancellor at various points in his career, like the rings of an old oak tree. One of his biographers, Juergen Leinemann, describes the patriarchal aspect of Kohl on a campaign session, wearing his woolen sweater, cutting enormous pieces of sausage for his advisers, and handing them each a piece on the point of his pocketknife. Woe to the wimp who does not eat.

And this being a German biography, Leinemann's book goes on to quote the philosopher Elias Canetti on his archetypal Mastereater King: "The fuller the monarch is, the better he feels. He will eat and drink with the chosen members of his entourage and what he puts in front of them, belongs to him. Even if he is not the one who eats most, his supplies are the biggest.... He could be the Mastereater if he wanted to be."[11]

Kohl's favorite dessert is said to be plum tart smothered in enough cream to sink the Austro-Hungarian Empire, though in recent years, he is said to go easier on the sweets, much to his regret. Indeed, Kohl occasionally could sound plaintively Bismarckian when he invited his guests to go on with the dessert, from which he unfortunately had to abstain.

Like millions of other Germans, every year Kohl goes to a health spa. For reasons of privacy, he chose Bad Hofgastein in neighboring Austria. Every year, the German press tried in vain to determine where exactly Kohl's rumored weight loss had occurred.

As big politicians have always done, Kohl used his physical size to dominate those around him. Henry Kissinger once remarked that when French President Charles de Gaulle, Le Grand Charles, entered a room, stomach shot out in front, you could almost feel the whole room tilt toward him. With Kohl, you start to worry about the floor construction, and other people in the room begin to look like garden gnomes.

Kohl is perfectly aware of this effect. He once noted with glee how the minister president of one German federal state almost had a heart attack whenever he had to be photographed next to Kohl.[12] Indeed, in certain situations, when Kohl strode into a room with all the bureaucrats and courtiers bowing and scraping, he could project the strength of a medieval monarch just back from a morning of wild boar hunting.

Kohl lore has it that once when, during a photo shoot in a park, one of Germany's leading photographers directed the chancellor to move toward him, Kohl did it with such determination that the photographer instinctively drew back, stumbled over his own legs, and promptly fell into a pond.[13]

FROM THE VERY BEGINNING, recalls Eduard Ackermann, Kohl established himself as a very different kind of chancellor. He rejected the idea that a politician has to be a good actor. "He always told us that you cannot shape me to act the part. You have got to take me as I am, and you have got to sell me as I am."

It took all the persuasive powers of one of his sons to get him to change from the heavy horn-rimmed glasses he used to wear, which looked like something Erich Honecker might have chosen, to the rimless ones he now wears. Kohl is fond of comfortable knitted cardigans, which he would immediately put on in his office when he had no visitors, along with a comfortable pair of slippers. The cardigan accompanied him everywhere he went as chancellor, in cars, planes, and so on. Once he was out of public view, off came the jacket, on came the knitted cardigan. One time an especially beloved specimen was accidentally left behind in a hotel in Athens; Kohl fretted about it for days, and voiced the suspicion that his staff had left it behind deliberately because it was so old and threadbare. He immediately acquired a new one.

As anybody who has followed Kohl on German television can testify, nobody could accuse him of being glib. As he once stated himself, "I am certainly not the embodiment of elegance." He is said on occasion to have been slightly envious of Francois Mitterrand who, in the classic Gaullist tradition of French grandeur, routinely referred to himself as "France" on TV.

Kohl's speeches, from a rhetorical standpoint, often sounded uninspired, except for involuntary moments of hilarity, as when he told East Germans that they would now be able to enjoy the "warm sofa of freedom." His archenemy, Franz Josef Strauss, once snidely remarked, "What fascinates me with Kohl's TV appearances is that they give the impression that anybody could be chancellor."

In short, Kohl was a bit of a speechwriter's nightmare. Even when he had a good speech, he could somehow manage to mangle it, droning relentlessly through the text without paying the slightest attention to verbal flourishes, pauses, and other dramatic fineries—rather in the Brezhnevian tradition. Even Kohl himself looked bored. A German TV channel in 1983 by mistake reran his New Year's speech from the previous year. The only reason people noticed, it was said, was that the chancellor wore the same tie as the year before. The chancellor's staff suspected deliberate sabotage on the part of the TV staff.[14]

On paper, some of Kohl's speeches—those dealing with Germany's past, for instance—were just as finely crafted as those of former President Richard von Weizsaecker, yet another elegant and refined German politician with what Gore Vidal would call "important hair" and with whom Kohl was often compared—invariably to his detriment, at least as far as style was concerned. Von Weizsaecker is a born orator whose movements are carefully choreographed; the camera never catches him from the wrong angle. As one of Kohl's former speechwriters ruefully notes, "If von Weizsaecker read aloud from the telephone directory, people would have thought they had heard a meaningful discussion of the development of communications technology."

Part of Kohl's problem was a certain linguistic laziness, a tendency to slur his speech; part of it was his Palatinate dialect, which lacks hard consonants, making his message sound less than urgent. But when an adviser suggested Kohl drop his native accent to sound more sophisticated, he was met with stony silence. Most observers agree that Kohl was much more forceful on the stump, where he could express himself freely and engage the audience. In one-on-one conversations, he can also be extremely forceful.

Most importantly, Kohl conveyed the impression that he cared more about results than about presentation. Paradoxically, for a country that has had a surfeit of demagoguery and overheated political rhetoric this century, Kohl's rather pedestrian personal style may not altogether have been a disadvantage. And at a time when politicians will do almost anything to prove themselves ordinary folks, there are things he would not do.

At the 1997 summit in Denver, when President Clinton gave Kohl a pair of cowboy boots, he refused to put them on, knowing that it would make him look ridiculous. And at a European summit in Holland, where the participants were issued bikes and enormous crash helmets, Kohl refused to play along. Helmut Kohl does not ride a bike; he rides in a Mercedes. As one of his advisers noted afterwards, he would not ride a bicycle even if the pope gave it to him. He did not need to prove himself a man of the people.

Postwar democratic leaders tend to fall into two categories. On the one hand, there are those who are concerned with the mechanics of government, making things run smoothly. On the other, there are those who are guided by a major vision, like a Konrad Adenauer or a Charles de Gaulle, a Margaret Thatcher or a Ronald Reagan, different as they may be from one another.

Helmut Kohl falls into the latter category: He was a big picture politician who had two or three major issues that he would push relentlessly, while leaving the details and the implementation to others. While Kohl's predecessor, Helmut

Schmidt, was technocratically minded, intimately concerned with the minutiae of politics, Kohl saw himself more as a generalist who set the course. At the same time, he kept his ear to the ground to ascertain what went on in the population.

As Wolfgang Bergsdorf points out, "Kohl concentrated on what is important, on the essential. He did not allow himself to be sidetracked and to be fragmented in many little pieces. Helmut Schmidt wanted to know what was going on in every ministry and in every corner of government. That is impossible."

Kohl was considered a hard taskmaster.[15] Recalls Horst Teltschik:

> On the one hand, it was exhausting because you had to work day and night for him. Sometimes I had to tell him I can't just shake my hand and the solution or the speech is ready. It really was the toughest time in my life.
>
> On the other hand, the trust he placed in me was breathtaking. He sent me to negotiate with Maggie in London, Mitterrand in Paris or Gorby in Moscow. I once asked him what I should tell Gorby. "You already know what I'm thinking. That's your job." He gave a lot of latitude.

Overall, Kohl seemed to be operating between two home-spun German proverbs that he is fond of quoting. One is "too many dogs spell the death of the hare," which means you should pick your battles with care, avoiding unnecessary conflicts. The other is "Many enemies, much honor," which means the states-man must lead from the front and make the really important decisions, however unpopular. Though the two may appear to be contradictory, they are not, upon closer consideration. Kohl was a cautious man who would take huge risks when he had to, a pragmatist who pursued a major vision.

This combination of caution and boldness, realism and idealism, political horse sense and high principle, was characteristic of Helmut Kohl. Says Wolfgang Bergsdorf, "He is a realist insofar as he can see what is politically feasible. He is also an idealist because, while he would not actually believe in a utopia, he does believe in what we Germans like to call a realistic utopia. That is to say, something that is on the borderline of the utopian but still within reach." Or as a German philosopher once put it, where there is a sense of reality, there also has to be a sense of possibility.

Like every politician, Kohl would track polls with great interest, but he did not govern by them. As he pointed out on numerous occasions, all the major decisions affecting Germany's postwar future were made against popular opinion. That was the case with the introduction of the new German Mark and the free market after World War II. It was also the case with the decision to integrate Germany into the West, most notably manifested in Germany's membership in NATO.

According to Kohl, it is vital for a statesman to know the difference between a seismograph and a compass, between populist rhetoric and responsible politics.[16] The job of the statesman is to make the right decision, even if it is unpopular.

Kohl's great political model and inspiration has been Konrad Adenauer, the father of postwar democratic Germany. Throughout his career, he presented himself as Adenauer's grandson. Rather endearingly, this was taken literally on one occasion by Spanish King Juan Carlos, who is used to thinking in bloodlines.

The other name that crops up frequently in conversations with Kohl is Ludwig Erhard. "I am a firm supporter of the market economy in the sense of Ludwig Erhard," says Helmut Kohl. "That is, an economic and social order that combines free enterprise and social harmony." Ludwig Erhard, of course, was Adenauer's cigar-chomping economics minister, the designer of the German economic miracle, whom caricaturists delighted in portraying as the archetypal capitalist. And so he was, and proud of it, too. A primary reason for Germany's success was that the country stuck to free market principles when trends in

Europe were going in the opposite direction. In Britain, for example, the postwar Labour government of Clement Atlee proceeded with large-scale nationalizations of British industry, thereby hastening Britain's decline. Germany's capitalism, however, was tempered by social responsibility and Christian compassion.

The same is true for Kohl, a practicing Catholic who believes in God and in the imperfection of man. He attends church regularly in Ludwigshafen, and many of his close friends belong to the clergy, including some of the men who shaped him back in Ludwigshafen in his youth.

But Kohl has never been the kind of politician who wore his religion on his sleeve. Says Michael Rutz, editor of the *Rheinischer Merkur* in Bonn, "To him it is private. A lot of people display their religion in public. That is not Kohl's way of being a Catholic." As to its influence on his politics, it is not as if the Ten Commandments entered into every piece of legislation, but he has said a Christian view of man informs his policies.

Kohl has been Konrad Adenauer's heir in foreign policy as well. In his time, Adenauer was criticized for being "the Allied chancellor," and some of the same charges were leveled at Kohl over the years. Adenauer, former U.S. Ambassador to Germany Vernon Walters recalls, was caricatured at the time as a man who would sit outside the Allied Commissariat with his brown-bag lunch, humbly waiting to be received by the High Commission—and, when called in to see the commissioners, would be careful not to step on the rug. In reality, nothing could be further from the truth. Adenauer stood up for German interests, but he also knew that those interests were defined by being firmly anchored in the West. Helmut Kohl is the same way; says Walters, "Helmut Kohl is a direct descendant of Adenauer, especially in his Western orientation."

On foreign policy, Kohl avoided the traditional trap of German chancellors—being either an Atlanticist or a Francophile—by being both at the same time. Kohl regarded the unity of Europe and the continuation of a common destiny with North America as the fundamental pillars of German foreign policy.

On one occasion, Kohl told former U.S. Ambassador Robert Kimmitt (1991–1993) that while France was Germany's closest ally—which could be taken in the geographical, cultural, or psychological sense—he considered America to be Germany's most important ally. In a typical Kohl image, he went on to tell Kimmitt that "America was like his pants and France was like his shirt." To which Kimmitt responded, " 'Well, Mr. Chancellor, you can go out without your shirt on, but not without your pants.' We got a good laugh out of that." Kimmitt hastily added, "Of course it is better to go out fully clothed."

As an Atlanticist, Kohl got on famously with every American president he had to deal with—Ronald Reagan, George Bush, and Bill Clinton. Even though Bill Clinton knew that Helmut Kohl and George Bush had enjoyed a close personal friendship, it took only one meeting to establish a good rapport between them. In contrast, Clinton never quite forgave British Prime Minister John Major for actively supporting George Bush in the 1992 presidential election, in which Major went so far as to send over political advisers to help the Bush campaign.

"This easy relationship had to do with the fact that Kohl came across as someone who generally liked Americans," says Leo Wieland, Washington correspondent for the *Frankfurter Allgemeine Zeitung*. Here he operated in sharp contrast to Helmut Schmidt, who got on famously with President Valery Giscard d'Estaign of France but could not stand Jimmy Carter.

Kohl's fondness for Americans dates back to the early postwar years, when his family was among the many needy European families who received CARE packages from the United States, millions of which arrived in the years after the war. This American generosity is something Kohl has never forgotten, and he has never failed to convey his deep sense of gratitude.

Says Kimmitt, "I think the relationship between Helmut Kohl and the United States was secured when he went on his first date with his future wife Hannelore, wearing a suit that had been contributed by a group of American charitable organizations right after the war. And when he talks about the CARE packages, he really knows what that meant. Today, you can still sense that emotional attachment."

The other pillar of Helmut Kohl's political worldview has been Europe. His whole life has been committed to the vision of a united Germany in a united peaceful Europe. Often he would take visitors into the backyard of his house in Oggersheim and point out that this piece of ground had for centuries been a battleground between the French and the Germans, back and forth. In fact, after the war, the French put up a sign outside the city of Mainz, where Kohl started his political career, proclaiming: "Mainz, General Headquarters of the French Army 1632–1651, 1718–1719, 1799–1814." A couple of days later, a sign appeared next to it that read: "Paris, Headquarters of the German Army, 1814, 1870, 1940."

"I first pledged allegiance to Europe when I was seventeen years old," says Kohl. In 1948, "German and French high school kids from various schools in Alsace and the Palatinate set out for the German-French border. We tore down the border posts and sang European songs. We were quite certain that a united Europe was just around the corner! Well, it turned out it did not come so fast. The border posts were hammered down again, and we were chased back over the border."

This spirit of enthusiasm for cross-border friendship was a distinctly new phenomenon. In his book *Ich wollte Deutschlands Einheit*, Kohl recalls how for centuries German children from his region had been taught to regard the French as the archenemy (and vice versa) in their early school years. Kohl also recalls his first trip to France after high school with a delegation of CDU representatives from the Palatinate. While their purpose was to visit French Foreign Minister Robert Schuman in Paris, Kohl and his fellow delegation members were treated like "lepers" by the French waiters. Part of what has driven Kohl is the determination that this centuries-old enmity must never rise again at the center of Europe.

But perhaps it is Kohl's view on German-German relations that most clearly showed both elements of his political character: the realist who adjusted to what the traffic could bear and the idealist who kept the dream of eventual German unification alive.

Back in Konrad Adenauer's day, unification had been on the top of the list of West German priorities. Adenauer predicted that the day would come when the Soviet system, due to its economic abnormalities, could no longer shoulder the economic burdens entailed in keeping Eastern Europe in subjugation and would therefore eventually have to accept a free Germany in a united Europe. Hence there was no question of having dealings with the puppet East German regime; nor would West Germany have diplomatic relations with states that recognized the East Germans.

But as time passed and the Soviet Empire proved more durable than expected and willing to take the necessary measures to crack down on rebellion, unification became more and more distant for most German politicians. And it started to dawn on Germans that German unification was not exactly a top priority for Germany's European allies; they were only paying lip service to the idea.

As for the Soviet position, it was expressed all too vividly by Nikita Khrushchev, taking certain liberties with the person of Konrad Adenauer in the process: "If you strip Adenauer naked and look at him from the rear, you can see clearly that Germany is divided into two parts. And if you look at him from the front, it is equally clear that his view of the German Question never did stand up, never does stand up, and never will stand up."[17]

The final blow was delivered in 1961 when the Berlin Wall went up, and President John F. Kennedy did nothing to tear it down, even though it was a flagrant breach of the treaty governing Berlin, which stated that there should be freedom of movement between the two parts of the city. The limits of U.S.

commitment to Germany became painfully clear. The United States was simply not willing to risk going to war over East Berlin.

Among the many people who were disappointed by Kennedy's lack of action was Willy Brandt, then-mayor of Berlin. The charismatic Brandt later became foreign minister in the so-called Grand Coalition of the CDU/CSU and the Social Democrats in 1966, and in 1969 he became chancellor in a Social Democrat–Free Democrat government. Brandt had decided that, since the nation's allies were unwilling to do anything about Germany's division, it was left to the West Germans themselves to recognize reality and find a way of living with the East German regime, however distasteful this might be.

Thus the policy of small steps was born, of cooperation with the communist regime on a variety of practical issues, such as visits by family members, with a view to bettering conditions for the East German population through trade and increased contacts. In time, this policy developed into Willy Brandt's *Ostpolitik*, or opening to the East, the policy of seeking improved relations with the Eastern bloc as a whole, which culminated in the signing of major treaties with Poland and with the Soviet Union in the beginning of the 1970s.

The casualty of these agreements, however, was the dream of German unification. Over time, all talk of unification stopped. Helmut Schmidt totally discarded the word from his vocabulary. As late as 1988, Brandt had called thoughts of unification the "living lie of the Second German Republic," and the coarchitect of Brandt's *Ostpolitik*, Egon Bahr, dismissed such talk as "political environmental pollution" and "irresponsible nonsense."[18]

Another effect of *Ostpolitik* was that West German officials tended to lose their sense of occupying the moral high ground when they spoke on behalf of all Germans. Instead, they become defensive and disoriented when dealing with the East German leadership. Wolfgang Seiffert, a former East German professor from the University of Potsdam who defected to the

West in 1978, noted, "Whoever has worked and lived under this regime is shocked to see the carelessness, naivete, insecurity, and lack of self-confidence with which the political elite of the Federal Republic confronts the elite of the GDR."[19] In fact, increasingly it was the East Germans who were on the offensive, delivering preposterous sermons to the West Germans on all the alleged deficiencies of the West German welfare state.

Talk of unification was seen as downright inflammatory and endangering the policy of gradual improvement between the two German states. The Social Democrats suggested that unification be removed from the West German constitution, so as not to offend the easily offended Erich Honecker. Even in Kohl's own party some suggested that the point be removed from the party's political platform.

Helmut Kohl, however, was one of the few who never gave up on Konrad Adenauer's dream of a united Germany. From the very beginning, he started reviving some of Adenauer's vocabulary, using phrases like a "split and divided Germany," and stating that such a split was unacceptable to Germans who wanted freedom and self-determination. Kohl's old speeches are spotted with the theme of the unnatural nature of the division. Again and again, Kohl spoke of the "intolerable border" and East Germany's abysmal human rights record. "We cannot and will not keep silent about the disregard for human rights even in our Fatherland," significantly using the term Fatherland to cover both states. He renamed his annual "State of the Nation" address the "State of the Nation in Divided Germany."[20]

On another occasion, Kohl reminded the West Germans that in the case of the East German regime, "we are not dealing with a freely elected government. Rather it is a political regime that holds two thousand of our countrymen political prisoners." He was immediately censured by the Social Democratic opposition for speaking in a manner that did not befit a chancellor of Germany and for "pandering to extreme right-wing votes."

Abroad, Kohl would make the same points. Kohl recalls a visit with Yuri Andropov in the Kremlin in 1983. "We were sitting in his study. Andropov was quiet, his foreign minister Gromyko was holding forth with the stern face of a schoolmaster. Then the general secretary interrupted him and said to me, 'Anyone who demands German unity is a warmonger.'

"I answered him, 'Mr. General Secretary, what would you say if your country was divided, and here, as is the case in Berlin, below the Kremlin, there was a Wall, your mother lived on the other side and somebody would call her a warmonger just because she wanted to be together with you?' Andropov looked at me and was silent. Gromyko immediately interjected, 'The division of Germany is the judgment of history. Whoever touches this puts peace at risk.'"

But at the same time, Kohl was always a realist. During his leadership of the opposition, from 1976 to 1982, he criticized elements of the Social Democrats' *Ostpolitik*, arguing that it signaled an acceptance of the status quo in Europe and the permanent division of Germany. However, when he came into power in 1982, Kohl adhered basically to the same course as regards contacts between divided German families and financial support for East Germany. Yet there were some notable differences.

Says Wolfgang Schaeuble, "With the Social Democrats, Honecker could hope that if he held out long enough and stuck long enough to his positions, he would eventually achieve concessions on fundamental principles. It became clear to Honecker that, with Kohl and the CDU, concessions on matters of principle were not to be had." Kohl insisted on reciprocity—Honecker had to give something in return.

In the early Kohl years, 1983–1984, private banks gave loans to the East Germans to the tune of one billion Marks. Cleverly, Kohl left their administration to Franz Josef Strauss, thereby achieving cover from attacks emanating from his sister party to the right.

Kohl's largesse paid off. East Germans below the age of sixty had not been allowed to travel to West Germany except in rare cases of family illness or to attend a funeral. In 1982 only 40,000 permissions were granted from a population of 17 million. By 1987 that figure had risen to 1.2 million.[21]

Kohl displayed his ultimate realist side in 1987 when he invited Honecker to West Germany. From September 7 to 11, Honecker became the first East German leader to visit West Germany since the creation of the two states in 1949. The possibility had first been raised during Helmut Schmidt's 1981 trip to East Germany, but the Soviets had twice vetoed the idea, exerting pressure on the intermediate-range missile issue.

Bergsdorf recalls Kohl's agonizing over the decision to allow Honecker to come to Bonn. "That was an extremely difficult matter for him to deal with. It was a subject that was brought up time and again in the evening discussions, and it took him months to finally come to a decision." What swayed Kohl in the end was the argument that the more people met in the two Germanies, the more difficult it would be for the regime in the East to survive. Wolfgang Schaeuble was then head of the Chancellery and was sent to receive Honecker at the airport. He recalls deliberately putting on his oldest and crummiest suit for the occasion, and national security adviser Horst Teltschik went on a well-deserved holiday.

For his part, Honecker's aims were clear: For all his fears about ideological "pollution" coming from the West, he could no longer do without the infusion of cash and loans from West Germany. His country had the highest standard of living in Eastern Europe to maintain but was hugely in debt. Cuts in Soviet oil deliveries had deepened the East German recession. The East German railways had even started to use the old steam engines again instead of diesel locomotives as a fuel-saving measure. Honecker's other main goal was to secure recognition of East Germany as a separate country.

For the seventy-five-year-old Honecker, who for decades had been an international pariah for supervising the building of the Berlin Wall, the visit was clearly a personal triumph. Though the West Germans stressed that this did not amount to an official recognition of the East German regime (the East German leader was only accorded an escort of seven police outriders instead of the fifteen normally accorded a head of state), to be received by the West German chancellor at all meant an increase of prestige and recognition. The visit conferred a measure of legitimacy on the East German leader. While Honecker was relaxed and smiling his thin-lipped and wintry little smile, Kohl had the distinctly uncomfortable look of a man who would rather be elsewhere.

Recalls Eduard Ackermann, "I observed him from a distance of a few meters when they stood in the receiving line before the *Kanzleramt*. If you knew him, you could see he was very upset, and that he was very conscious that there were many people who could not understand why he was welcoming the man who had deprived eighteen million Germans of their freedom." Especially difficult was watching the East German flag go up. Like Kohl, many Germans were obviously uncomfortable when the national anthem of East Germany was played in front of the Chancellery. Still, according to one poll, 93 percent of the population favored the visit.

Kohl made up for his discomfort by inflicting some on Honecker during the state dinner, which was broadcast on East German television. During it, Kohl condemned the Berlin Wall and demanded that the East German leader permanently abolish his border guards' shoot-to-kill orders. (On his best behavior, Honecker had suspended them during his visit.) Kohl also expressed his hope that some day "the whole German people should be allowed to choose unification." Protocol demanded that Honecker sit through the speech and applaud politely at the end.

The visit and the speech demonstrated that for Helmut Kohl, the East German regime was something he had to deal with, but at the same time it also showed that he was not willing to regard it as permanent. The distinction is important.

Though he had followed the policies of his predecessors, Kohl saw them as temporary means. Many may have scoffed at his constant repetition over the years of the need for a united Germany, which at times seemed to sound monotonously like a Tibetan monk with his prayer mill. But it meant that he was mentally prepared for a change in the relationship when the opportunity arose.

3

ENEMIES

KOHL'S SOLIDITY, lack of pretension, essential *Buerger-lichkeit*, may have made him a vote-getter with middle-class Germans, but it did nothing to endear him to the German media and intelligentsia. Even though he was regarded as belonging to the more liberal wing of the CDU when he came to power in 1982, and even though in just about every other country Kohl would have been regarded essentially as a Social Democrat, his critics at home lost no time painting him a black reactionary.

The political spectrum on the right in Germany is extremely narrow. In the United States, a typical political spectrum goes from libertarians to paleoconservatives, to neoconservatives, to Reagan Republicans, to country-club Republicans, from Southern Democrats, to New Democrats, to neoliberals, to liberals, to socialists. In France it is from the radical left-wing Jacobins to the National Front's Jean Marie le Pen.

Not so in Germany. Here the Right, even the bourgeois Right, has been taboo since World War II. There are no similar limitations on the left side of the spectrum, where it is perfectly respectable to be Trotskyite, Spartakist, anarchist, or other exotic persuasions. For instance, a fierce public outcry arose when at the height of the terrorist wave in the 1970s, the Bundestag passed a law designed to prevent left-wing terrorist sympathizers from holding public sector jobs. (It should be emphasized that this law was introduced by a Social Democratic–led government.) Since there is no real Right in Germany, the Left had to invent one, and so they seized on Helmut Kohl.

According to Christoph Stoelzl, director of the Deutsches Historisches Museum in Berlin, the 1960s and 1970s in Germany were a time of great illusions and even greater delusions. The protest movement of the day was completely unconnected to reality. Indeed, for all its bloody deeds, the Baader-Meinhof terrorist group was straight out of the nineteenth-century German Romantic school. While the Red Army faction and its sympathizers obviously constituted an extremely small group, some of their political views resonated in the youth movement at large (and among older radicals as well). If Americans think that the 1960s were bad, the generational conflict that beset Germany was every bit as ferocious. This postwar generation rose up with a vengeance against its parents, who, because of the Nazi era, commanded no moral authority.

German society reacted to the challenge from the radicals not with counterarguments but with well-intentioned, if misplaced, attempts to understand their bitterness and fury. The youth movement, in return, showed its lack of appreciation immediately by labeling this attitude "repressive tolerance." Respected older intellectual figures like Heinrich Boell went so far as to question the right of the republic to defend itself against terrorism. Boell viewed the violence of terrorists such as

Ulrike Meinhof and Andreas Baader as less worrisome than "the lies and propaganda of the fascist press."[1]

Equally preposterously, people on the left in Germany identified with the civil rights movement in America, deluding themselves that the situation in Germany somehow resembled that of the United States. The fact that there were no blacks in Germany, and that the Turkish guest workers who were there had come of their own volition and desperately wanted to stay (and bring their families as well) seemed of minor importance.

But they did not stop here; they identified with the poor downtrodden wherever they thought they could find them in the world. As Dorethea Soelle, a church activist, put it at a 1983 conference of the Council of Christian Churches in Canada: "Our San Salvador is in militarist West Germany, which is the place where our struggle should proceed. This is our Vietnam, our Soweto, our San Salvador, our battlefield for justice and peace."[2]

Into this morass Helmut Kohl strode briskly in 1982 with a call for spiritual and moral change, a call that his enemies immediately seized upon. Some ridiculed it, others saw it as a sinister plan to impose a right-wing ideology on Germany. In part, Kohl reacted to his predecessor Helmut Schmidt, who had stated that the job of the chancellor was not to preach moral values, but to implement pragmatic policies. Schmidt had, in fact, called himself the "first civil servant" of the German state, indicative of a rather limited view of the office.

Kohl, for his part, was of the opinion that politics was more than mere pragmatism, that if Germany wanted to keep its position as a leading industrial nation, it had better rediscover some of its traditional values, such as honesty and hard work, freedom and justice, which had made its economic success possible in the first place. To have seen this as rabid right-wing ideology was way off the mark.

Says Stoelzl, "When Kohl in 1982 promised a spiritual and moral change, although he might have wanted more, this meant nothing more than going back to the common sense of the great majority of the population. This was not a conservative revolution."

But even a return to normalcy seemed preposterous to the generation that had been able to indulge its left-wing fantasies while living off the accumulated wealth of its parents, who had rebuilt German prosperity after the war. The reason Kohl aroused such strong antipathy after the left-wing idealist binge of the 1960s and 1970s, according to Stoelzl, was that with his solidity and his roots, he reminded everyone of what they were trying to forget—that real life involves work and responsibility, taking care of your children and your family. He spoke not just about freedoms, but also about obligations, not just about rights, but also about duties. Kohl was the embodiment of common sense after years of romanticism and escape.

Indeed, Kohl quickly became a kind of national dart board for the 1960s generation. This generation of young men and women who were on the long march through German institutions now found themselves in positions of responsibility, and had long since been tamed; the Volkswagen Beetle and the Velo Solex moped had been exchanged for a Mercedes Benz; the squatters and the activists had moved into their own villas. In a kind of Freudian way, Kohl acted as a surrogate father figure. Pointing a finger at Kohl, every schoolteacher with the liberal newsweekly *Die Zeit* under his arm could delude himself that he still belonged to the avant-garde.

Needless to say, the intellectuals and the German media were at the forefront of the assault. In order to understand the relentless attacks directed at Helmut Kohl, an American audience should recall the media reaction to Ronald Reagan, who shared some of Kohl's easy-going and amiable characteristics. Throughout Reagan's political career, the media treated Reagan voters as if they did not know what they were doing. (In 1994, when the heirs of Reagan captured the U.S. Congress, ABC anchor Peter Jennings described it as a "temper tantrum.") Or, alternatively, they were seen as flinty-hearted egotists, devoid of compassion for the less fortunate in society.

In both the United States and Germany, intellectuals and the press tend not to look favorably on conservative politicians for the simple reason that very few writers are conservatives themselves. In the United States, surveys have shown that almost 90 percent of the journalists in the country's main newsrooms vote Democratic and are generally out of tune with mainstream America. Similarly in Germany, a great majority of the media—some 80 percent—regard Social Democratic and Green positions favorably.

But in Germany this phenomenon goes a step further. Despite the country's extensive social welfare net, which is supported by liberals and conservatives alike, being a conservative in Germany is seen by many on the left as not only a sign of mental deficiency but also as something infinitely more sinister. Says Stoelzl, "Normal people who believe in law and order in Germany are defined as Nazis. It is nonsense, of course, but there it is."

Some of it comes down to intellectual snobbery. After all, few things will make people repress their own middle-class origins more readily than a university education. Thus from the very beginning Kohl was mocked in the papers as the *"Birne,"* or "pear," which alludes to the chancellor's shape and also carries the overtones of a dim bulb. The campaign recalls the one waged with deadly effect against French King Louis Philippe in the nineteenth century by caricaturist Daumier, whose most famous cartoon of the king shows his head gradually transforming into a pear. And that was comparatively mild stuff. One critic, wheeling out the heavy artillery, labeled the chancellor "an imposition on Germany as a cultural nation."

Among Germany's heavyweight intellectuals, the most prolific of Kohl's critics was author Guenter Grass, whose contempt for Kohl was almost visceral. Of all the self-important German left-wing intellectuals, Grass is surely the most self-important. With his huge drooping moustache, grandfather pipe, and old sweater, Grass looks docile enough. This is, after all, a man who has chosen the snail as his literary emblem. But when the subject turned to Helmut Kohl and the state of Germany democracy, the snail became apoplectic.

Like his fellow author, the late Heinrich Boell, Grass has tended to see postwar Germany as a police state, a sham democracy, "a dictatorship of money" with neo-Nazis about to take over any minute, if they have not already done so. One critic perceptively compared Grass's own political development, or rather stuntedness, to that of the hero of his most famous book, *The Tin Drum*, the boy Oscar Matzerath, who willed himself to stop growing when the Nazis took over and witnessed the cruelties of war from his child's perspective while hammering away on his drum. Grass himself is forever stuck in the twilight shadows of the Third Reich, and forever banging his drum about imaginary demons without noticing or being willing to notice that the world around him has changed.[3]

Apart from fashionable self-loathing, in their constant harping on the Hitler years, leftists such as Grass found a convenient weapon with which to attack and delegitimize Kohl's moderately conservative middle-class values and the market economy itself. Using the vocabulary of the Nazi era as a weapon for the task goes beyond the rules of civilized debate in a democracy. Furthermore, by using such words lightly, it cheapens them, depriving them of any real meaning.

Among the print media in postwar Germany, the most influential has been the weekly magazine *Der Spiegel*, which has routinely portrayed itself as a savior, educator, and guarantor of German democracy, without which Germany could not have returned to the family of respectable nations. *Der Spiegel* held this position for decades, though with time it has lost some of its impact due to competition from other publications. But with a circulation of about one million, it remains a publication that cannot be overlooked. Most politicians are hesitant to challenge it; to be on *Der Spiegel*'s hit list is not a healthy place to be.

Der Spiegel is a prime example of what some call the angst industry in Germany, which is made up of a triad located in Hamburg—*Der Spiegel*, *Die Zeit*, and the "human interest" magazine *Stern*—or what Kohl refers to as "the Hamburg complex of the press." In common, they have a highly skeptical attitude toward power, which, given Germany's history may be reasonable enough. Yet in the case of *Der Spiegel*, skepticism reaches an almost hysterical pitch; any kind of power is suspect, including power exerted within a democracy. In *Der Spiegel* a minor local problem is immediately blown up to be a national crisis, while a national crisis becomes instant *Goetterdaemmerung*.

Licensed after the war by the British in 1946 and based on the *Time* magazine model, *Der Spiegel* and its founder and publisher Rudolf Augstein soon showed that they had their own political agenda. Thus the *Time* analogy is misleading. As opposed to American weeklies, which at least make a pretense of objectivity with careful sourcing and plenty of facts, no such attempt is made in *Der Spiegel*. Openly polemical, fact and opinion mix freely in *Der Spiegel*'s pages, and in a time-honored European tradition, sourcing is minimal. You have to take the news on trust.

Despite the publisher's stated nonsocialist views (he is a Free Democrat), *Der Spiegel*'s editorial line is decidedly left of center with a weakness for environmental affairs. Its style, known as Spiegelese, is instantly recognizable, a cynical, insinuating, sarcastic, and streetwise tone, to which is added a hefty dollop of moral rectitude.

The style is a reflection of the personality of its publisher, a man of restless intellect who has written biographies on figures as diverse as Frederick the Great and Jesus Christ. Coming originally from a strict religious background, against which he rebelled in *A Man Called Jesus*, 1972, Rudolf Augstein challenged the historical basis of the Bible and went on to inveigh against reactionary Catholics, who, in his opinion, ran Germany and blocked social change.

On foreign affairs, despite the early British support for the magazine, Augstein remained a German nationalist, which he combined with a deep sympathy for Russia. Always backing the underdog, which in the Cold War he believed to be the Soviet Union (a rather large underdog, one should have thought), he has always been hostile to American power in the world. Early on, Augstein proved himself an ardent enemy of Konrad Adenauer's Western orientation and the integration of Germany into the Western defense alliance.

Augstein was one of the main cheerleaders when in 1969 the Free Democrats formed a government with the Social Democrats. Not surprisingly, his favorite chancellor was Willy Brandt, and *Der Spiegel* became a conveyer belt for his views, especially the opening to the East. In 1974 one of the magazine's editors, Gunther Gauss, was appointed West German representative in East Berlin.

Accordingly, Augstein hit the roof when the Free Democrats switched allegiance in 1982 and threw their weight behind Helmut Kohl. For sixteen years, Augstein waged war against Kohl. Kohl once referred to *Der Spiegel* as "representing a Hamburg sewer rather than reality" and advised people "to save their money and enjoy life." Its covers are famous for their depiction of the chancellor; one from 1986 shows a tiny little Kohl figure under a gigantic headline screaming "The Minus Chancellor," while a post-unification cover from 1994 shows his head on a locomotive relentlessly barreling ahead under the headline "The Power Machine."

For two decades Kohl did not grant the magazine an interview, knowing that it would make no difference in the weekly's biased treatment of him. Why help a magazine devoted to his downfall? He even refused to read *Der Spiegel*. As it was still Germany's leading magazine, and hence could not be overlooked, he would get around his own ban by leaving the unpleasant task to his press spokesman, who summarized parts for him.

Compared to *Der Spiegel*, the weekly newspaper *Die Zeit* is a much more refined product. It has none of the in-your-face wiseguy tone of *Der Spiegel*, but politically it takes similar positions—liberal-left and Social Democrat—and its editorial line was decidedly anti-Kohl.

Its publisher is Marion Graefin Doenhoff, the grande dame of German newspapering and a member of Germany's old Prussian nobility. She saw her brother and many of her family friends killed after the unsuccessful attempt on the life of Adolf Hitler in 1944. After the war she lost all the family lands in East Prussia and escaped on horseback from the advancing Soviet troops.

Trained as an economist before the war, and nicknamed the Red Countess because of her socialist leanings, she has a way of getting things wrong. When Ludwig Erhard declared the currency reform in 1948, she immediately pronounced it a "disaster" for Germany. The currency reform turned out to be the foundation of Germany's economic rebirth, but this did not seem to register with the countess.

At heart, despite all her socialists leanings, Doenhoff identifies with the kind of nationalism that represents the old Germany, the real Germany within the officer corps. (She has written an elegant and elegiac memoir about her childhood in East Prussia, which, incidentally, Kohl admires.)[4] Today, approaching ninety, she still writes. Where Augstein mixes his intellectualism with wiseguy smartness, Doenhoff tends to opine with all the vacuity of the Very Virtuous.[5]

Die Zeit's editor-in-chief until 1992 was Theo Sommer. He had been picked decades earlier by Doenhoff as one of her promising young men. Under his stewardship, *Die Zeit* continuously editorialized about how the East German regime was a peace-seeking and well-meaning state that the Federal Republic should help and understand; the paper roundly criticized Helmut Kohl for constantly bringing up the unification issue.

Since unification and the opening of the East German archives, interesting revelations about *Die Zeit's* editorial practices have surfaced. In 1986 the magazine ran a series of articles about life in East Germany, later published in book form under the title *A Journey Through the Other Germany*. The archives embarrassingly reveal Sommer eagerly agreeing to downplay the significance of the Wall and other unpleasant aspects of life in East Germany and instead stress its stability and full employment. In short, the articles amount to acceptance of the journalistic terms imposed by the East German regime.

A few quotes from Sommer will give the flavor: "Life in the GDR means life under Erich Honecker. The citizens in the other German State regard him with a quiet kind of reverence. That always comes through in conversations. Honecker carefully avoids any kind of personality cult.... On the other side, a system has been created that in many ways surpasses ours. There is no unemployment. On the contrary, managers complain over lack of manpower."[6]

The picture emerging from the articles was of a state that was essentially benign and nonthreatening, if a little boring. The series was influential in shaping not only the West Germans' view of East Germany, but also international opinion. Sommer has since admitted in general terms that his view of East Germany was wrong, but he never apologized for the series.

In all fairness, notes Kohl adviser Wolfgang Bergsdorf, it should perhaps be pointed out that *Die Zeit* was not the only publication that was taken in by the East German line. "There are hundreds of journalists," he says, "who chose to close their eyes and not see the human rights violations committed in the GDR, all in the interest of defining peace and good relations with those in power." At the same time, these people were deeply upset about human rights violations in Chile and South Africa. In fact, the further away, the greater the righteous indignation.

To rarefied personages like Doenhoff and Sommer, Helmut Kohl was a petit bourgeois Catholic and an unworthy leader of Germany. America stood for vulgar consumerism, as opposed to Prussian virtue and thrift, the kind of stern frugality of the rich which the countess was brought up on. As she describes it in her memoirs, it was considered wasteful to put butter *and* marmalade on a piece of toast, in order to save and keep up the family's vast estate. In this view, life under East German communism was a character-building exercise: The East Germans were the true Germans.

How did Kohl respond to these press attacks? In his time as prime minister of the Rhineland-Palatinate, he was used to favorable reviews in the local press as an up-and-coming politician, so the onslaught of the national media came as something of a shock. Kohl was known for his "angry glare" at journalists whom he found impertinent, and he took a certain pleasure when the press had to eat its own words.

Eduard Ackermann, who as press secretary occupied an exposed post in the war with the media, recalls, "In the old days, the way a question was phrased could irritate him and throw him off his guard." Over time, he became more equaniminous, but this did not prevent him from saying a question was truly stupid if he found it so.

For the proper perspective, it should be remembered that Konrad Adenauer was ridiculed by the intellectuals for having a vocabulary of five hundred words. And Kohl was surely no more sensitive than Willy Brandt, who when faced with jokes and media attacks assigned a psychologist in the Chancellery to delve into the mystery of why people would criticize him.[7]

Given all the vitriol expended on him during his years in office, one may wonder how Kohl survived for so long. The answer lay partly in his understanding of and connection to the ordinary German voters and partly in the fact that Kohl was a formidable political tactician and infighter, something that was often not understood by his opponents—until it was too late. "Helmut Kohl's survival skills were highly developed," says Wolfgang Bergsdorf. "If there was a rat that threatened to gnaw the wood of the chair he was sitting on, he could smell that rat right away." Kohl's political enemies and rivals tended to have one thing in common: the belief that they were smarter than he was. For the life of them, they could not understand that he, not they, occupied the chancellor's chair.

Thus Kohl's cheerful exterior, the jolly giant with a zest for the good life and cheerful company, concealed a sometimes ruthless politician with a sizable ego and a prodigious memory for past slights, as a number of political rivals have discovered over the years. As any leader will realize, regicides are always waiting in the wings. (Mrs. Thatcher in Britain comes to mind; after three election victories she thought she could go "on and on and on," only to be brought down by the mousy men of her own party.) Closer to home, Kohl had the cautionary example of Helmut Schmidt, who was popular as chancellor but not in control of his own party. Indeed, at regular intervals throughout Kohl's career, there were claims within his own party that he had become a liability and that it was time for him to make way for somebody more appealing.

Kohl's CDU is full of people who underestimated Kohl and lived to regret it—who woke up one day and found themselves relegated to exile in distant and fog-filled provinces in the new eastern Germany. One such is the prime minister of Saxony, Kurt Biedenkopf, a man of great intellect and wit, who fought a series of early battles with Kohl about the direction of the CDU and lost—and harbored a huge grudge. At predictable intervals, Biedenkopf would jump up and down in his palace in Dresden overcome with the injustice of it all.

Another example is Lothar Spaeth, the once-popular prime minister of Baden-Wuerttemberg and in 1989 considered a serious rival of Kohl. Former U.S. Ambassador to Germany Richard Burt once asked Spaeth if he meant to take on the chancellor. "I've thought about it and it scares me," came Spaeth's reply.

"Why does it scare you?" asked Burt.

"Because on weekends, when he comes down to Baden-Wuerttemberg, and we go around to CDU winefests, he knows more people by name in my state than I do."

Predictably, the Spaeth challenge never emerged, and today Spaeth is CEO of Jenoptik in Jena, Thuringia. Kohl was not merely the leader who sat in the Chancellery and greeted visiting potentates and other dignitaries, he was a grass-roots politician who lived and breathed politics. "He was not just a wholesaler of politics, he was a retailer, who understood that people plus policies equal politics," notes Richard Burt.

Someone who immediately recognized Kohl's staying power was U.S. Ambassador Vernon Walters, who was appointed to Bonn in the spring of 1989. In one of his very first meetings at the embassy, he ordered every reference in embassy telegrams to the "bumbling and stumbling chancellor" removed. "No one stumbles and bumbles his way into the Chancellery and remains there for sixteen years," says Walters. "The competition is very great. A lot of people are looking for that job." From then on, all embassy telegrams were to carry his signature. Kohl once told Walters, "My enemies have underestimated me since I ran for the city council in Mainz. And they still do it in the federal Chancellery. I hope they continue to do it."

Another key to Kohl's survival was that he was the ultimate party man. He served his way all the way to the top through a long line of positions and knew every aspect of the party, including where all the skeletons were buried. While all chancellors run the risk of ending up as prisoners of their own staff and the rigid Bonn power structures—political Robinson Crusoes in splendid isolation—Kohl counteracted this by keeping close contact with local party officials at the grass-roots level throughout the country, making him in effect his own main adviser. On important questions he conferred with his friends among the clergy back in Ludwigshafen to get opinions that were not influenced by self-interest.

His favored instrument for doing business was the telephone. Kohl liked to call lowly CDU officials throughout small-town Germany with the words "Helmut here, how are things in Hinterpfaffenhofen?"—the German equivalent of Glockamora—and they would not be the least bit surprised. It was once said of him, and only half in jest, that if he got President George Bush on one line and a party official on the other, he would put Bush on hold.

It was indeed amusing to see how opposition newspapers like *Die Zeit*, on those intermittent occasions when it decided to take the chancellor seriously, managed to make his manner with a telephone sound almost Machiavellian. Like some latter-day Caesare Borgia with a telephone, Kohl was shown plotting and scheming, compartmentalizing people, sucking them dry for knowledge while telling them little, so that in the end only the man at the center of the web had the whole picture. It certainly is a frightening image, for those who are easily frightened.

As is common with politicians whose views journalists do not share and whose success they accordingly do not quite understand, Kohl's career has been dismissed as pure luck—as was, one recalls, Ronald Reagan's. As Kohl himself freely acknowledges, no politician gets anywhere without luck, but it has to be combined with tenacity. Ronald Reagan was successful only in his third attempt to capture the White House.

At a superficial glance Kohl's career on paper may have a certain inevitability to it, but Kohl has seen his share of setbacks. Although in 1976 he scored the second-highest election result in postwar German history, he lost the election just 300,000 votes short of an absolute majority, this out of forty-two million votes. In 1980 Kohl suffered another disappointment when the CDU/CSU candidacy for chancellor instead went to Bavaria's Franz Josef Strauss, Kohl's alleged ally—and always rival.

More than with anyone else, Kohl fought with Strauss, also known as the "King of Bavaria," who used to refer to Kohl as a "mere office holder." After Kohl's defeat in the 1976 general election, Strauss stated, "Believe me, Helmut Kohl will never become chancellor. At the age of ninety, he'll write his memoirs, *Forty Years as a Chancellor Candidate*."

All things out of Bavaria are bigger and louder than elsewhere in Germany, rather like Texas in the United States. Bavarians tend to be extremely independent-minded folks. When Adenauer went to Bavaria for the first time, he came by train and was greeted by a delegation of CSU officials who greeted him with the words, "Mr. Chancellor, we have not come here to say 'yes' and 'amen' to everything that you come up with." To which Adenauer calmly responded, "Gentlemen, 'amen' is not necessary." But things had changed since Adenauer's paternalistic days, and Franz Josef Strauss was definitely not among the amen types.

Strauss's folksiness masked a keen intelligence and a ruthless political ambition. As a former minister of defense and of finance, Strauss commanded respect for his enormous expertise and knowledge, more than Kohl would ever claim for himself. Much of Strauss's analysis of the German economy in the late 1970s and early 1980s was right on the mark. It was the way he sometimes expressed his analysis that scared people away. Similarly, when Strauss started toying with the idea that Germany should have its own nuclear deterrent, a lot of people got rather frightened.

With a gargantuan ego, Strauss was a baroque figure who once described himself as "a Hercules who carried the world on his shoulders." In Strauss's mental universe, Winston Churchill was just a quarrelsome politician who owed his career to Adolf Hitler, while Konrad Adenauer was a competent lord mayor of a minor town who had been lifted from obscurity after the breakdown of the Third Reich. Strauss was forever bemoaning the fact that he himself lived in such uneventful times, which did not call for the greatness he embodied.

Some of Strauss's resentment of Kohl was due to genuine disagreements over policies and strategy. CDU and its Bavarian sister party CSU are both based on Christian values, a much-needed component of political life after the Nazi period. But the CSU generally lies to the right of the CDU on the political spectrum. While Kohl might be considered a middle-of-the-road Democrat in the United States, Strauss could have passed as a Republican. For decades, the two quarreled over every issue, from the economy to *Ostpolitik*, with Strauss demanding more reciprocity from the East Germans.

From Strauss's side, however, the rivalry between the two was in large part a personality clash. Strauss could not quite get used to the idea that somebody other than himself held the title of chancellor. His hatred of Kohl verged on the irrational, and it clearly clouded his political judgment. He never missed an opportunity to vent his contempt for the chancellor.

Kohl and Strauss also differed on election strategy. Strauss always regarded the Free Democrats as untrustworthy and wanted to go for a clear CDU/CSU majority government in the 1980 elections. Kohl meanwhile had learned from his own defeat in 1976 that obtaining a clear majority was not politically feasible and that, therefore, cooperation with the Free Democrats was the only way for the conservatives to regain power.

When Strauss was chosen as chancellor candidate for the 1980 election, Kohl gave him his full backing. Instead of sulking and returning to the Rhineland-Palatinate, Kohl stuck it out, the ultimate party loyalist. Not even Strauss could accuse Kohl of destroying his chances. Accordingly, when Strauss suffered a humiliating defeat, the second worst result in CDU/CSU history, proving once and for all that he was an unviable candidate, Kohl was there to take over again as chancellor candidate for the opposition in Bonn.

When Kohl became chancellor in 1982, he made it clear to Strauss that the heavyweight ministries such as foreign affairs, finance, and economy would not be an option for him. Instead, Strauss was offered a beefed-up defense portfolio, which he turned down and which he was meant to turn down. Kohl did not want the Wild Man from Bavaria in his cabinet.

Despite the insults, Kohl always tried to have a good working relationship with Strauss because he needed his support to keep the Right from joining up with nationalist parties like the Republikaners. According to Ackermann, "Kohl surely clenched his fist in his pocket many times, but he put up with it. Easy it wasn't, of course."[8]

Kohl himself, in a moment of exaggerated enthusiasm, once described the relationship with Strauss as a *Maennerfreundshaft*, a "friendship among men," but it could best be described as an armed truce. The two would go for long walks in the Bavarian mountains, hashing out pressing issues. Along the route, Strauss would place photographers at strategic locations to document how the chancellor came to Bavaria to seek advice and guidance.

The results of these walks would vary considerably depending on who was doing the retelling. Whereas Kohl usually stressed the picnic aspects of these trips and waxed lyrical about the impressive Bavarian landscape, in the belief that this was a confidential conversation, Strauss invariably claimed to have won some gigantic concession from the chancellor.[9]

When Franz Josef Strauss died in 1988 and was given a funeral worthy of a Bavarian king, Kohl gave a most moving tribute to him. When you have triumphed over people in life, you can afford to be generous at their death.

THE OMINOUS TERM *Maennerfreundshaft* has also been used to describe the other key political relationship in Kohl's career, the one with Hans-Dietrich Genscher, leader of the Free Democrats.

While Genscher's party was still in coalition with the Social Democrats, Kohl started cultivating him, knowing that he would need his support to form a government one day. Kohl needed Genscher in order to have a majority, and Genscher needed Kohl to continue to play a national role after the demise of the Schmidt government. Like all marriages of necessity, it was an uneasy one.

Genscher, whose trademark big ears have earned him the nickname "Jumbo" among caricaturists, is an intriguing character. Growing up in the city of Halle in Saxony, during the war Genscher served as a plane spotter at an anti-aircraft battery. He had just completed Pioneer school when the war ended. Genscher was taken prisoner by the Americans and then turned over to the British. When the Western Allies left Saxony, which was to become part of the Soviet Zone, Genscher, rather than taking the offer of going with the British, chose to go back to his mother in Halle, where he went on to study law.[10]

But in 1952 it became clear to Genscher that the law was not highly regarded in the new East German regime. Accordingly, he and a couple of friends packed their suitcases as if going on holiday, went to Berlin, and took the S-Bahn from the Eastern part to the Western part, avoiding the East German ticket control, something that in the days before the Berlin Wall was still possible. From Berlin, he went to Bremen, where he settled and quickly established himself professionally and politically as a member of the Free Democrats.

During Genscher's time as minister, first as minister of the interior under Brandt, then as foreign minister, Genscher demonstrated an uncanny ability to hog the limelight. He jetted around the would as no German foreign minister had ever done. And Helmut Schmidt once joked that he hardly dared take a holiday for fear that Genscher would jump into his chair.

Genscher assiduously propagated the myth of Genschman— the superdiplomat who indefatigably traveled the world in search of peace, the man who invented the "working funeral," as when he held meetings with U.S. Secretary of State George Schultz and his British counterpart, Sir Geoffrey Howe, at the funeral of Pakistani President Zia ul Haq.[11]

For years, Genscher was the most popular politician in Germany, precisely because of his tendency to give a great segment of the population the peace pablum they so wanted to hear. Once, *Stern* magazine asked its readers, if they were stranded on a desert island with a politician, with whom would they prefer to be stranded? The majority responded: Hans-Dietrich Genscher.

The interdependence between Kohl and Genscher as coalition partners has prevented an honest airing of differences; mostly, one has to read between the lines of this long and complicated relationship. Genscher's political survival skills were legendary. One of Henry Kissinger's favorite jokes describes how two German Luftwaffe aircrafts collide somewhere in the Atlantic. Investigators discover that Genscher was aboard both of them. What's more, he survived.[12]

Partly because of Genscher's constant need to keep up the political profile of his tiny party, partly because of his own vanity and personal ambition, which had been strengthened by a long and life-threatening battle with tuberculosis,[13] Genscher quickly started making his own personal foreign policy. This was often at odds with the chancellor's. On several such occasions, Genscher refused to go along, and Kohl had to give in. For instance, when in 1989 Germany had to decide on the modernization of short-range missiles, Kohl favored going ahead with the NATO modernization program, but Genscher dug in his heels and modernization was scrapped.[14]

As a counterweight to Genscher and his minions at the Foreign Ministry, Kohl established his close associate, Horst Teltschik, as his national security adviser in the Chancellery, sending a clear message that ultimately this was where German foreign policy would be made.

The nature of the Kohl–Genscher relationship is illustrated by their respective books—mainly that they have very little to say about each other. In 1995 Genscher published his mammoth memoirs, *Erinnerungen*, which Foreign Ministry officials had the grim duty of learning by heart (the honest ones admit they never quite made it through). In the book, Genscher emerges as the omniscient master strategist who can predict every development months in advance. Kohl's role, on the other hand, is pretty much reduced to signing what he is told by the Foreign Ministry.

By contrast, Kohl in his book carefully avoids addressing major policy differences between himself and his foreign minister. Indeed, he does not mention Genscher at all, except when it is absolutely unavoidable, limiting himself to a few veiled remarks about his foreign minister's prima donna complex.

Of all Kohl's battles, his fight with former President Richard von Weizsaecker, whose relations with Kohl go all the way back to the days in the Rhineland-Palatinate, has been the most discrete. Von Weizsaecker owes his whole career to Kohl, becoming mayor of Berlin from 1981 to 1984, and later president of the Bundesrepublik from 1984 to 1994.

The two were continually engaged in a kind of political shadow boxing. In Germany, the presidency is largely a ceremonial role, which the patrician[15] and eloquent von Weizsaecker over the years developed into a strong platform for moral leadership, becoming the nation's conscience, so to speak. He spoke movingly about Germany's special responsibility after World War II.

But there were certain differences between Kohl and von Weizsaecker, according to Richard Burt. Von Weizsaecker was always more nationalist than Atlanticist, more skeptical about the United States, preferring a European option for Germany. "Particularly during the missile debate, von Weizsaecker was a little 'wobbly,' to use Margaret Thatcher's term. I doubt if von Weizsaecker had been chancellor, he would have seen the missile deployments through."

Toward the end of his term in office, in 1992, von Weizsaecker got carried a little too far in his lofty idealism, overstepping the bounds of the Bundespresidency. He took to writing about the sordid rough-and-tumble of everyday politics; "I am convinced," he wrote, "that our state is dominated by two things: the hunger for power to achieve election victory and the hunger for power in the political leadership task of implementing content and concept," comments that were clearly aimed at Kohl.

On another occasion, von Weizsaecker acidly spoke of career politicians as "generalists with a special knowledge of how one destroys political opponents." Again the target of this comment was never in doubt; "generalist" was one of the words Kohl frequently used to describe himself.

Why this animosity, which some might call ingratitude? Probably it had something to do with class; von Weizsaecker, with all his talents, can be pretentious and preachy, belonging to the Protestant part of the CDU. Says Richard Burt, "I know von Weizsaecker had people around him constantly telling him he should be chancellor rather than this oaf from the Palatinate, that he was really the symbol of the greatness of his country. Kohl made von Weizsaecker. What does von Weizsaecker do in return but quietly piss on Helmut Kohl. I think he saw Kohl as a mediocre intellect and as a kind of crass politician, and I think his mistake was that he let people know that, and it got back to Kohl."

Though Kohl never criticized von Weizsaecker in public during the latter's time in office, von Weizsaecker's sniping, according to close Kohl associates, did not sit well with the chancellor, and along the way the two ceased to be on speaking terms, only addressing each other when absolutely necessary. The Social Democrats, of course, did their utmost to exploit the differences between Kohl and von Weizsaecker.

WITH FRIENDS LIKE THESE, one might well ask, did Kohl really need enemies? But of course they existed on the other side of the political spectrum, too. In particular, Kohl did not think much of academic types with cushy state sector jobs, people who joined the Social Democrats out of self-interest more than devotion to the workers' struggle. However, despite the youthful brawls and Kohl's famous battle cry from the 1976 election campaign that he would fight the Social Democrats "on land, on water, and in the air," he was well aware that in a country with a history like Germany's, political discourse had to be kept within civilized boundaries.[16]

Throughout his career, Kohl had cordial relations with many leading Social Democrats. As prime minister of the Rhineland-Palatinate, Kohl once sent his friend, the mayor of Bremen, a case of Rhine wine with a small card attached to the effect that since the Social Democrats seemed to have little idea how to handle money, Germans might as well get used to the idea of going back to the old barter system.

During most of his period in office, however, Kohl was blessed with an opposition in tatters, much like the Labour Party in Britain during the Thatcher era. Though not quite as colorful as the British Labour Party (and with considerably better dental work), the Social Democrats for a long time seemed bent on self-destruction.

Having beaten the mild-mannered Hans-Jochen Vogel in the 1983 election, Kohl won again in 1987. By the previous year,

Kohl had wiped out inflation, and for the first time in twenty-seven years prices fell. The election itself was a less than brilliant performance, and Kohl squeezed by with a narrow margin. He could thank a particularly inept opposition for helping to make that possible.

Kohl's 1987 opponent was Johannes Rau, the prime minister of North Rhine Westphalia, a "feel-good" Social Democrat whose selection as candidate was an attempt on the part of the party to project a more moderate and avuncular image. Rau was a member of the Evangelical Church Council and read the Bible every morning, which earned him the nickname Brother Johannes. He wore a Helmut Schmidt–type skipper's cap throughout the campaign to signal his moderate credentials. Still, Rau could not paper over the deep fissures in the Social Democrats between the more moderate camp and Oskar Lafontaine's more radical left-wing on issues such as NATO and the relationship with the United States.

Some Social Democrats thought they had a chance of gaining power in 1987 by forming an alliance with the Greens. Rau, to his credit, opposed this alliance, though his party's Lafontaine wing lambasted him for his opposition to teaming up with the Greens. At the same time, the Greens were steering further left, coming up with proposals to legalize sex between adults and children and offering free karate lessons to women.

Throughout Kohl's years in office, his steadiness, imperturbability, and optimism were the key factors in his winning. Invariably, Kohl slumped in midterm, and his party lost important state elections as Germans grumbled about this and that, and why didn't the government do something about it. Yet, when it came to the actual decision in federal elections on who should run Germany, the voters cast their support behind Kohl. The more alarmist the opposition sounded—the more they raved about the manifold impending catastrophes threatening Germany—the more trustworthy and father-like Kohl looked. This made it seem like a choice between Kohl or Chaos, which suited Kohl just fine.

4

KOHL AND THE PAST

HELMUT KOHL'S PERIOD IN OFFICE coincided with a renewed focus on World War II. One reason was the fortieth and fiftieth anniversaries of the great battles and the end of the war; these were the last commemorations that veterans of the campaigns could be expected to see, and the celebrations therefore took on a special urgency. The half-century mark, moreover, had a resonance that could not be ignored.

With all these commemorations, the Germans found themselves confronted over and over with the legacy of the Nazi period, and with a vehemence that left Bonn reeling and occasionally wondering if its record as a member of the Western community of democracies, a pillar of NATO and of the European community for more than four decades, counted for nothing.

Dealing with World War II and its legacy is undoubtedly one of the most delicate issues facing a German leader. It is a given that his every word and every action are seen through a certain prism. Like his predecessors, Helmut Kohl had to tackle a set of historical problems particular to Germany, not just in relation to the country's international partners and allies, but equally importantly in a dialogue with the Germans themselves.

The late CSU leader Franz Josef Strauss once stated with characteristic bluntness that Germans should not be "the permanent penitents of history." "While I was a passionate opponent of Nazism," Strauss insisted, "the German people should not be forced to go through life wearing sackcloth and ashes. Without denying the lessons of history, we must finally step out of the shadows of the Third Reich. We need a normal, self-confident national identity."

Unlike Strauss, Kohl did not seek to relegate the Nazi period to the nation's attic. Kohl notes that throughout his years as chancellor he had to deal with the Holocaust on a daily basis. What Kohl objects to is what he terms the rather "strange picture" of Germany, particularly in the U.S. media, which seems to be stuck on the image of Germany as a nest of Nazis and anti-Semites. "Two-thirds of today's Germans weren't even born at the time of the war," he says.

Kohl himself was fifteen at the end of the war, not old enough to carry responsibility for it, but old enough to realize the disaster the Nazis had wrought on his country. He had seen the devastation, the charred bodies, and the maimed soldiers. Kohl's wife had also felt the effects of the war. Hannelore Renner, Kohl's high school sweetheart, whom he married in 1960, was the daughter of an engineer in Leipzig, the head of the team that developed the Panzer Faust, the Wehrmacht's hand-held tank killer. When the allied bombing of Leipzig became heavy, she was sent to the countryside as a nurse's helper and took care of the steady stream of wounded coming from the Eastern front. When the Soviets closed in on Germany from the East, the family went West, where she ended up in Ludwigshafen as a displaced person.

Even so, Kohl has insisted that Germany cannot forever remain paralyzed by the past. He asked his angst-ridden fellow Germans to be less uptight about themselves, to accept that they live in a normal democracy and have a right to feel proud about their country. In a 1987 election speech, Kohl addressed young voters: "Don't let yourselves be convinced by some jackass that patriotism has something to do with Nazism or National Socialism. Love of fatherland is a virtue that becomes every people, the Germans as well." Needless to say, he was immediately accused of having violated a taboo in order to please the far Right.

In his definitions, Kohl is very careful to distinguish between patriotism, which is a positive feeling, a belief that one's country has something to offer the world, and nationalism, which he calls "a kind of arrogance and megalomania."

According to Professor Christoph Stoelzl, director of the Deutsches Historisches Museum in Berlin, Kohl sees today's Germany not as some kind of misty Germanic nation of yore, living in Teutonic oak forests, but as a Western democratic country, a people who share a common past, present, and future. His is a common Western definition of the nation-state, the way an American, a Briton, or a Dane might define it. There is nothing chauvinist or aggressive about it, certainly nothing compared to the chauvinism, say, of France today, which is found both on the right and on the left of the political spectrum.

Still, Germany's past is undeniably a minefield of historical divisiveness. Kohl's 1984 visit to Israel illustrated the difficulty of negotiating this minefield. Then he talked of the "grace of a late birth" in a speech before the Israeli Knesset. Immediately, German magazines like *Der Spiegel* accused him of trying to duck German responsibility for the war. Kohl was also accused by the Left of seeking to portray Germany as a victim of Nazism, which was apparently miraculously freed from itself. Another way to read his comment on "the grace of a late birth" is as a bit of introspection, gratitude that he had not been faced with the wrenching moral dilemmas of his parents' generation.

Part of Kohl's dilemma as chancellor was how a nation deals not only with guilt but with defeat itself. Following World War II, the nations of Europe dealt with their war experiences differently. In France, for instance, passivity or collaboration with the German occupiers was the norm. General Charles de Gaulle, after a few years of collaborator-hunting in liberated France, decided that the country could not afford an extended period of internal strife and recrimination. "France needs all its sons and daughters," he insisted, and he allowed the myth to grow that all Frenchmen had somehow taken part in the resistance, even if some seemed to have operated under cover so deep that not even the resistance was aware of their contribution.

In Italy the easy solution was "Blame It on Benito"—Benito Mussolini. All responsibility for the war came to an end when he and his mistress were strung upside down from a lamp post in 1943. Instead, the Germans became the enemy. In Austria, where the population had joyously accepted the annexation to Germany in 1938, the Allies allowed the myth to develop that Austria had been Hitler's first victim, though a more willing victim would be hard to find. Indeed, the Austrians made the best Nazis of all. Hitler, Eichmann, and Kaltenbrunner were from Austria; 40 percent of the staff in the death camps were Austrian, as were 70 percent of Eichmann's staff.[1]

But in Germany, where it all started, there could be no luxury of pretense. Defeated and occupied, the Germans had to build a democratic society from scratch. Thus in the 1950s and 1960s the West Germans concentrated their energy on building prosperity and security. Questions of German national identity were dropped like hot coal, and over time Germans became more "European" than anybody else.

But by the 1980s the Kohl government came to realize that no other European country—neither Great Britain, nor France, nor Belgium, nor Italy—was prepared to give up its own national identity for the sake of the European idea. Germany is practically the only nation where the blue

European Union flag, with the circle of yellow stars, can actually be seen flying from private homes, rather than the national flag.[2]

Something else had happened in the meantime. A lack of direction, an insecurity, had developed among young Germans, manifesting itself in various ways: self-hatred, nihilism, cynicism, and rampant self-righteousness. The constant dwelling on the crimes of the Nazi past and the failure to provide positive national ideals had unfortunate effects fifty years after the end of the war.

When Americans, for instance, are asked the question in polls, "Are you proud to be an American?" 80 percent will answer yes. Put the same question to Germans, and a mere 15 percent will give an affirmative answer. This, in the opinion of psychologists and sociologists, is unhealthy. When traveling abroad, many young Germans often avoid mentioning that they are German. Says a close Kohl adviser, "There is no country in the world I know, and I travel a lot, where I found so much self-hatred as in Germany."

To some extent this is a legacy of the 1968 student revolt. The young men and women of that generation undertook a legitimate airing of the Nazi war past, which had been ignored by their parents' generation, but they did not end there. As noted above, they used the Nazi past as part of a deliberate effort to delegitimize the very foundations of modern German democracy.

Prominent left-wing intellectuals argued that German history and culture carried the latent seeds of disaster and were tainted for good. Ignoring positive aspects of German culture, they traced a direct line from Frederick the Great, through Bismarck and Kaiser Wilhelm, to Adolf Hitler. With Nazi crimes in the background, they argued, the most the postwar German state could hope for was a patriotism based on the values enshrined in the German constitution, a patriotism limited to the postwar era, a so-called constitutional patriotism.[3]

But in the view of many historians, this kind of minimalist constitutionalism advocated by the Left or the transnationalism of the European idea is not enough; it is too abstract to be the basis of a durable and politically stable state. People do not generally think in abstract terms when they think about their country, and one of the problems in West Germany was precisely this slightly antiseptic quality of life, the absence of symbols of national identity.

"Some measure of patriotism is necessary for a country," says Elizabeth Noelle-Neumann, founder of the Allensbach Institute. "National pride is insolubly connected with self-respect and a sense of purpose, direction, and worth, confidence in the institutions of your country, even confidence in your family. People who say they have no pride in their country also tend to express negative attitudes about other vital aspects of their life. People who have lost their value system are helpless, easy to sway in almost any direction."

Kohl, with his instinctive sense of what goes on in the population, knew that there was a vacuum in terms of German history and national identity, a vacuum that begged to be filled. The Weimar Republic, it should be remembered, also had its constitutional patriotism, which turned out to provide no emotional protection against the assault of communism, on the one hand, and Nazism, on the other.

The particularly German political confusion and psychological insecurity manifested themselves in a variety of ways. Consider, for instance, how a large segment of young German intellectuals fervently espoused the Palestinian cause. Some have seen this as an attempt to evade the German stigma by pointing to alleged Israeli mistreatment of Palestinians. The shelling of Beirut by Israeli forces in 1982—an attempt to force out the Palestinian Liberation Organization (PLO)—was suddenly compared to the destruction of the Warsaw Ghetto. As the *Green Calendar: An Almanac for Environmentalists* put it in 1983, "Jewish mercenaries are preparing for the 'final solution of the Palestinian question'.... The Nazi crimes and

neo-Nazi smears pale in significance beside the Zionist atroci-
ties.... Many people are asking themselves when this criminal
association known as Israel will finally die out."[4]

Similarly, the eagerness with which young Germans turned
against the United States during the Vietnam War can be traced
to the same roots, as can their anger against the United States
over the treatment of Indians and blacks, equating slavery with
the Holocaust, and their fury over the dropping of the nuclear
bomb. These young Germans were trying to obtain absolution
for the crimes of their fathers by convincing themselves that
other nations, the United States and Israel in particular, were
no better than Germany during World War II.

American readers should not be altogether unfamiliar with
these problems. The United States is a country founded on an
idea, and it is currently experiencing some of the same currents,
an attempt to deprive it of much of its concrete history and
replace it with vague notions of political correctness and multiculturalism. The result has been a loss of national cohesion in
the United States, a disdain for the shared symbols of the past.
The Founding Fathers have become irrelevant Dead European
White Males; instead of the Declaration of Independence and
the Constitution, history classes focus on slavery, the mistreatment of Native Americans, and so on. This attack on the country's historical heritage causes a steady erosion of the ties that
bind Americans together, and instead highlights the issues that
divide them. In the United States as in Germany, it takes more
than an idea to keep a nation together.

But with their historical background, can Germans have a
normal patriotism, as Kohl has insisted they must have? One of
the difficulties facing anyone trying to foster a feeling of
national pride in Germany is that, since World War II, the
German language itself has more or less been disqualified as a
vehicle for such sentiment, having been hijacked and debased
by the Nazis. Words cast long shadows in Germany.

The word "fatherland," for instance, which is a perfectly
normal word in other European countries, in German immedi-

ately conjures up visions of soldiers in steel helmets marching off in search of a little extra living space. Another is the word *Heimat*, one of Kohl's favorite words, which he uses with great frequency, an emotional word that means both one's home and where one feels spiritually at home. Unfortunately, this word was also heavily exploited by Nazi propaganda to create a sentimental patriotic ideal, a sense of belonging, a nostalgia for a better past.[5]

Kohl's course, which he followed consistently throughout his time in office, did not seek to diminish the past, but to confront it openly—and at the same time look to the future. Kohl attempted to reclaim Germany's past by stretching back before the Nazi period, but he never implied that Beethoven in any way made up for Hitler. Nor did he ever agree with revisionists who tried to equate the bombing of Dresden with the bombing of Coventry. The Nazi regime, he repeatedly stated, was solely responsible for World War II.

What Kohl did do was to try to emphasize what was good about Germany's past as well as what was bad, a challenging balancing act, to say the least. Germans do have great accomplishments. This is the land of Goethe, Schiller, and Beethoven, and of Frederick the Great. Besides being a skilled general, Frederick was a major Enlightenment figure, a musician and architect, a thinker who was passionate about freedom of expression and religious tolerance, a man who admitted political refugees from all over Europe—French Huguenots, Dutchmen, Poles, and Protestants. In fact, Frederick was much admired by contemporary philosophers, including Voltaire, who journeyed to his court to pay tribute and became a friend. In this sense, Frederick was the opposite of Hitler, the dictator, the man without law.

In a highly symbolic gesture, Kohl in 1991 presided over the reburial of Frederick the Great. As the Soviets advanced on Berlin in the last months of World War II, Frederick's remains were dug up and smuggled to the West, out of the Soviet zone. The reburial was a major occasion: A horse-drawn wagon carried the king's coffin from Potsdam to his castle, Sanssouci. The coffin, draped in Prussia's black and white colors, was placed on a silk-draped bier surrounded by an honor guard, and some eighty thousand people, Kohl among them, filed past during the day. At midnight the coffin was lowered into the ground. In accordance with the king's last wishes, he was laid to rest alongside his beloved whippets.

The occasion sparked protests that Kohl was celebrating Prussian militarism, and there were dire warnings that Prussians would start wearing monocles again and that ordinary people would have to step off the pavement into the gutter whenever meeting an officer. But most Germans saw this as a historical occasion, not a chauvinist relapse. Said Kohl before the event, "As with many great historical figures, the light and the dark sides of Frederick lie close together."

The same can be said about Bismarck, the Prussian junker who in the past century unified the kingdoms of Saxony, Bavaria, and Prussia—and a number of smaller principalities— to form modern Germany. By throwing Prussia into a series of wars (and winning them), ending with the victory over France in 1871, Bismarck managed to encourage a nationalism that united the German states under the banner of Emperor Wilhelm I. Wilhelm announced the birth of the Second German Reich in the Hall of Mirrors in Versailles in 1871.

Though he forged Germany out of "blood and steel," the Iron Chancellor was actually an extremely cautious man who warned his countrymen against overconfidence, concerned that Germany through arrogance would seek to dominate Europe, which he knew could have disastrous consequences. More than anything, he feared two-front wars, and a lot of his energy went into preventing them through a host of secret alliances. At the start of the twentieth century, the strutting chauvinism of Wilhelm II did precisely what Bismarck, by then long since dead, had feared: Germany became involved in a two-front war.[6]

Kohl's effort to return Germany to what he called "normalcy" or "mental balance" had its ups and downs and on occasion landed him in hot political waters. One success story was the symbolic meeting in September 1984 between Helmut Kohl and French President Francois Mitterrand at Verdun, where 650,000 soldiers had fallen during World War I. The photo of the two leaders holding hands is both somber and moving. The meeting was designed to parallel a similar meeting in 1963 between Konrad Adenauer and Charles de Gaulle, who attended Mass together at the Cathedral of Reims in celebration of a friendship treaty between Germany and France.

The 1982 Bitburg incident, on the other hand, is a prime example of how such things can go wrong. In an effort to highlight the good relations between Germany and the United States, Kohl invited President Reagan to join him at a wreath-laying ceremony at the Bitburg cemetery. Unfortunately, it turned out that the cemetery contained the graves of Waffen SS soldiers, which had been overlooked because they had been covered by snow. The blunder caused a huge controversy and a major embarrassment for the Reagan administration. The German Left accused Kohl of trying to rehabilitate the SS, and Reagan got caught in the middle and could not back out because it would mean the German chancellor would lose face. A visit to the concentration camp Bergen-Belsen was included to dampen the criticism, which it failed to do. What was meant as an opportunity to create goodwill ended as a public relations disaster.[7]

Another example of the perils of Kohl's balancing act was his trip to Poland in 1989; reconciliation along the French model was still very much on his mind. The plan had been to conduct a joint German–Polish Mass on the Annaberg, the site of fierce fighting between Polish and German forces in World War I. The program had to be rethought, however, after the Polish government of Tadeuz Maziowiecki, a fellow Catholic, let Kohl know that the gesture might be too risky. Fighting might even erupt between Poles, who had fought the Germans in World War II, and parts of the Silesian German minority, which might use the visit as an opportunity to demonstrate their

German roots. (The communists were busily fanning the flames.) Instead, the Mass was held at Kreisau, the center of the Prussian resistance (small as it was) to the Hitler regime.

Kohl's period in office also coincided with the so-called Historians Debate in the mid-1980s. The debate itself was a blunt response to the self-loathing imposed on Germans by the 1968 generation, and it escalated into a major fight over the nature of National Socialism, national identity, and the political agenda of the Kohl government itself.

The key figure here was Berlin philosopher Ernst Nolte. Nolte's essay, "The Past That Will Not Go Away," published in June 1986 in the conservative *Frankfurter Allgemeine Zeitung*, was the opening salvo in the dispute, which revolved around historical revisionism. One of the essential questions concerned the Holocaust, not whether it happened, but whether it was similar in kind to other twentieth-century terrors or entirely unique, an event without precedent or comparison.

In his article, Nolte disputed the uniqueness of the Holocaust and suggested that Joseph Stalin's death camps and the murder of millions of Kulaks were forerunners of Hitler's "final solution." He pointed to other murderous campaigns, such as the killing fields of Pol Pot's Khmer Rouge regime in Cambodia.[8]

Nolte argued that National Socialism could be seen as a bulwark against the terrors of Soviet communism and suggested outrageously that Hitler declared war on Stalin to protect the heritage of Western civilization. Even more bizarrely, he further cited as a reason for Hitler's hatred of the Jews a declaration made by Jewish leader Chaim Weizmann in September 1939 that Germany's Jews would fight on the side of England. Wrote Nolte, "This fact might justify the consequential thesis that Hitler was allowed to treat the German Jews as prisoners of war and by this means intern them." This is appalling: after six years of his people's systematic persecution by the Nazis, Weizmann's support for Britain could hardly be received as a surprising provocation.

Understandably, Nolte's arguments caused a storm of protest, both at home and abroad. Nolte and his supporters were accused of being engaged in an exercise in "comparative genocide," exhibiting the Genghis-Khan-was-not-a-gentleman-either syndrome. As one critic put it, determining which was worse, the "pastoral" extermination by the Khmer Rouge or the mechanized genocide of the Nazi death camps, is hardly a matter one can reduce to a question of efficiency.[9]

Nolte's critics, among them Marxist philosopher Juergen Habermas, argued that, by comparing the Holocaust to other massacres, Nolte downplayed the barbarity committed by Hitler. Nolte's arguments would make genocide, if not common, then at least a recurring twentieth-century phenomenon, thereby removing the specifically German stigma. Nolte's critics pointed out that the unique aspect of Hitler's programs was the plan to systematically wipe out a whole people, including the old, the infirm, women, children, and infants. Compared to this, Stalin's terror was more random and "democratic" in nature—everybody was scared stiff of Joe Stalin.

In Germany, Nolte's essay was immediately pounced on by the German Left, who declared it a sign of a new mood brought on by the Kohl government. In essence, they were trying to pin Nolte's views on Helmut Kohl. "It was argued that all this came about because there had been a change in government, because Kohl had called for a change in value consciousness," recalls Hermann Schaefer, director of the Haus der Geschichte in Bonn. "With Kohl's promise to pay more attention to moral values in Germany," notes Schaefer, this attempt to minimize the Holocaust was interpreted as "an alleged attempt on the chancellor's part to create a new historical consciousness, reflecting a more conservative strain of thought."

Anyone who has read Kohl's statements and speeches will realize that the connection simply wasn't there. Every speech he has made on the subject of the war has stressed the unique horror of the Holocaust and the need never to forget it. In April 1987, for instance, Kohl stated, "We know that the crime of the genocide in its cold, inhuman planning and deadly efficiency was unique in the history of mankind. We never want to forget the Nazi crimes. We shall resist every attempt to suppress or play them down."

Though Kohl was acutely aware of the pitfalls in his search for a sound German patriotism and of the attacks it exposed him to, he persevered. The danger of allowing this permanent German pessimism to go unaddressed was simply too great. Among some young Germans, the heavy emphasis on guilt could produce a backlash and make them seek refuge in extreme nationalism. Or it could result in anti-Americanism.

As part of his efforts to strengthen historical consciousness in Germany, two museum projects were close to Kohl's heart: the Haus der Geschichte in Bonn and the Deutsches Historisches Museum in Berlin. The former covers the period from 1945 to the present, and is situated on Konrad Adenauer Alle, a few minutes' walk from the Bundestag and the Chancellery, while the latter covers the history of the Germans in its entirety. It was originally meant to be built right next to the old Reichstag building close to the Wall, but after unification it was settled permanently in the former East German historical museum in the old armory on Unter Den Linden. A new wing designed by architect I.M. Pei, whom Kohl personally talked into taking on the project, will be added.

Talk of a museum devoted to the postwar German state had been going on in Bonn for quite a while. Former Bundespresident Walter Scheel from the Free Democrats complained in the 1970s of the danger that Germany was becoming a "country bereft of history" and spoke of the need for what he called an Exhibition on the Federal Republic in Bonn. Helmut Kohl took up the idea and made it one of his priorities. In his opening statement as chancellor on October 13, 1982, Kohl announced the founding of a museum that would document the development of postwar German democracy.

The idea behind the Haus Der Geschichte, according to its director Hermann Schaefer, was to recognize the historical significance of the first stable, democratic state in Germany, one that grew out of the death of Nazism. "It was one of the intentions of Kohl to make our children and grandchildren conscious of the roots of our democracy," says Schaefer.

As Schaefer points out, many young Germans take their freedoms and their material wealth for granted without realizing the foundation of laws and institutions upon which they rest. This was brought vividly home to him in 1980, when he and a group of West German students visited the grimy port city of Rostock in East Germany on a research trip. One evening the group chanced upon an East German merchant marine sailor in a town square, and a discussion ensued about conditions in the East and the West. The sailor explained how he had often been to port cities like Hamburg and Bremen and had thought of jumping ship. What had kept him from doing so was the fear that he might not be able to find a job.

"Certainly, you can find work in our country, but you won't be able to change anything politically," answered a young student from the West German group, implying that apart from the difference in material wealth, the two systems were pretty similar. "To me, that was so symptomatic of the way our young people are unaware of what our system has to offer," says Schaefer. Accordingly, the museum painstakingly describes the country's economic and political successes and the sacrifices it took to achieve them, starting with the so-called "rubble women" who painstakingly cleaned up the debris of Germany's bombed-out cities, brick by brick, stone by stone.

The idea behind the museum in Berlin, which Kohl threw his full support behind when negotiations had become deadlocked in the mid-1980s, was to give a comprehensive view of the history of the Germans and to come to an understanding of the common past of Germans and Europeans. According to its director Christoph Stoelzl, "German history is a mixture of dizzying heights and abject lows, of evolutions and breakdowns, of cuts and gaps, a hot and cold experience, the tremendous contributions of the Enlightenment age to European literature and culture on the good side, of neurosis, aggression, and the black hole of the Holocaust on the dark side."

From the beginning the two projects aroused fierce controversy. On the Left, they have been seen as part of a nefarious right-wing scheme to hijack history, to establish "a cultural hegemony." Kohl was accused of wanting to rewrite history and impose an official government interpretation of the past, of wanting to create a monument to the greater glory of himself and his party—"the World of Germany According to Helmut Kohl," as one newspaper headline derisively put it.

Another accusation was that by dedicating the Bonn museum to the development of the postwar German state, Kohl was somehow trying to sweep the Nazi past under the carpet. In the case of the museum in Berlin, the argument was made during the planning stages that, set in the context of the whole of German history, the Holocaust would somehow be seen as less important. Both points were picked up by the American media.

As for the charge that Kohl wanted to impose a single official view of history, says Schaefer, that is off the mark. "Kohl knows there is no government history and that history can be seen from different perspectives. For a historian like Kohl, this goes without saying." Besides, German law forbids the government from interfering with the academic freedom of museums.

What both museums seem to do is give a mainstream interpretation of history, and also point out where differences among historians do occur. But, says Stoelzl, "If you look at history through the values of the German constitution, which is similar to the American and the French, people of good will come to interpretations which are rather close to each other."

As for the charge that Kohl wanted to relegate the Holocaust to convenient forgetfulness, anybody who has actually seen the Bonn exhibition will know that this is simply not so. The first exhibit consists of an American jeep parked among the rubble, symbolizing the German defeat. But the museum does not actually start in 1945, but in a section called "the ever present past," which immediately backtracks to 1933 and explains how the catastrophe came to happen, how Hitler came to power. It also presents footage of concentration camp survivors and their personal histories.

The exhibit then demonstrates how the Nazi past has hit Germany in waves over the decades: in the 1950s section, it shows interviews with victims over the question of compensation. In the 1960s segment, it shows the Frankfurt trial of Auschwitz guards, which resulted in parliament prolonging the statute of limitations for Nazi crimes indefinitely.

It further shows intellectuals discussing the murder of the Jews, and why their parents' generation did not do more to resist Hitler. In the 1970s, it shows the reaction to the TV mini-series *Holocaust*, which had a deep emotional impact in Germany. And in the most recent past, it shows attacks by right-wing groups on asylum seekers. For a museum accused of wanting to paper over the past, it does a mighty poor job of it.

As for the Berlin museum, it seeks to anchor Germany firmly in European thought and points out the price Germany and the rest of Europe have paid whenever Germany has deviated from this path. The consequences have been exacerbated by the fact that Germany is more powerful than any other European state, and it has more neighbors. Whenever Germany has elected to follow a purely national policy, its neighbors have reacted by forming military alliances against it.

The museum makes clear the historical points at which things have gone wrong for Germany: the failure of the German states to democratize in 1848, due to resistance from the kings and the aristocracy; Germany's late emergence into nationhood; the attack on France in 1870 and the capture of Alsace-Lorraine, which, though not a strategic defeat, left deep wounds in the French psyche; and of course World War I, during which the German leadership cynically sacrificed hundreds of thousands of young men.

What the organizers of the museum do not buy into, however, is the Left's argument that German history is permanently sick and inevitably headed for catastrophe—the direct line from

Frederick the Great to Adolf Hitler thesis. It also points out that none of these events was predetermined.

As presented by the museum, Bismarck, for instance, was a ruthless politician who played a power game designed to give Germany prominence among the European countries. But it also shows the statesman who knew where to stop. Had World War I not been declared, the expected landslide election for the Social Democrats in 1917 would have brought further parliamentarization to Germany. And if the victorious allies after World War I had not imposed a punitive peace on Germany, Hitler might not have come to power. Only with Hitler's assumption of power in 1933 could war be said to have become inevitable.

Nor is it true that the Holocaust is somehow made to look smaller when viewed against the backdrop of the whole of German history. The opposite is the case. While national historical museums often run the risk of ending up as art galleries, glorified exhibitions of national treasures that engender a certain plump complacency in the visitor, encountering the shocking contrast between the Good Germany and the Bad Germany in the Berlin museum is meant to inspire the visitor to think, and to think hard.

Looking back over the documentation of the historians' debate of the mid-1980s, much of the agenda behind the attacks seems as much a concern with present-day politics as with the past. Many of the accusations were founded in the fear that these museums, particularly the one in Berlin, might represent an "aggressive challenge to the East German and the Soviet systems," "a threatening fist," as left-wingers put it, pointed in the direction of East Germany. The Berlin radical newspaper *TAZ* complained that the Bonn exhibition portrayed West Germany as a "superior civilization" when compared to East Germany.

All this became linked with the *Historikerstreit* and with the allegation that Kohl somehow shared the revisionist views of Ernst Nolte. Add to that Ronald Reagan's fight against total-

itarianism, and it became a giant right-wing conspiracy to desta-
bilize peace in Europe. Oliver Stone could not have thought up
a kookier argument.

In one sense the critics were right, of course. A museum
that would point out the human rights abuses of the East
German regime would be perceived by the Communist leaders
as a challenge, just as the very existence of a free West Berlin—
or the existence of the Federal Republic itself, for that matter—
represented a threat to their regime.

Today, at a time when Germany's neighbors worry that a
united Germany might be tempted to go its own way as in the
past, a museum like the one in Berlin, which shows the price
Germany has paid for going wrong in the past and which
emphasizes Germany's roots in Western thinking, can only be
helpful. Such efforts become even more important for the former East Germans, who were kept in historical ignorance by
the communist regime.

"The Americans have always complained that we Germans
did not love our institutions," says Karl Dietrich Bracher, the
grand old man of German contemporary history, who was
involved in organizing the Bonn project. "We loved our country,
our landscapes, our people of great genius, our culture, our
music, and so on. But not our democracy, not our parliament.
The museum's purpose is precisely to strengthen the tie
between the people and German democracy."

5

UNIFICATION

ONCE WHEN ASKED what was the most difficult thing to handle as prime minister, Britain's Harold Macmillan responded in his inimitably languid manner, "Events, my dear boy, events." The year 1989 was certainly a year of "events." When faced with events, the test for the statesman, as opposed to the mere politician, is not just to react, like a firefighter trying to control a blaze, but to get ahead of the events and shape them.

In his handling of German unification, Kohl proved that a determined individual can make a huge difference. This is eminently clear from Kohl's own account of the crucial years 1989–1990, *Ich wollte Deutschlands Einheit* (*"I Wanted Germany's Unity"*). The title loses something in translation; in German it suggests a strong element not only of wishing for it, but of willing it, too.

What makes Kohl's achievement even more remarkable is that he had to fight for unification under extreme time pressure on both the home front and the international front, and the two battles had to be fought simultaneously. If unification had been allowed to drag out, the window of opportunity might have closed.

"The inner and outer change of course that the Soviet leadership under Mikhail Gorbachev carried out from 1985 on was a crucial precondition for the revolutionary changes in Central and Eastern Europe between 1989 and 1991," says Helmut Kohl.

As 1989 progressed, the events in Eastern Europe picked up speed. It became a favorite sport among Eastern Europe's dissidents to quote Gorbachev and *Pravda* chapter and verse on the virtues of reform to their own nations' officials. In Poland, strikers had taken over the Lenin shipyard in Gdansk in the fall of 1988, barricading the entrances and forcing the Communist government to hold round-table talks with the protesters. Elections in June 1989 were won overwhelmingly by Solidarity members wherever they were allowed to compete. This resulted in a power-sharing arrangement between the labor union and the government. It was the first time ever a Communist government had given up its undisputed monopoly on power.

In Hungary, the most easy-going of the East European nations, reform started within the Communist Party itself. On June 28, 1989, in a symbolic gesture that was attended by Hungarian Foreign Minister Guyla Horn and Austrian Foreign Minister Alois Mock, Hungarian border guards started cutting the barbed wire along the border with Austria. The Iron Curtain that had divided Europe since the end of World War II was breached.

This news had an immediate and direct impact on East Germany. During the summer East Germans started out for Hungary, a traditional holiday spot, and before long reports had it that East Germans were crossing into Austria without the proper papers. By August their numbers were growing dramatically; the Hungarian government estimated the number of East Germans in the country at some ten thousand. And more in Romania and Bulgaria would be transiting to Hungary.

Initially, Hungarian border guards would stop East Germans who wanted to cross into Austria, and make an entry in their papers. This meant that they would be criminally prosecuted when they returned to East Germany. But then, increasingly, the border guards would just turn their backs and let the East Germans pass. In one celebrated instance, a crowd of nine hundred East Germans who had attended a picnic sponsored by Otto von Habsburg and Hungarian reformist leader Imre Pozgay literally waltzed over the border.[1]

The East German government protested to Budapest, citing the standing 1969 agreement between the two Warsaw Pact allies, which obligated the Hungarian government to return any East German citizen who tried to cross the Hungarian border into any third country without proper permission.

Predictably, the state-controlled East German media went ballistic, accusing the Hungarians of "gross interference in the internal affairs of the German Democratic Republic," and claiming that "the Hungarian action amounted to an organized trade in human beings under the guise of humanitarian solutions." The media also alleged that the refugees had been drugged by Western security services and were clearly leaving without knowing what they were doing.

Fanciful though it was, this reaction was rather unimaginative compared to the hyperventilating language the East Germans had used back in 1961, before the Berlin Wall went up. In those days, they had warned refugees exiting to the West through Berlin that East German women invariably would end up in brothels for Allied soldiers, while the men folk would go straight into the French Foreign Legion. More seriously, East German Minister for State Security Erich Mielke was said at one point to have contemplated the idea of sending East

German troops into Hungary in a coordinated operation with fellow hardline regimes in Czechoslovakia and Romania.[2]

The West Germans approached the Hungarians and asked them to help find as humane a solution as possible. Hungarian Foreign Minister Guyla Horn was said to have certain reservations, worrying that the Soviets would retaliate against him personally and demand his dismissal. It took the Hungarian ambassador to Germany, Istvan Horvath, three days to allay Horn's fears. Then the issue was submitted to the approval of Miklos Nemeth, the prime minister.

After intense deliberations, the Hungarians stated that they would like discussions with both the East Germans and the West Germans. The East Germans declined on the grounds that Erich Honecker was ill after a gall bladder operation, but the West Germans were eager to talk. Foreign Minister Horn and Prime Minister Nemeth flew to Bonn on August 25. On August 31 Horn flew to East Berlin to inform the East German government that, in the absence of constructive East German ideas, Hungary was forced to seek its own solution to the problem.

Clearly, the Hungarian government no longer regarded the 1969 agreement as valid in the changed atmosphere of the day, and the agreement was officially suspended on midnight of September 10. Camps were set up in Hungary, and reception centers for the refugees were established in Bavaria, which borders Austria. The East German government was allowed to send counselors to Hungary to try to talk their countrymen into going back to East Germany. But the counselors did not have much success. Television showed deliriously happy East Germans leaving by the busload, throwing their pitiful East German Marks out the window.[3]

Meanwhile, Kohl had to deal with a challenge from within his own party. Indeed, the year had not started well for Kohl. His party had lost important local elections, and the ritual cry had gone up again that it was time for Germany to elect a new chancellor. CDU members under the leadership of a Kohl protégé and friend, CDU General Secretary Heiner Geissler, were staging a revolt against his leadership, claiming that he had become autocratic in his control of the party and was using steamroller tactics against any political dissenters. Geissler wanted the party to move more to the left, become Greener, more fashionably multicultural. The revolt could hardly have come at a more inconvenient time.

To make matters worse, Kohl was also hit by a prostate condition, for which his surgeon recommended immediate surgery. Kohl knew that he had to face his challengers at a CDU party conference in Bremen on August 22, or his political career might be over. This he did, heavily fortified by pain-killers, and Geissler had to step down as party secretary. Again Kohl had displayed his iron determination to prevail. His surgery took place immediately afterwards.

An even trickier situation was developing in Czecho-slovakia. After East Germany, Czechoslovakia was generally regarded as the most repressive of the East European regimes; a permafrost had descended after the short Prague spring of 1968, which had been squashed by Warsaw Pact troops. The government was led by Milos Jakes, who had been dubbed a man for all seasons except spring. Like the East German government, Jakes regarded reform as anathema and (correctly) as a direct threat to his government's political survival. East Germans who had tried to cross the Czech border into Austria had been seized by border guards and beaten up. Some had drowned by trying to swim across the Danube, which around Bratislava forms the border between what is now Slovakia and Austria.

Slowly, East Germans started assembling in the West German embassy in Prague. Their tiny abandoned Trabant cars were found scattered all over the city. Within a few weeks, nearly five thousand East Germans occupied every inch of space at the embassy and its grounds—men, women, and children camping out in increasingly unsanitary conditions. Clearly, the situation was becoming intolerable. Pictures went around the world of Czechoslovakian police trying to drag away refugees desperately clinging to the fence surrounding the embassy—not the best publicity.

"The situation had become untenable for the GDR," recalls Rudolf Seiters, then the chief of staff at the Chancellery. The East German regime was under strong pressure on all fronts. They were under economic pressure, the country being on the verge of financial collapse. They were under pressure from the Soviets, whose foreign minister, Eduard Shevardnadze, argued that the refugees should be allowed to leave on humanitarian grounds. And they had the fortieth anniversary of the founding of the German Democratic Republic coming up.

On September 30 the Chancellery got word from the permanent East German representative in Bonn, Horst Neubauer, that, although the West Germans had no right to admit East German citizens to their embassies, the East German government was willing to let the refugees go in the interest of deescalating the situation. He now wanted to negotiate the procedure. In an attempt to save face and assert their sovereignty, the East Germans insisted that the refugees be put on sealed East German trains and travel over East German territory to West Germany. That way, the East German regime could pretend that they had been expelled as undesirables and antisocial elements from the workers' and farmers' paradise.

In order to reassure the refugees in the embassy, who were unlikely to believe the promises of their government, it was decided that they would be accompanied by officials from the West German government. Kohl had wanted to go to Prague himself but was denied permission by his doctor, as he was still recuperating from his prostate operation.

Instead, on September 30 Genscher and Seiters flew to Prague. Initially, Genscher had objected to being accompanied by anybody from the chancellor's office. But Kohl was not about to let him get away with that, given the momentous nature of the occasion. An agreement had been reached between the Foreign Ministry and the Chancellery that no advance notification would be made to the press. But the plane was hardly airborne before the announcement was made from the Foreign Ministry that Genscher was on his way to Prague—with no mention at all of the chancellor's office. In his memoirs, Kohl dryly remarks that the foreign minister seemed to claim all the laurels for himself.[4]

In what Genscher has since described as the greatest moment in his career, he and Seiters announced from the balcony of the West German embassy in Prague that a breakthrough had been achieved in the negotiations and that the refugees would be allowed to leave.

The East Germans' attempt to save face by using their own trains turned into another public relations disaster for the GDR. At stations throughout East Germany, police had to keep people back from trying to jump on the trains.

Equally unrealistic was the expectation of the Honecker government that this would end the situation. Recalls Seiters, "There was a vague hope on the part of the GDR that after the five thousand people had left the embassy, things would go back to normal. They did not, of course. A few days after the five thousand had left, the next five thousand refugees were already in the Prague embassy." To this add two thousand who were outside the embassy compound trying to get in, again with the Czech police using force to keep them away. And another three thousand to four thousand were on their way.

When Seiters tried to call Honecker about the situation, he was told that the East German leader was not available. He then called Czech Prime Minister Ladislav Adamec, who announced that the border to the GDR would be closed and the second wave of refugees permitted to go to West Germany. This ended the refugee crisis at the embassy in Prague. But for East Germany's leaders it was only the beginning.

Emboldened by events in Eastern Europe, an increasing number of East Germans started taking to the streets at home. There were mass demonstrations in East Berlin, Leipzig, and Dresden, most embarrassingly during Mikhail Gorbachev's visit to celebrate the East German state's fortieth anniversary on October 7. Despite police brutality, the demonstrations were always peaceful so as not to give the Communist government any excuse for a Tiananmen Square–type solution. Indeed, in Leipzig the hospitals had been filled with extra beds, and additional supplies of blood plasma had been requested in preparation for a crackdown.

It was clear that the East German authorities had no idea how to handle the situation. While Honecker wanted to clamp down, Gorbachev ruled this out during his visit. He told Honecker in a famous line, "We have to move with the times; otherwise life will punish us." He also informed members of the East German Politburo that it was time for the seventy-seven-year-old Honecker to go. On October 18 it became official. After eighteen years at the helm of one of the most repressive regimes on earth, Honecker would step down. The official reason for his resignation was poor health.

Honecker's successor was his party secretary for security, Egon Krenz, known as the man with the phoniest smile in East Germany and a severe drinking problem. Krenz was the consummate apparatchik, Honecker's right-hand man. Visiting China in the summer of 1989, he had complimented the Chinese leaders on the massacre of the demonstrating students in Tiananmen Square. Krenz emphasized that the East German constitution must be respected as well as its socialist foundation and that the East German press must not become "a forum for anarchistic and leaderless chattering." Later, Egon Krenz tried to take credit for the fact that no Tiananmen Square happened in East Germany. Krenz, however, was obviously a transitional figure. Recalls Seiters, who went to Berlin to get an impression of the new East German leader, "He was not convincing. He was not a credible figure."

The end came faster than anyone could have predicted. In a move designed to take the lid off the pressure, the GDR Politburo agreed to ease travel restrictions. On November 9 a clearly unprepared Gunther Schabowski, East Berlin's

Communist Party chief, who had been sent to announce that East Germans would henceforth be allowed to travel, was asked on live television when the new rules would take effect. "Now, I guess," was his hesitant reply. What he forgot to mention was that the East German authorities would still demand exit visas. The result was an immediate mass convergence at the checkpoints at the Wall. Border guards, who had no orders, simply let people through.

The Berlin Wall, for close to thirty years the visible symbol of Soviet repression in Europe, had been broken by an unprepared remark, probably the only unscripted remark in the history of East Germany. On November 13 the East German Volkskammer elected the alleged reformist Hans Modrow to be prime minister, someone who was portrayed as a mini-Gorbachev.

NO ONE COULD HAVE FORESEEN the fall of the Berlin Wall, and Helmut Kohl does not pretend to have done so either. Like other Western leaders, he had no forewarning that the East German regime would collapse so fast. In fact, on November 8, the day before the Wall fell, the chief of West German intelligence, Hans-Georg Wieck, assured the other guests at a Washington, D.C., party that he did not foresee unification within the next ten years.

On November 9, Kohl was on an official state visit to Poland. During the banquet at Radziwill Palace, he was told that hundreds of people were streaming through the checkpoints in Berlin. Back at his hotel, he watched the television images, and knew immediately that he had to be in Berlin. Kohl recalled how Adenauer in one of his few political missteps had failed to show up in Berlin when the Berlin Wall went up in 1961. To fail to be present when it came down was unthinkable.

The next morning, having laid a wreath at the monument to the 1943 Warsaw ghetto uprising, Kohl informed his Polish hosts that he had to leave for Germany at once. The trouble was how to get there in time. Kohl had hurriedly been scheduled to speak at a CDU rally at the Kaiser Wilhelm Gedaechtniskirche in Berlin, but soon learned that Berlin's Social Democratic Mayor Walter Momper, in what Kohl regards as a bit of political chicanery, had planned an earlier rally at the Schoeneberg City Hall. Kohl would have difficulty making it in time. Not to be at the city hall, however, would be to let the Social Democrats take all the credit, and Kohl was not about to let that happen.

The problem was that the German air force plane on which Kohl had arrived in Poland could not fly directly into Berlin from Warsaw. Owing to the access rules governing Berlin, the West German air force was allowed neither to traverse East German airspace nor to land in Berlin. Instead, the plane had to fly the long way, via Swedish airspace to Hamburg. Once Kohl was back in West Germany, U.S. Ambassador Vernon Walters put a U.S. air force jet at his disposal to go to Berlin. He got there at the very last moment.

On his arrival in Berlin at the Schoeneberg City Hall, Kohl found a solid phalanx of Social Democrat luminaries lined up waiting for him on the balcony, including the honorary chairman of the Social Democratic Party, Willy Brandt; Mayor Walter Momper; Hans-Jochen Vogel; and of course Kohl's ubiquitous foreign minister, Hans-Dietrich Genscher, who had managed to get there before him. To make matters worse, the crowd was hostile, with nary a Kohl supporter in sight. In this less-than-friendly setting, Kohl praised the peaceful nature of the East German demonstrators, noted the spirit of freedom enveloping the whole of Europe, and urged caution. "We want to pursue this course with warm hearts and cool heads," he said.

The occasion was certainly a tense moment, as Kohl describes it in his book. In the middle of the rally, there was an urgent telephone call for Kohl from Mikhail Gorbachev. In an attempt to get Soviet troops to intervene, the KGB and the Stasi, East Germany's secret police, collaborated in sending false messages to Gorbachev that the situation in Berlin was getting out of hand and that Soviet military installations were being attacked by angry crowds. Gorbachev wanted to know whether this was true.

Catcalls and rowdy behavior from a small group of hostile left-wing demonstrators interfered with the momentous force of the occasion. For Kohl to have left the balcony at this point and talked to Gorbachev would have looked as though the chancellor were giving in to demonstrators. Instead, one of Kohl's aides was instructed to tell Gorbachev that the reports were fabrications and to give him the chancellor's personal guarantee that no such attacks would take place. After that, Gorbachev made it clear to the East German rulers that there would be no Soviet interference.

Kohl cites the incident as a prime example of the importance of trust between statesmen. "To this day, I am very grateful to Gorbachev for not listening to the agitators," Kohl wrote in his memoirs.

Kohl's guarantees to Gorbachev, however, gave Chancellery officials sleepless nights. Recalls one adviser, "I can remember how nervous we were. For instance, someone whose father or son had been killed by Soviet soldiers might be tempted to hurl a Molotov cocktail. Or what if an agent provocateur had done it? That is what we feared the most." Fortunately, nothing of this kind happened, but the official is convinced that had Markus Wolf, head of the notorious East German espionage service, not retired by then, such incidents would have been orchestrated.

Another awkward moment came when Mayor Momper in his speech said that this was not a question of *Wiedervereiningung*, of reunification, but of a *Wiedersehen*, of the separated German people seeing each other again. He also spoke of the "people of the GDR," which was certainly not how Kohl felt about his fellow Germans living behind the Iron Curtain. The later rally, planned by Kohl's own party at the Kaiser Wilhelm Gedaechtniskirche, was a much more harmonious and dignified affair, but not deemed important enough to be carried on television.

That same evening, Kohl telephoned Margaret Thatcher to try to convey some of the joyous atmosphere in Berlin. Mrs. Thatcher was less than enthusiastic about the news.[5] Then he called George Bush, who responded in a much more positive manner. The next day phone calls followed to Francois Mitterrand and to Mikhail Gorbachev. Again, Kohl assured the Soviet leader that West Germany did not want chaos in East Germany.

But while Kohl did not want chaos to break out next door, neither did he want the status quo preserved. His efforts can best be described as moving the process along in the desired direction while trying to prevent it from spinning out of control.

Negotiations began immediately between the Kohl government and the new East German government of Hans Modrow. It soon became apparent to Kohl, however, that Modrow and his people were stalling to gain time and to obtain West German aid to keep them afloat economically. Meanwhile, they showed little evidence of being willing to undertake the needed political and economic reforms.

On November 28, 1989, Kohl stood up in the West German Bundestag to proclaim his Ten Point Plan for a unified Germany. His intention was to channel political developments. His vision as set out in the Ten Point Plan outlined steps to "develop confederative structures between the two states in Germany in order to create a federation, a federal order." This was to be a gradual and measured movement that would eventually lead to unification some time in the future. No specific timeframe was suggested.

Kohl's plan recommended setting up joint committees to coordinate efforts in the fields of the economy, crime prevention, and the environment. It stressed a major expansion of economic aid to East Germany provided, of course, that economic reform was initiated and free elections were held— elections that would include nonsocialist parties. The plan left contentious issues like membership in NATO and the Warsaw Pact untouched. It further stated that German unification should be achieved as part of European integration. The plan made unification synonymous with Kohl.

Throughout this crucial phase, Kohl made decisions only in the presence of a very small group of close advisers, who during weekends would send their proposals by courier to him in Oggersheim. In his memoirs, Kohl describes how the final draft of the Ten Point Plan was hammered out by his wife Hannelore on a portable typewriter, with Kohl himself adding the final touches. He did not even inform his own foreign minister and coalition partner, Hans-Dietrich Genscher, probably out of fear that the latter would create confusion with his usual talent for ambivalence and fuzziness. And, as Kohl later remarked, if he had relied on study groups and commissions, the Germans would probably still be waiting for unification.

The importance of the plan was that, for the first time, the goal of German unification was spelled out. It was a bold and risky move, and Kohl put all his prestige on the line. If the plan misfired, as it easily might have done, Kohl would be open to criticism at home and abroad. He could have been the German chancellor who upset stability in Europe.

The plan was immediately criticized abroad, mostly by the British and the French; Kohl was censured for not having informed his Allies before delivering it. President Bush had been informed a few hours in advance, and the European Allies were told while Kohl was actually delivering the speech. The British declared angrily that unification was not on the agenda, and French diplomats muttered about a "surprise attack."

The Bush White House was also somewhat annoyed, but it kept its misgivings to itself. Then–National Security Adviser Brent Scowcroft recalls, "We thought by that time that we had established a relationship of confidence, so he would be prepared to confide in us, and he did not. I was a little nervous from the standpoint that if the chancellor would not tell us ahead of time on a matter of this importance, then we would never know what he had in mind."[6]

Scowcroft suggested to President Bush that he bring this up when he talked to Kohl right after the speech. The president, however, chose not to, and immediately threw his support behind Kohl.

Kohl's answer to these objections is typically straight-forward. If he had revealed his intentions in advance there again would have been a thousand objections. Furthermore, the plan did not contain anything that had not been official NATO policy for decades.

PERHAPS THE MOST IMPORTANT point in the process of reunifi-cation, after the Berlin Wall fell on November 9, was Kohl's landing in Dresden airport on December 19. A huge throng of people had assembled to get a glimpse of the West German chancellor. Later in the evening, following a meeting with Hans Modrow to discuss the future of East Germany, Kohl took a short walk from the Hotel Bellevue in Dresden across Neumarkt Square to the ruins of the Frauenkirche. The church had been destroyed by Allied firebombing in World War II.

Along the way, the crowds were overwhelming. People carried the East German flag, but with the center cut out where the communist symbol of a hammer and a pair of compasses used to be. (Excepting that symbol, the East and West German flags were the same.) And the banners no longer sported the slogan *Wir sind das Volk* ("we are the people"), as they had in the early days of the uprising, but *Wir sind ein Volk* ("we are one people").

In front of the Frauenkirche, a small podium had been set up, and the television lights were on. The scene was reminis-cent of a nineteenth-century Caspar David Friedrich painting with the black and ruined church brightly lit against dark rolling clouds and a sky streaked with lavender and green. The crowd was going wild, chanting, "Helmut, Helmut." One of Kohl's major concerns was that the crowd should not become overenthusiastic and get out of control. He urged patience:

"When the historic moment allows it, let us have unity in our country."

As Kohl tells in his memoirs, one particular worry during that evening was that the crowd would break into the first stanza of the *Deutschlandslied*, the German national anthem. Since World War II, the first stanza, beginning *"Deutschland, Deutschland ueber Alles, ueber Alles in Der Welt,"* had not been sung because of its association with the war. Having East Germans sing about "Germany above all in the world" would have made an unfortunate impression abroad. (The German national anthem today starts with the third verse, which is about freedom.)

In order to prevent the crowd from singing that first stanza, Kohl's people frantically tried to arrange for a church cantor and a choir, who, at any sound of the *Deutschlandslied*, would lead the crowd immediately in singing a psalm instead. It turned out to be impossible to arrange this at such short notice, and fortunately it was not necessary. The true significance of these moments in Dresden, as Kohl describes it, was that for the first time he sensed that German unity could be brought about not in ten, five, or three years, but right away.

Indeed, it soon become clear that even Kohl's Ten Point Plan was being overtaken by events. Despite appeals from the Kohl and the Modrow governments, East Germans were still leaving in record numbers. The figure for January 1990 was 73,729. Some two thousand to three thousand people were leaving every day, and, just as before the construction of the Berlin Wall, it was the young and the best educated who voted with their feet. Whole sectors of East German society, like industry and hospitals, were left undermanned; in some areas, mail delivery stopped.

To provide essential services, East German authorities called on conscripts from the military, but the society was hemorrhaging. It became clear that the Modrow delegation that arrived in Bonn on February 13 for discussion had only paid lip service to the idea of a joint venture; it had done nothing to introduce property rights to allow profits to leave East Germany.

Indeed, Communist ineptitude in handling the situation was staggering. The disbanding of East Germany's feared secret police, the Stasi, was proceeding very slowly. And it did not help when somebody in the party suggested the creation of a new security service to protect the country from alleged neo-Nazi activity. (Curiously, Nazi graffiti had suddenly appeared on the Soviet World War II memorial, which was normally heavily guarded.) Understandably, many concluded that the Communists might try to grab power again.

The other factor was sheer impatience on the part of the East Germans, who felt they had been paying the price for losing World War II for more than forty years. They wanted freedom—now.

Meanwhile, the pressures on the Kohl government for decisive action were mounting in West Germany itself, where the continuing exodus was giving rise to different concerns. The Kohl government all along wanted to avoid a "reunification on West German soil," as the phrase had it, which would worsen an already serious housing shortage and stretch the social welfare system beyond the limit.

East Germans, who were granted automatic citizenship and became eligible for the same social benefits as West Germans, were filling up empty army barracks, campgrounds, and school gymnasiums. Some were even lodged in the sleazy hotels in Hamburg's Reperbahn red-light district, where business was slow because of concerns about AIDS. In one resettlement center in Bremen, eighty-seven men had to share one, hopefully sturdy toilet. This type of situation tends to make Germans very unhappy.

Kohl realized that another grand gesture was needed. In order to prevent the people of Leipzig from coming to the Deutsche Mark, the Deutsche Mark had to be brought to them. To send a strong signal and to restore public confidence, on February 6 Kohl decided to offer the East Germans the ultimate gift: the German Mark. As Kohl writes in his book, he was aware that this was an unprecedented decision and one that economists would find controversial: "I was of course aware that this was a most unusual offer without precedents, one that you could not read about in the economic textbooks. As one of the most stable currencies in the world, the Deutsche Mark was the foundation of our prosperity. We had to be careful how we dealt with it. Even so, I considered social stability in the GDR a correct priority. What we did not know at the time, of course, was the catastrophic state of the GDR economy."[7]

Some 180 billion Ost Marks had to be replaced. Various possibilities had been discussed. In the old days, before travel restrictions were lifted, one Ost Mark officially equaled one West German Deutsche Mark. On the black market at the time, however, the ratio was 10:1. First there was talk of a 5:1 exchange rate, then a 2:1, and finally a 1:1 rate. The Kohl government was particularly concerned about fears among East Germans about the value of their savings (estimated at the time to be around ten thousand Ost Marks per person).[8]

Fearing that their nest eggs would vanish into thin air, East German savers started to withdraw their money from the banks and spend it on anything tangible, from clunky Czechoslovakian refrigerators to Meissen porcelain figures. It was therefore regarded as crucial to assure the East Germans that their savings, pensions, and social benefits would be safeguarded.

A new cabinet committee on unity, headed by the chancellor, had been set up to deal with adopting a single currency, as well as with the political, legal, and economic aspects of unification. Because of the rapid deterioration of the situation, the date for free elections in East Germany, first set for May 16, had to be moved forward to March 18.

But while trying to give the East Germans hope for the future, the Kohl government continued to refuse substantial aid to the Modrow government before the election, so as not to prop up the communists. Kohl insisted that all serious discussion would have to wait until East Germany had a democratically elected government. Thus, when Modrow asked for $9 billion in financial aid, a so-called contribution to solidarity, the Kohl government turned down the request on the grounds that it was futile to fund a system that still refused to make fundamental changes.

As could perhaps be expected, segments of the West German press complained how the Mighty Kohl was riding roughshod over Modrow, this obviously undernourished and modest little man. The Kohl government did, however, approve $3.6 billion in carefully earmarked aid for immediate infrastructure upgrades such as road repair and a new telephone system, but none of that money would be at the Communists' disposal.

As for the political unification of the country, the question facing Kohl was precisely how this should be done. How could one merge what for more than forty years had been two separate states? Serious constitutional questions were involved. Basically, there were two options, a simple one and a complicated one. The simple one, which would speed up the process of monetary union and economic reform, was for the East to adopt the entire corpus of West German law. Under Article 23 of the West German constitution, the Basic Law, parts of Germany outside the Federal Republic could accede to the Basic Law without further ado.

The second, more complicated solution—which could have involved years of legalistic wrangling—would be to write a whole new charter. This approach, needless to say, was initially favored by the East German government—and by the West German Social Democrats, who protested that Bonn could not just take over East Germany.

But as Kohl explains in his book, this argument was rejected for a number of reasons. One was the time pressure. Such a revision would take at least two years to accomplish, and Kohl repeatedly compared his situation to that of a farmer who has to get his harvest in before a thunderstorm breaks loose. He knew that he did not have the luxury of time.

That Kohl was right in choosing the quick way to unification was amply demonstrated by the coup attempt against Mikhail Gorbachev in August 1991, when a group of hardline conspirators seized the Kremlin and arrested Gorbachev and his family at their dacha on the Black Sea. The coup was badly bungled, but it did indicate the dangerous instability within the Soviet Union.

Equally important, as Kohl points out in his book, the West German republic, founded on the ashes of World War II, had been the creation of men and women who had been through extraordinary tests. They had survived the war and in many cases Nazi persecution, imprisonment, and concentration camps. Some had gone into exile. After the war, they had worked with the Western Allies to create a new Germany. Though of differing political persuasions, they had a shared vision of what the country should be.

Kohl doubted that a similar vision and commitment could be found in today's Germany after decades of life in a prosperous welfare state, and after the divisions caused by the youth movement and the Cold War. He thought it would be unwise to throw away a constitution that had proved its worth for more than forty-one years, especially since Germany had thrown away so many constitutions in the past. Rather, Kohl saw it as a ploy on the part of those who had never liked the Federal Republic to fundamentally alter the nature of the country, a bid to create a more collectivist, neutral Germany.

From the very beginning, Kohl's major problem was the opposition Social Democrats, who resisted the idea of unification. For years, the Social Democrats had been trying to cozy up to the East German regime. They had conducted their own party-to-party relations with the governing East German Socialist Unity Party. Indeed, they had had their own foreign policy; they had signed agreements on nuclear and chemical weapons free zones with the East German government, disregarding the government in Bonn. In other words, they had behaved like a classic example of a disloyal opposition.

Federal states run by the Social Democrats even refused to give contributions to the running of the Salzgitter Archive, which recorded all incidents involving the shooting of East German escapees by border guards, as well as other human rights crimes of the East German regime. Needless to say, the East German regime was forever pressing to have this archive closed down. In his memoirs, Kohl takes a dim view of these Social Democratic positions.

At the same time, while hobnobbing with the East German bigwigs for years, the Social Democrats had studiously avoided any kind of contact with ordinary East German people. Shortly before the fall of the Wall, East German union boss Harry Tish was an honored guest of the Social Democrats (the East German unions were, of course, run by the state, as in other communist countries). So when the Wall came down in November 1989 and the refugees from the East really started to pour in, the Social Democrats were caught by surprise and were at a total loss as to which course to follow.

First, they thought a permanent solution would be two federated states. Not prepared for the collapse, they hoped it was possible to stabilize a new kind of Social Democratic East Germany. Thus, in the beginning, the Social Democrats were in favor of lavish credits for East Germany without any strings or preconditions attached, which would have been prohibitively expensive and would have drawn out the end-game.

"THE WHOLE YEAR OF 1990 was a campaign year," recalls Michael Roik, one of Kohl's key campaign strategists in the Chancellery. It started with Volkskammer, that is, with parliamentary elections in the still existing East Germany. State elections in West Germany followed in the autumn, and the all-German national elections came in December 1990.

The first and only free elections in the history of East Germany were held on March 18, 1990. The Social Democrats were widely favored to win since this was considered old Social Democratic territory, going back to the time of the

Weimar Republic. Some preelection polls gave the Social Democrats 53 percent of the vote, and they were hard at work organizing.

Pessimism extended far into the ranks of Kohl's closest advisers. Recalls one of them, "Everybody expected the Social Democrats to be victorious in the Volkskammer elections, and we were all convinced that, after the German Bundestag elections, Germany would be Red for decades because Saxony and Thuringia were the old bulwarks of Social Democracy." Kohl took the opinion poll jitters with great calm. "You people do not know how ordinary people think and feel. I do."

Accordingly, Kohl threw himself into the election with customary gusto. Priority one was to set up a party organization in East Germany. Here Kohl had to rely on the East German version of the CDU, which had been part of the East German power structure and was therefore tainted. However, with the dizzying speed of developments, the West German CDU found it had no choice. To better its chances of electoral success, the CDU entered an alliance with two other groupings, the *Demokratischen Aufbruch* (Democratic Awakening) and *Deutsche Soziale Union*, to form the *Allianz fuer Deutschland*— the Alliance for Germany. This was all Kohl's brainchild, even down to selecting the name.

The partnership was not without its problems, since these were new and untested politicians. The chairman of the new CDU-East, Lothar de Maizière, for instance, had made some rather peculiar statements ten days after the fall of the Wall. He had announced in an interview that he held socialism to be one of the most beautiful visions of human thought and that the demand for democracy did not mean a demand for getting rid of socialism. He had also opined that German unity was not the theme of the hour, but something his children or grandchildren would experience. These comments were not exactly helpful and led to a certain skepticism in the Chancellery as to his usefulness. There was also a fair amount of infighting among East German politicians over who was going to have what responsibilities.

In other words, it soon became clear that all the organizational efforts had to come from the West, as the Eastern politicians obviously had no experience with democratic politics or electoral campaigns. That meant that all the leaflets, posters, and newspapers spelling out the program for the Alliance for Germany and explaining the rudiments of the market economy had to be produced in the West.

In the election, Kohl, the old campaign worker who as a teenager had put up posters himself in hard-to-reach places (and undoubtedly had torn down a few of the opponents') took a keen interest in the minutest details, such as the kind of glue used for the posters in the East—he wondered whether it was strong enough. Accordingly, campaign workers had to bring a pot of glue to the Kanzleramt and demonstrate to the chancellor that the glue indeed was up to the task.[9]

No weapon in politics is stronger than turning an opponent's own words against him. Particularly effective was a pamphlet produced by the CDU filled with statements from leading Social Democrats on the subject of unification. It reminded everybody of Social Democratic Party elder Egon Bahr's 1988 statements that had dismissed all talk about unification as "Sunday speeches" and sheer "political pollution," "objective and subjective hypocrisy that poison us and others."

The pamphlet also reprinted photographs of Social Democratic leader Oskar Lafontaine with his great friend Honecker, which had graced the front page of the Communist Party organ *Neues Deutschland* a record five times. There was also Lafontaine's repeated calls for the recognition of East German citizenship.

Kohl's great advantage, says Michael Roik, was that "in contrast to other people, he did not have to rewrite the speeches he had been giving in the sixties, seventies, and eighties." Kohl had had a coherent position on East Germany all the way through.

Six rallies were planned for Kohl across East Germany—at Erfurt in Thuringia, Chemnitz in Saxony, Magdeburg in Saxony-Anhalt, Rostock in Mecklenburg-West Pomerania,

Cottbus in Brandenburg, and Leipzig in Saxony. The first of these rallies was on February 20 in Erfurt in the south. "It was a crucial event, because we had no experience running a campaign in a country in which people had suffered forty years of dictatorship. For others, it went all the way back to 1933," says Roik.

Roik accompanied the chancellor in his car, and they were not sure what to expect. There might be only five thousand people to see Kohl and ten thousand people from the Socialist Union Party, who would be well organized to protest. But the tense mood in the car brightened considerably when on the motorway to Erfurt they saw people on the bridges waving welcome banners and slogans.

When asked how many people might be expected to turn up, the accompanying escort of East German security people had suggested perhaps a few thousand, but when Kohl arrived, the city square in front of the old church was filled to the edges with 150,000 people. Some had punched holes in the roof of an adjacent house to get a look at the chancellor. It took Kohl and his entourage thirty minutes just to get from their cars to the podium.

The scene was repeated in Rostock. Occasionally, the German habit of punctuality could be a bit unnerving. "Sometimes fifteen minutes before the rally started, the meeting place was quite empty," recalls Roik, "and we were a bit nervous whether they would show up." They did. On the dot. The East German attitude was that if the chancellor was set to appear at five, then five would be the time to show up.

During the six meetings, Kohl appeared before at least 1.2 million East Germans—that is, every tenth East German voter saw him in person. At the final rally in Leipzig, Kohl addressed some 300,000 people in front of the opera house, the biggest rally since the end of World War II.[10]

One potential embarrassment occurred just days before the election: A top official in the CDU-East, Wolfgang Schnur, was found to have Stasi connections and had to step down. Social

Democrats scornfully pointed out that the CDU-East was just part of the old power structure. Kohl's people dealt with the situation immediately and contained the damage. "It was not so great a shock to them as to us, perhaps," says Roik. "They had known the regime for a long time." Just after the election, the Social Democratic Party–East leader also had to drop out for similar connections.

Until the very end, the papers predicted a Social Democratic victory. But this time, it was a distinct advantage to campaign for a party that did not have the word "Social" in its name. The Social Democrats received only 21.7 percent of the vote, while the Alliance for Germany got 47.7 percent. Asked in the exit polls why they voted as they had, the East Germans said they had voted for the chancellor. The intellectuals from Neues Forum, who had been in the forefront of the revolution but who wanted a socialist state based on a "third way" between communism and capitalism, garnered even less of the vote.

For reasons of unity, a grand coalition of all the democratic parties was thought preferable, and such a one was duly formed under Lothar de Maizière. On April 12 the Volkskammer voted in favor of the accession of the five New Laender to West Germany through the Basic Law's Article 23.

GERMAN UNIFICATION ITSELF took place on October 3. The day before, Kohl had flown into Berlin with his wife and close associates, including Genscher. At a concert at Schauspielhaus on the Gendarmanmarkt, East German conductor Kurt Masur directed the Leipzig Gewandhaus Orchestra in the "Ode to Joy," the final movement of Beethoven's Ninth Symphony. For the occasion, the word "Freude," joy, had been replaced with "Freiheit," freedom. At midnight the German flag was raised, fireworks lit the sky, and the crowds broke into the German anthem.[11]

Throughout this fourteen-month period—from the flight of the East Germans in the summer of 1989 to the day of German reunification on October 3, 1990—Kohl and his men were subjected to uncommon pressures. Says former Kohl adviser Horst Teltschik, "What kept us going was the excitement, the feeling that we were living in a historic moment which we could shape and settle peacefully." Occasionally, Kohl would grouse about the workload, chewing up his advisers, wondering aloud how previous chancellors had organized their work, and complaining that everything rested on his shoulders. To which Teltschik would calmly respond that Kohl would not have had it any other way.[12]

As late as two months after Unification Day, the Social Democrats were still conducting a rearguard action against Kohl's policies, clearly out of touch with the prevailing popular mood. One of the few Social Democrats who grasped intuitively what was about to happen was Willy Brandt. Kohl is kind to Brandt in his book, seeing him as the only member of the Social Democratic leadership with a desire for unification. But Brandt had given up hope of unification.[13]

The Social Democrats' candidate in December's all-German elections, Oskar Lafontaine, was his usual quick-witted and abrasive self. But next to Kohl, Lafontaine with his fancy floral tie looked about as statesmanlike as Roman Polanski. Lafontaine lacked the required gravitas for the time, allowing himself on one occasion to be introduced by a punk rock group named Fury in the Slaughterhouse (the name alone would have a slightly unsettling effect on the German middle-class voters, who much prefer the oom-pah-pah sound of the traditional brass band). Not even the sympathy engendered by a knife attack by a deranged woman, who stabbed Lafontaine in the neck at a rally, had any effect.

Lafontaine kept prattling about post-material values and "an ecological modernization of industrial society," which may have sounded fine in the West, which had enjoyed material prosperity for forty years, but for the former East Germans—who had gone without the simplest material comforts for decades and who had to wait seventeen years for a plastic Trabant car—it was not the cleverest tactic. At the time, the former East Germans were understandably the most materialistic people on earth.

In the end, Lafontaine had been forced to accept unity, but most had the feeling it was a sour duty for him. In fact, he was practicing the ancient political art of speaking out of both sides of his mouth. While he was telling the East Germans that they should be asking for more money and that the government was not doing enough for them, he was telling the West Germans that unification was going to be an extremely costly affair.

Lafontaine had also insisted that a unified Germany could not be a member of NATO. In an instance of political payback, Helmut Schmidt, no doubt recalling Lafontaine's comment that he was fit to run a concentration camp, stated that his fellow Social Democrat did not deserve to win. "If we Germans fail to craft lasting good fortune from the windfall of unification, then we court our own damnation."[14]

The Germans showed their gratitude by giving the CDU three election victories in one year—the East German Volkskammer elections, local state elections in West Germany in the autumn, and the all-German parliamentary elections, which Kohl won handily. It was the culmination of an incredibly intense year, one that earned Kohl a place among the first rank of European statesmen.

6

UNIFICATION
AND THE ALLIES

GERMAN UNIFICATION was not just a domestic issue, but one that also involved the whole system of strategic alliances in Europe. Helmut Kohl had to deal with the reaction of Germany's European allies and neighbors, as well as the United States and the Soviet Union. This was no less challenging than controlling domestic developments.

Almost half a century after World War II, many Europeans were still concerned about the prospect of a reunited Germany of some eighty million people, which would once again be the dominant power on the Continent. For the Soviet Union, it was a question of giving up East Germany, its most prized vassal state. And for the United States there was concern over whether Germany—NATO's key country, where 250,000 American troops were stationed, along with American nuclear weapons—would remain within the alliance. A reunited but neutral Germany, maneuvering between East and West, would be a sure recipe for trouble in Europe.

In early 1990 things were moving fast. Kohl had announced his Ten Point Plan the previous November 28, and in February his working group on *Deutschlandspolitik* had started to meet in Bonn. He had already produced plans for an economic and monetary union.

The view in Germany had always been that the key to reunification lay in Moscow. On February 10 Kohl and Genscher traveled to Moscow to meet with Mikhail Gorbachev. There, they received his commitment in principle to respect the decision made by the Germans themselves. "The Germans must decide how to solve the question of German unity," Gorbachev told them. When Kohl returned triumphantly to Bonn, he announced he had received "the green light" from Gorbachev on unification. In principle, Gorbachev might have given his assent to unification, but the question remained: under what conditions?

To provide a framework for negotiations between NATO and the Warsaw Pact, U.S. Secretary of State James Baker had come up with a formula for discussing the external aspects of unification in the so-called Two Plus Four model, which involved the two Germanies, plus the four Allied victors of World War II—the United States, Britain, France, and the Soviet Union.

The Two Plus Four idea was launched at a crucial NATO meeting on February 13, 1990, in Ottawa. The meeting had initially been called to discuss Open Skies agreements between NATO countries and the Warsaw Pact, allowing flying over each other's territories, but turned into a forum for intense debate over Germany's future.[1]

In the beginning, the Soviets contended that German unification could happen only if Germany became neutral; Gorbachev stuck closely to the old line that the Federal Republic of Germany should act as a bridge between East and West.

But at some point Gorbachev came to the conclusion that he could not afford to keep his external empire and the Soviet Union going at the same time; one had to be sacrificed to preserve the other, however painful this would be. Giving up East Germany, the prize of World War II, was risky for Gorbachev's own career because much of the military brass would be opposed. Resorting to military means in Europe, however, would cut off the economic assistance from the West that he so desperately needed. The question for Gorbachev was how to get the best deal possible.[2]

Kohl and Gorbachev had had some rocky moments in the past. In a 1986 interview with *Newsweek*, at a time when everybody was trying to judge what the new Soviet leader was up to, Kohl had compared Gorbachev's public relations skills to those of Nazi propaganda chief Joseph Goebbels, a remark he had to apologize for. By 1988, having changed his mind about the Soviet leader's seriousness on domestic reform, Kohl had started to support Gorbachev's economic experiments.

At an early stage, it had become clear to Kohl's men that Moscow had no clear idea how to deal with the German question. Says Kohl's national security adviser at the time, Horst Teltschik, "If you follow the statements of Gorbachev, Shevardnadze, and other Soviet leaders, you recognize that there was a discussion going on over what to do. There were no final decisions, neither positive nor negative, which was good for us. As long as the discussion in Moscow was going on, there was a chance of a solution."

Thus there were notable differences in tone between the statements of Gorbachev and Shevardnadze. Recalls Teltschik, "If one reads Foreign Minister Shevardnadze's announcements, they were much tougher than everybody else's." Shevardnadze's advisers, whom Kohl's men referred to as the Soviet Foreign Ministry's "German mafia," consisted of hardliners like Valentin Falin and Alexander Bondarenko, old hands who had served as advisers to Shevardnadze's predecessor Andrei Gromyko, Old Iron Pants himself, who knew only one word and that was

"*Nyet.*" Therefore, Teltschik counseled that everyone pay more attention to the statements coming from Gorbachev and less to Shevardnadze's.

On Gorbachev's part, it was a question of a gradual retreat, with Shevardnadze fighting a rearguard action at every turn. Among other things, Shevardnadze accused Kohl of forcing the issue by playing "rapid chess," a rather ironic complaint coming from the Soviet side, whose people were supposed to be masters at the chessboard. "Some politicians would like to play a political game of rapid chess with a five-minute time limit," Shevardnadze complained in a speech to the Canadian parliament on March 16, 1990. "Is this a sensible thing to do when peace and the security of nations... are at stake?"

Gorbachev's retreat on the NATO question went through a number of stages in May and June of 1990, starting with the immutable declaration that only a neutral Germany could gain reunification. Then the Soviet position became that the Western part of Germany could remain a member of NATO but that the Eastern part would remain in the Warsaw Pact. (This, of course, was a bit unrealistic given that the Warsaw Pact was dissolving before his very eyes. Never having been a voluntary club, its members were stumbling over each other to leave and join NATO.) The next fall-back position was that a unified Germany would be allowed to join NATO only after five years—after U.S. and Soviet troops had withdrawn. Without the American presence, however, there would not have been much of a NATO to join. Finally, it came down to one thing: money—how much the Germans were willing to pay for their unification.

It was during a later trip to the Soviet Union, starting July 14, that Kohl got the go-ahead for a unified Germany to remain within NATO. Kohl spent one day in Moscow and two days with Gorbachev at the resort spa of Zheleznovodsk in the Caucasus mountains. Here the two sweater-clad leaders hammered out the last details and removed the final obstacles to a unified Germany by year's end. Kohl received Gorbachev's promise that a united Germany was free to join any alliance of its choice.

At the "sweater summit," as it came to be known, Kohl's trusty cardigan became a potent symbol, expressing more than any grand statement could have ever done; it conveyed the image of the nonthreatening German as the leader of a comfortable and civil society.[3]

Always the spoilsport, Genscher was ready with a couple of sour comments, even on this occasion. In the evening, Kohl and Genscher withdrew to their separate cottages. Genscher demonstratively ordered beer, as if to drink champagne would somehow be "undignified." Champagne was something one drank only after an election, he noted. This was of course a thinly veiled criticism that Kohl was engaging in triumphalism. When Kohl the next day forced Genscher to accept a glass of wine and drink a toast to Germany in front of the photographers, Genscher's comment was, "When forced by circumstances, even the Devil drinks wine."[4]

The deal Kohl struck with the Soviets included the following: The Soviets would pull out of East Germany over a four-year period, and a united Germany would remain a member of NATO. In return, Germany would continue its voluntary renunciation of nuclear, chemical, and biological weapons. Its armed forces would be limited to 370,000 (down from 490,000). Germany would help finance Gorbachev's restructuring of the Soviet economy and give large contributions to the construction of housing for the returning Soviet troops who had been stationed in East Germany, 385,000 in all.[5]

Right up to the last minute, the Soviets kept upping the price. Kohl initially thought he had an agreement to pay eight billion Deutsche Marks, only to be presented with new demands of sixteen billion and then of eighteen billion, until the figure was finally settled at twelve billion Marks. Much of it was, of course, wasted; it simply disappeared, skimmed away by corrupt Soviet officials. And this aid was only part of a total amount of some seventy billion Marks (about $45 billion) that the Germans have pumped into the former Soviet Union in connection with unification—not exactly the Louisiana Purchase, but still a very good deal.[6]

Throughout, dealing with Gorbachev was tricky. He may have held all the low cards, but he did have extremely broad popular appeal in the West. The ongoing danger was that Gorbachev might prevail with his megaphone diplomacy; he was literally coming out with a new proposal every second day. An offer of quick unification in return for German neutrality, Kohl notes in his book, would be attractive to many Germans, both East and West.[7]

Before setting off for his final July visit to Moscow and the Caucasus, Kohl had informed U.S. Ambassador Vernon Walters that Gorbachev had invited him to come to talk things over regarding NATO. Walters recalls that Kohl told Gorbachev before leaving, "Mr. Secretary General, I know what you are going to offer me. You are going to offer me German unity in return for Germany leaving NATO. We will not buy German unity at that price because we are going to get it anyway."

The Soviet Union was not the only problem for Kohl, however. Despite the West's commitment to German unification, which had been a stated goal since the creation of NATO, some of Germany's alliance partners seemed distinctly less than enthusiastic at the prospect when the possibility became real. As historian Alfred Grosser once remarked, "The Western Allies only want reunification as long as it is impossible."

The sharpest criticism of unification emerged in Britain. British tabloids drew parallels to Hitler's march into the Ruhr district in 1936, and warned that this was the last chance to stop a new catastrophe.

Which was exactly what Margaret Thatcher tried to do. The Kohl–Thatcher relationship had never been exactly cordial. Mrs. Thatcher, who prided herself on being able to make up her mind about people in five minutes, had never taken to Helmut Kohl. Legend has it that once, in 1984, when Kohl was on one of his slimming-down visits to Austria, Mrs. Thatcher was staying with the British consul in Salzburg. Grasping this remarkable opportunity, she arranged for a two-hour meeting with the German chancellor. Mrs. Thatcher, as may be recalled, has a fondness for the monologue, and proceeded to lecture Kohl on what's what in the world, with an interpreter struggling to keep up.

One hour into the meeting, Kohl suddenly excused himself, muttering that affairs of state demanded his urgent attention, whereupon he quickly departed. A surprised Mrs. Thatcher was left behind with nothing much else to do than to go on a shopping expedition in Salzburg. Here, in a sidewalk cafe, she suddenly spotted the chancellor leisurely reading the newspaper while enjoying an enormous cream pastry and a cup of coffee.[8] British officials have denied the incident ever took place, dismissing it as pure myth. But one close Kohl adviser says with a glint in his eye, "It could have happened."

What is indisputable is that relations were cool between the leaders of England and Germany. The words used to describe it ranged from "indifferent" and "businesslike" to the more ominous "intense, full, and frank," which normally meant that Mrs. Thatcher was on the warpath.

In his memoirs, Kohl describes one of his meetings with the Iron Lady: "She could be exceedingly friendly when one was invited to her country seat. She set great store on always pouring out the tea herself. But from one moment to the next she was suddenly prime minister again and kept her distance. If the atmosphere got too frosty, she picked up the teapot and poured out again. It took me some time to understand that she regarded the willingness to compromise as weakness.

"More than once, we had terrible rows," he continues. "It generally happened like this—she talked unbelievably fast and hardly let me get a word in edgewise. And if I did say something, she would break in and say, 'Don't interrupt me.... You talk all the time.'"[9]

Occasionally, Kohl would treat the prime minister with good-humored indulgence. He tells how, during a March 1990 visit to St. Catherine's College, Cambridge, Mrs. Thatcher pointedly wondered aloud why the chancellor always spread a large white napkin across his chest. Kohl replied that it was really meant as a white flag—a symbol of his surrender before the Iron Lady.[10]

Kohl ascribes Mrs. Thatcher's bitterness over the prospect of German unification to Britain having lost its empire and seeing Germany the winner at the end of the century.[11]

As expected, Mrs. Thatcher immediately started a rearguard action to slow the unification process, trying her level best to "handbag history," as a headline in the *Sunday Times* of London put it. She reminded the Kohl government of the Allies' rights and insisted that this would require "massive consultations" with them over a long period of time. When criticized for her strident remarks, she would only reply that she was saying aloud what everybody else was thinking. She was right, of course—up to a point. After all, in 1988 Italian Prime Minister Julio Andreotti had stated flat out, "God save us from the eventuality of German unification."

It is an indication of the British leader's instinctive fear of Germany (she was fourteen when war broke out in Europe) that Mrs. Thatcher, who together with Kohl had been the two main pillars against Soviet tyranny in Europe, now wanted to retain some Soviet influence as a counterbalance to Germany. In February 1990 she called President Bush, suggesting that the Soviets be allowed to stay on in Germany without any specific termination date. "One had to remember," she told Bush, "that Germany was surrounded by countries, most of which it had attacked or occupied on mainland Europe in the course of this century. Looking well into the future only the Soviet Union—or its successor—could provide such a balance... to German dominance in Europe."[12] She was clearly toying with the idea of recreating the old pre–World War I triple alliance between Britain, France, and Russia against Germany.

On March 24, 1990, Margaret Thatcher invited a group of international experts on Germany to her country estate,

Chequers, to discuss the implications of German unity, or as she once put it, "the Teutonic lust" for reunification. A memo describing the meeting, written by her private secretary Charles Powell for limited distribution in the British Foreign Office, showed up in the press a few months later. The memo sought to predict future German behavior in Europe by looking hard at the country's past.[13]

At the meeting, Mrs. Thatcher and her team of experts discussed what were deemed some of the less amiable German characteristics evidenced in the period from Bismarck up to 1945. These included insensitivity, self-obsession, a strong inclination to self-pity, and a longing to be liked. To this were added angst, aggressiveness, bullying, feelings of inferiority, neurotic self-assertion, chauvinism, sentimentality, and a tremendous birthrate.

According to the memo, postwar Germany was clearly different; it was a democracy, and, moreover, Germany had done its best to confront its past and make up for it. But still unanswered was the question how a civilized nation had allowed itself to sink to such depravation as during the Hitler period, and whether some of the same traits might not reemerge in the future, decades from now. A unified Germany, it stated, was not necessarily the same kind of country as the Federal Republic. There were material inequalities that could provide a breeding ground for political extremism after unification. And besides, how genuine was Germany's commitment to European ideals? Was it just a ruse to obtain unification?

The upshot of the meeting—and the conclusion of the memo—was that despite these apprehensions unification had to be accepted: Germany's democratic record since 1945 had been excellent. And to be nice to the Germans would be wise, precisely so as not to stir up those feelings again.

This conclusion notwithstanding, British Foreign Secretary Douglas Hurd would emerge from meetings with Mrs. Thatcher warning his cabinet colleagues that they had better not bring up the subject of Germany with her, rather like Basil Fawlty warning his staff for God's sake not to mention The War in the popular television series *Fawlty Towers*.

Kohl himself regarded Mrs. Thatcher as a throwback to an outmoded type of leadership. Though she claimed to carry on the Churchillian tradition, he believed she was in reality pre-Churchillian, as Kohl once informed her to her dismay. He thought she was stuck on traditional European notions of balance of power, all of which had done nothing to prevent war in the past, while he himself was post-Churchillian in his devotion to the European idea. Indeed, Kohl often quoted Churchill's speeches of 1946–1947 calling for a united Europe, and the copy in the Chancellery library is heavily underlined.

As early as 1942 Churchill stated that one day he hoped to see the economy of Europe studied as a whole. "We hope to see a Europe where men of every country will think as much of being a European as of belonging to their native land, and wherever they go in this wide domain will truly feel 'Here I am at home.'" Elsewhere he addressed directly the question of integrating Germany into the European context. "In a continent of divided national states," Churchill said, "Germany and her hardworking people will not find the means or scope to employ their energies.... Germany will once again become a menace to her neighbors and to the whole world.... But on the wider stage of a United Europe German industry and German genius would be able to find constructive and peaceful outlets."[14]

THE FRENCH REACTION WAS more subtle than that of the British. Of all of Germany's European relationships, the most notoriously prickly was with the French. Konrad Adenauer gave Kohl some useful advice on this topic, which stood him in good stead over the years: "When you are dealing with the French," Adenauer said, "bow once to the German flag and twice to the French one."

Kohl's counterpart during these years was Francois Mitterrand. Though of opposite personalities—Kohl congenial, down-to-earth, and solidly middle-class; Mitterrand cerebral, aloof, and socialist—the German media made much of the chancellor's personal rapport with the French president. The two went for highly publicized walks in the Alsace-Lorraine, and, both being keen students of history, they swapped reading lists. Occasionally, though, Mitterrand would let a catty remark slip out. "How inelegant he is," Mitterrand was once overheard remarking about Kohl.

With the prospect of unification, the French president's attitude cooled considerably; France was becoming worried about its diminishing role in Europe. That the so-called friendship between statesmen should never be assigned too much weight was illustrated in 1994, two years before Mitterrand's death, when one of his closest advisers for a decade, Jacques Attali, published the third volume of his diary, entitled *Verbatim*, covering this period. This gives a rather different picture of the relationship between Mitterrand and Kohl, and of the gulf between Mitterrand's public utterances and his private thoughts.

In *Verbatim* Kohl is portrayed as cool and calculating, masking his intentions until he suddenly becomes ruthless. Mitterrand, meanwhile, emerges as a pompous pedant who thinks he can outsmart the Germans and is instead outsmarted by them. Up until almost the end, he does not believe that unification will happen: "People who talk about German reunification understand nothing. The Soviet Union will never allow it," Mitterrand stated in October 1989.

When Mitterrand realized that events were gaining momentum, he flew to the Soviet Union twice—to Kiev in December of 1989 and to Moscow in May 1990—to try to persuade Mikhail Gorbachev to hold the line in East Germany. And he became bitter when he found that these attempts were in vain. According to Attali, in July 1990 Mitterrand burst out, "There you are! Gorbachev, who so urgently implored us not to give in to Kohl, is letting him have everything, doubtless in exchange for a few more Deutsche Marks. We shan't be able to hold out much longer."

With his highly developed sense of political intrigue, Mitterrand even speculated that Kohl and Genscher may have cleverly divided up the roles between themselves in a good cop–bad cop routine, with Kohl making the blunt moves and Genscher smoothing out behind.

For Mitterrand, the outcome of German unification would be war, and he saw the European Union as the only means of holding back Germany. "A reunited Germany presents a double danger for Europe. By reason of its power, and because it would lead to an alliance of Great Britain, France, and the Soviet Union, it would be certain war in the twenty-first century. We must create Europe very quickly in order to defuse German reunification.

"We must dissolve Germany in a European political union before Kohl hands over power. Otherwise German arrogance— Bavarian this time, not Prussian as before—will again threaten the peace of Europe," he stated in October 1990.[15] Mitterrand singled out Bavaria in particular because it harbors millions of expellees from former German-occupied areas of Poland and the Czech Republic.[16]

In his own book, as perhaps would be expected, Kohl goes lightly over the differences with Mitterrand, dismissing Attali's memoirs as fabrication. But the fact remains that Mitterrand did visit Gorbachev in December 1989 and in late May 1990, long after a common Western position on unification had been agreed on. And Soviet notes of these conversations corroborate in general terms what Attali wrote. Mitterrand had also visited East Germany in December 1989, when he told the Modrow government that "it would be dangerous to question the existing borders" between the two Germanies, which was certainly not regarded as helpful in the Chancellery. He also supported the Polish demands for endless assurances on the border question between Poland and Germany.

Kohl's frustration with the French maneuverings behind the scenes during this period are revealed in a couple of outbursts in face-to-face meetings with the French president. In one instance, Kohl asked the French leader point blank if Germany's postwar record as a solid democracy and its close partnership with France were of no importance.

Similarly, when a Polish diplomat told Kohl that Mitterrand and Mazowiecki were playing a game of ping-pong over the German net, Kohl responded with exasperation, "The old game. That you can, of course, do. In fact, we can all make the same stupid mistakes we did back then." In order to overcome British and French reservations, Kohl worked constantly to reassure them, especially the French, about his commitment to Europe.

But perhaps the most anxious of Germany's neighbors was Poland, a result of the country having served as the doormat of Europe down the centuries, a place where the French, Germans, and Russians would pass through to and from various wars, sometimes wiping it completely off the map. After World War II, the entire country was shifted westward. Poland got Silesia, eastern Pomerania, and the southern part of East Prussia, which are all east of the Oder-Neisse River and had all belonged to Germany before the war (the river is now the border). But it lost a large part of eastern Poland, which the Soviet Union wanted to keep for itself. The Poles worried greatly that a united Germany might again raise the question of borders.

The Polish government no doubt remembered the Silesian expellee organization that in 1985 coined a slogan at a rally: "Forty years after, Silesia remains ours," a slogan they had to change through pressure from Bonn. There had also been articles in their exile newspaper expressing the hope that German troops might again recapture Silesia.

Prime Minister Mazowiecki clearly demonstrated the level of concern in Warsaw at this time when he said that some Soviet troops might have to stay on in Poland as a counterweight to Germany—this after forty years of hated Soviet occupation, which the Poles were longing to end. Accordingly, the Poles demanded to be present at the Two Plus Four Talks, but were turned down. After French intervention, however, an agreement was reached by which Poland would be allowed to participate in the talks when they related to Poland's western border.

To a certain extent, the border dispute was a phony issue, and that was how the American side perceived it. Says Philip Zelikow, who at the time was in charge of European policy at the National Security Council, "No one in the U.S. government doubted for a minute that Kohl would respect these borders. We considered it inconceivable that Germany would actually reopen the Oder-Neisse border question." However, for a long time, Kohl avoided committing himself totally, seeking refuge in the legalistic argument that a final decision on the border question would have to be taken "by the government and parliament of a united Germany."

Most analysts saw Kohl's hesitation on the Polish border issue as an attempt to pacify German expellees, the beery guys at the *Stammtisch*, his favorite table, in the pubs in Bavaria. In a possibly tight December election, Kohl would need every vote he could get. Kohl wanted to keep them from voting en masse for the ultra-nationalist Republican Party.

Genscher, of course, pounced on the issue with glee, accusing Kohl of damaging Germany's image abroad, and there was some truth to this. The issue was in danger of spinning out of control. Pressure from abroad and some further arm-twisting from Genscher brought results; Kohl unequivocally reaffirmed the Poles' right to "live in secure borders which will not now or in the future be questioned by us Germans."

This was passed as a resolution in the Bundestag on May 21, 1990. Later, on June 21, both German parliaments voted "affirming the inviolability of the frontier existing between [Poland and Germany] now and in the future and undertake to respect each other's sovereignty and territorial integrity without restriction." The Germans had forever given up any claims to Polish territories east of the Oder-Neisse border. Still, Kohl's handling of the Poles was perhaps the least elegant of his unification moves.

THROUGHOUT THIS PERIOD, Kohl's partner in unification was George Bush. Of Germany's NATO Allies, the United States was the only one that truly backed German unification. George Bush's attitude toward Germany was one of respect for what German democracy had achieved. It is best summed up in Bush's words, "At some point you should let a guy up."[17]

At the time the Berlin Wall was breached, the administration naturally had been concerned over how the Soviets might react—about overloading the circuits in Moscow and the potential rash actions of border guards, who were suddenly faced with huge crowds of people wanting to enter West Berlin. But once that particular crisis was over, there was no serious debate about the desirability of unification itself within the administration.

Says President Bush:

> *Indeed both the British and the French and other Europeans too had serious reservations about German reunification. They did not want it to happen too fast. They were far more concerned about Germany's past than I was…. I felt that Germany had learned its lessons and that history would not repeat itself.*
>
> *I think there were such reservations inside our administration, but my own view was that Germany had paid its dues in terms of being committed to democracy. I did not feel that a united Germany would seek hegemony. I did not feel that Kohl would opt for Germany, once united, staying out of NATO, and I felt that a united Germany would recognize existing borders. I confess to some worry about how the Soviets would react, but I stayed in very close contact with Gorbachev, giving him reassurance, telling him that he had indeed stated that the Germans should decide this important matter by themselves, telling him too that we*

were not seeking to take advantage over the USSR on this matter.

The Americans played a crucial role in persuading the French and the British to accept unification. On this point, says Robert Kimmitt, former U.S. ambassador to Bonn, "We made it crystal clear that we were not going to change our position, and there was no advantage to be gained from probing the U.S. for soft spots in our positions." One factor in the different reactions of the Americans on the one hand and the British and the French on the other could be that, unlike Britain and France, the United States had never been bombed or occupied by the Germans and hence did not have the same deep-seated fears. The United States considered a divided Europe a bigger threat to peace than a unified Germany.

Outside the Bush administration, however, voices in the United States advised going slowly on German unification. Among them was former Secretary of State Henry Kissinger, who argued that Germany would not be ripe for unification for another ten years. In the past, Kissinger had occasionally expressed the view that if Germany was too weak, it was destabilizing, and that if it was too strong, it was also destabilizing. This he summed up in the words "too big for Europe, too small for the world."

But Kissinger at this point seemed motivated more by fear of upsetting the delicate relationship with the Soviet Union than by fear of a united Germany. Kissinger proposed a confederated Germany in which NATO forces would be cut drastically, and a disarmed Eastern part integrated in NATO. This idea was rejected by the Bush administration as amounting to a second Yalta, carving up Europe with the Soviets one more time, and this at a time when there was no need for making concessions since the Soviet Union was collapsing from within.

At crucial moments, such as when Kohl laid out his Ten Point Plan and afterwards at the Malta summit with Gorbachev, the Bush administration shielded the chancellor. Throughout,

Washington had only three provisos: recognition of the existing border with Poland, continued German membership in NATO, and continued U.S. troop presence in Germany, though at lower levels than in the past.

There is no doubt that personality and mutual trust, which Kohl so stressed, played a crucial part here.

"I had worked with Kohl since he came into office," says George Bush. "I knew him well when I was VP. I worked with him on the deployment of the Pershing missiles. I was at his side during a ferocious demonstration in Krefeld, Germany. I believe Kohl trusted me. I know I trusted his word. Kohl's strength and his personality helped a lot. I felt that standing for a united Germany, whatever the pace of things, was the right thing to do; and that was made easier because of my confidence in Helmut Kohl. Kohl is a very strong leader, and I never felt that he would go back on his solemn word, given to me on matters like the borders and NATO membership."

For his part, Kohl knew from years of working with Bush that he could be trusted implicitly: "I think it is above all wisdom and humanity that moved George Bush to support us Germans in the unification of our country. We will always be grateful to him and the American people."

Robert Kimmitt sums it up: "There was what I might call the coincidence of character on both sides of the Atlantic. We were fortunate and history was fortunate to have two individuals who knew each other so well. On this side, in George Bush, you had someone who not only was a foreign policy expert, but having been vice president under Ronald Reagan and before that director of Central Intelligence, he was someone who knew Helmut Kohl well and that generation of German leaders.

"If we had had a newly elected Michael Dukakis in the White House or a newly elected Oskar Lafontaine in Bonn, and people had not had time to know each other, things might have been a lot more difficult," says Kimmitt.

The Americans were distinctly less enthusiastic about Kohl's foreign minister, Hans-Dietrich Genscher, who claimed credit for being the first Western statesman to urge his colleagues to take Gorbachev at his word. Like Reagan officials during the missile debate, high-ranking Bush officials had the unsettling feeling in 1990 that Genscher might be willing to settle for less from the Russians than what was actually achievable, such as unification in exchange for German neutrality. This suspicion was reinforced by Genscher's continuous talk of alliances withering way and of replacing NATO with a new collective security system in Europe.

Seeing a distinct parallel between this stance and Genscher's behavior during the missile debate, National Security Adviser Brent Scowcroft strongly opposed the idea of allowing NATO to be replaced. "We thought that was an abomination," he recalls. "We could not have accepted it." Again, an old refrain among U.S. policymakers can be heard: "Genscher is a mystery to me. I'm not sure what he had in mind," says Scowcroft.

The Americans were not the only ones who felt that Genscher was undercutting the Western position. Says Horst Teltschik, "Genscher was always ready to put forward concessions to the Soviets." For instance, Genscher argued that the former East Germany could not be part of NATO as this would be the end of unification. The implication was that two-thirds of Germany would be in NATO and one-third outside, not exactly a feasible proposition. And Genscher immediately seemed amenable to the idea proposed by the Soviets that internal and external negotiations about Germany's future should be separated. This would have allowed the Soviets to drag the process out and continue to play a role after internal unification had been achieved. Thus Germany would not be sovereign on its own territory. Genscher was immediately reined in by the Chancellery.

On the question of future German troop reductions, Genscher suggested as a starting position a ceiling for the future German army of some 350,000, while Kohl opted for 400,000 to give himself some bargaining room. Kohl eventually got the Soviets to accept the figure of 370,000.[18]

Indeed, muses Teltschik, "Genscher was publicly discussing concessions to the Soviets who had not even asked for them yet." On one occasion, he proclaimed that "no Bundeswehr troops, whether assigned to NATO or not, could be stationed on the territory of the former East Germany." Making concessions before they are asked for seems a rather peculiar way of conducting diplomacy.

At best ambiguous and at worst counterproductive, Genscher's speeches during unification often undermined Kohl. Accordingly, they had to be constantly "clarified" or corrected from the Chancellery. Soon a pattern developed wherein the chancellor had to rein in his foreign minister, causing the latter to retaliate by making sharp little remarks and unflattering leaks to the press about his boss. One of Genscher's wittier comments referred to Kohl's penchant for invoking the grand sweep of history. Genscher was leaving the White House after a meeting with George Bush, and, as somebody helped him into his coat, he noted slyly: "You see here the mantle of history. Many only touch it. I wear it."[19]

Over time, the relationship between Kohl and Genscher deteriorated to such a point that Kohl would publicly correct his foreign minister and then shut him out of key political decisions, even important international meetings.

Indeed, Genscher's mission to Prague in September 1989 marked the pinnacle of his career. Since that time, no important decision was made in the Foreign Ministry. Unification became a *Chefsache*, a matter for the boss. Foreign Ministry diplomats complained about being reduced to messengers, a kind of glorified postal service.[20]

Still, when Genscher suddenly retired in 1992 after eighteen years on the job, he was widely hailed as a visionary and a statesman. The *New York Times* headlined its article, "Kohl Gets German Spotlight, But Genscher Had the Vision," and gave him most of the credit for unification.

THE OTHER PERSON WHO is given credit beyond his due for the outcome of unification is Mikhail Gorbachev. Right up to the present, many Germans look on Gorbachev as the man who set Germany free and ended the division of Europe. According to one poll, 92 percent credit Gorbachev with unification. This is obviously wrong. Gorbachev did not voluntarily give up East Germany, or the rest of Eastern Europe, for that matter. "Our people will never forgive us if we lose the GDR," he once told the Soviet ambassador to East Germany, Wjatscheslaw Koschemassow. What happened was that Gorbachev lost control over the forces he had set in motion. Nor did Gorbachev believe in the free market; he believed that the socialist system could be reformed and saved by installing Gorbachev clones in the various republics and vassal countries.

What broke the Soviet Union was first and foremost Ronald Reagan's defense budgets, a fact that German historians and diplomats mostly overlook, and Reagan's determination to meet the Soviet challenge throughout the world.[21] That was the heavy lifting. Add to this President George Bush's quiet, largely unheralded, but enormously skillful diplomacy in Europe, which won the end-game.

What Gorbachev can be given credit for is being a realist. Though force was used by the Red Army in the Baltics and in the Caucasus republics of the Soviet Union when they broke from the Soviet Empire in 1991, Gorbachev did not lash out in Eastern Europe, as some leaders in his position might have done. Overall, Gorbachev did not have the stomach for bloody solutions, which is not the worst characteristic a man can possess.

As for the Germans' own contribution, with the German penchant for theories and intellectual neatness there are historians today who see the reunification of Germany as a great synthesis of two approaches: the Adenauer approach of being tough on the Soviets and the Brandt approach of opening to the East—a Hegelian balance of opposites. This is clever nonsense.

Thus German Social Democrats have tried to claim credit for the fall of the Berlin Wall, claiming that their *Ostpolitik* made the first small holes in the structure. In this view, which is based on the concept of traditional Soviet insecurity about its borders and the memories of the battle of Stalingrad, it was essential that Moscow be put at ease, reassured that there was nothing to fear from Germany.

Some historians, like Walter Laqueur, have pointed out, however, that the Soviets in the 1970s were not exactly mortally afraid of the Germans, and needed no psychological reassurance that German revanchism was no longer a danger. What the Soviets wanted was the money that came with *Ostpolitik*, and the weakening of Western resolve. Furthermore, as noted, the Social Democrats were prepared to prop up the failed socialist regime in East Germany forever and to accept the permanent division of Europe.

Did the Kohl government itself help the East German regime live longer than necessary? In his early years as chancellor, Kohl did extend massive loans to East Germany. Here is what Kohl has said on the matter: "People are always wise after the fact, and after 1989 it would be easy to say that had it not been for this first billion and then the second, the GDR would have become destabilized a lot more quickly, which would have unified the two countries sooner. I do not believe this, for a very important reason: The Soviet Union was in a completely different situation. At the time, it was still very strong militarily and diplomatically. And the decision would have been very different under Brezhnev and Andropov."[22]

7

FOREIGN POLICY
AFTER UNIFICATION

GERMAN UNIFICATION CHANGED the power structure in Europe. A united Germany is destined to take its place as first among equals of the European nations; its sheer size and economic strength dictate as much. This is a clear departure from the post–World War II situation. Ever since joining NATO in 1955, Germany had been a dependent. Though for strategic reasons the key country, it remained a junior partner. With 250,000 American troops stationed in Germany, the German people could feel safe, as could their neighbors.

The same subordination used to hold true in the European context, in which West Germany had allowed the French to take the lead in the European Coal and Steel Community in 1952. The organization, which grew into the European Community and later into the European Union, was strongly supported by the Americans and inspired by the vision of French diplomats Jean Monnet and Robert Schuman.

Although it was clear to both Charles de Gaulle and Konrad Adenauer that the key to peace in Europe lay in reconciliation and cooperation between France and Germany, the French continued to have mixed feelings about their old adversary. French novelist Francois Mauriac spoke for many of his countrymen when he said that he was so fond of Germany he was glad there were two of them. The existence of a rival German state and the threat from the Soviet Union ensured that Bonn would follow the lead of France.

Thus the division of labor in the European Community was clear: The political initiative was mainly left to France while Germany supplied the economic power. France was the driver, Germany was the engine.

Today, Germany, with its eighty million inhabitants, no longer needs to defer reflexively to the wishes of its allies, giving it more room to maneuver, "to shape and move things," in Kohl's words. Helmut Kohl stressed the need to "take a bigger role and new responsibilities" in the community of nations. Developing a role in relation to its European neighbors and the world community at large—one that befits a united Germany's size and national interests, yet at the same time is sensitive to the facts of history—was how the Kohl government saw the challenge. It is a question of balance.

Says Kohl, "I think, as a German, one must show an understanding for these mixed feelings. Older people in France, the Netherlands, or Poland—to mention only a few countries which in World War II had to suffer especially hard during the German occupation—have not forgotten the injustice that was inflicted upon them, even if they are ready to shake hands with Germans as a gesture of reconciliation."

Adds Joachim Bitterlich, Kohl's national security adviser, "Germany after unification has to familiarize itself with its new status step by step, it has to grow into its new role. We have to learn to play it better psychologically than has been the past

German tradition." In this effort, the Kohl government was greatly encouraged by the Americans, who wanted Germany to pull a bigger load.

This idea, however, was regarded rather ambivalently not only among Germany's neighbors, but also among the Germans themselves. After fifty years of subordination and self-imposed pacifism, German society was far from ready in 1990 to step into this more active role. The resulting growing pains were evident throughout Germany's foreign policy during the early part of the decade.

Unification thus led to immediate concern among other Europeans that the Continent's great power would begin to forge its own path. One British commentator worried that the Germans were getting "too big for their jack boots." The London *Sunday Telegraph* made much of the symbolic significance of Frederick the Great's statue in Berlin: "In the center of Berlin, where the new government will take its seat, stands again the monument of Frederick the Great on horseback, with his arm pointing eastward in the direction of Silesia.... In a unified Germany many things will happen that would have been unimaginable in Bonn."

The instruction that German diplomats were henceforth to conduct more official business in their own language was much commented upon, too, sending shivers down the spines of the international diplomatic community, that imagined being forced to learn German by some merciless Frau Bluecher look-alike.

"The time when a German secretary general in NATO wrote a letter to his own government in English is over," says one Kohl adviser. This actually happened one time; the secretary general in question was Manfred Woerner, who later offered the rather lame excuse that his German-speaking secretary was not on duty that day.

The unspoken—or in some cases not-so-unspoken—fears in Europe were that Germany would return to its traditional role of maneuvering between East and West, with the usual disastrous consequences. Those with a sense of history recalled the Prussian–Russian military pact of the Napoleonic Wars, and the treaty of Rapallo between the USSR and Germany in 1922. They pointed to the Reichswehr's relationship with the Red Army in the 1930s, which contrary to the Treaty of Versailles allowed German troops to train on Russian soil. And, of course, there was the Molotov–Ribbentrop Pact of 1939, which carved up Poland and the Baltic states between Germany and the Soviet Union and set the stage for World War II.

Similarly, on the economic front, Kohl's government was accused of going solo, of ruling with the Mark. During the early phase of unification, when fears of inflation grew in Germany due to the massive expenditures to rebuild the eastern part of the country, the German Bundesbank in 1992 raised interest rates without informing its European partners.

With the Bundesbank increasingly playing the role of the central bank for Europe, any moves it made had a ripple effect throughout the Continent. Pegged to the Mark in a tight currency band, other currencies were forced to follow suit, and national banks throughout Europe were none too happy about it. The strain created a major European currency crisis in 1992, when the British were forced to drop out of the currency band, the French franc and the Danish krone plummeted, and the Swedes were reduced to raising their interest rates to 500 percent overnight to defend their currency. Many Europeans grumbled about having to pay for Germany's high interest rates and thus help finance the rebuilding of East Germany.

In short, as Germany emerged from unification, the question posed by uneasy Europeans was whether the fears expressed throughout 1990 were coming true. Were they witnessing the beginning of a Fourth Reich, as the more alarmist headlines put it?

THE FIRST TEST OF GERMANY'S resolve on the international stage came with Iraq's invasion of Kuwait in the summer of 1990—that is, before unification was complete. Germany's role in the Gulf War was hardly that of an emerging great power, a far cry from "the partners in leadership" vision that George Bush had optimistically proclaimed in 1989. It offered instead clear evidence of confusion among Germans about their international responsibilities. As Joachim Bitterlich puts it, "The Gulf War came too early. The Germans were still hiding themselves."

Some of the reasons for Germany's reticence to engage militarily were obvious, others perhaps less so. Some were emotional, some military, some constitutional. It was certainly true that if President Bush had a hard time getting congressional approval for U.S. military action, the obstacles facing Kohl in the Bundestag and among Germans generally would have been insurmountable at the time. Still, the fact that Germany, a power heavily dependent on the flow of Gulf oil, was unable to send its troops to fight alongside the Allies who had protected its soil during the Cold War did not go down well in Washington, London, or Paris.

Germany, of course, endorsed all the obligatory UN resolutions relating to the occupation of Kuwait, and the government condemned Saddam Hussein's aggression publicly. Helmut Kohl, however, tried to urge caution on President Bush—this at the same time as Mrs. Thatcher was telling him not to "go wobbly."

Many Germans held to the view that the 1949 West German constitution, the Basic Law, prevented German troops from being deployed outside the NATO area, a legacy from World War II. The uproar over the Gulf War in Germany was huge, both within political circles and on the streets. January 1991 saw massive peace demonstrations in German cities, and appeals from the Chancellery not to damage Germany's image abroad as a reliable ally went unheeded. In a statement, the Kohl government urged protesters at a huge rally in Bonn on January 26 "not to be blind to who is responsible for this war, in view of the worldwide attention this assembly will attract. Demonstrators bear a heavy responsibility for Germany's reputation in the world." Even so, hundreds of thousands of demonstrators denounced American policy and the fact that

American troops had been allowed to depart from bases in Germany.[1]

On February 13 the American Embassy in Bonn was raked by automatic weapons fire from across the Rhine. No one at the embassy was hurt, but 262 empty shells were found. Afterwards a communique was sent to the police in which the Red Army Faction took responsibility for the deed, denouncing the U.S. imperialist war on Iraq, accusing NATO of genocide, and proclaiming "international solidarity of the tenderness of peoples."[2]

Theo Sommer of *Die Zeit* wrote that the Persian Gulf War "turns out to be a last, almost spastic twitching of U.S. supremacy which resurrects the reflexes of the Cold War." In the Bundestag, Bjorn Engholm, party chairman of the Social Democrats (who had obviously not been reading *Die Zeit* or watching the virulent signs of the demonstrators on television demanding that Germans "Oppose the U.S. Aggressors") declared, "It is wrong to place those who are demonstrating because they are deeply shocked by the war in an anti-American corner. There is no just war."

Accordingly, Kohl had to announce that Germany could not send troops to the Gulf, citing the German constitution—an interpretation that legal scholars said was far from clear. By January 14, days before war broke out, the German parliament was still issuing resolutions appealing to Saddam Hussein to withdraw from Kuwait.

The Gulf War demonstrated once again how politically confused the younger German generation had become. Germany, like every other European nation, had a vital interest in seeing the regional ambitions of Saddam Hussein stemmed. There was also an obvious moral side to the conflict: Iraq, a big nation, had launched a war of aggression against a small country, Kuwait. Thus Operation Desert Storm was a multinational effort to ensure collective security, based on the principles and the resolutions of the United Nations. To any politically sound person, this was indeed a just war.

But this seemingly clear-cut question of good and evil came into conflict with decades of pacifism taught in German schools, where war had been portrayed as a primary evil, no matter who was fighting or for what reason.

What did help change the mood in Germany was the sight of Arab missiles raining down on Jewish cities, which finally produced a sense of unease and gave rise to second thoughts. It was especially true because German firms, in circumventing export restrictions, had been doing brisk business with Iraq, helping build up Saddam's stocks of chemical weapons.[3] A German delegation headed by Hans-Dietrich Genscher was dispatched to Israel to show support, and Germany ended up contributing 5 million Marks (a little more than $3 million) to victims of Scud attacks in Israel.

Overall, Germany's financial contribution to the Gulf War Alliance was significant. Over 1990–1991, it amounted to 18 billion Marks ($12 billion), of which some 10 billion Marks ($6.5 billion) went to the United States. To put this in perspective, the total American contribution by 1991 was $21 billion.

In other words, Germany's role in the Gulf War did not bespeak any great appetite for military adventures or, for that matter, a desperate urge to recreate Rommel's Afrika Korps. But the crisis had opened a debate about Germany's ability to use military force. In the unsettled post–Cold War 1990s, other opportunities soon arose to ponder the question further—in Somalia, Haiti, and Bosnia.

IN THE YEARS THAT FOLLOWED, the Kohl government took a series of small steps, which it hoped would accustom the Germans to a more active international role. They were careful steps indeed. First came the German contribution of military hospitals to the UN operation in Cambodia in 1992, intended to restore hundreds of thousands of Cambodian refugees in camps across the Thai border.

The invasion of Somalia in December 1992 was another instance. This was Kohl's friend George Bush's last act in office. The purpose, at least initially, was to deliver humanitarian aid to a starving population, held hostage by gangs of drugged-out thugs controlled by local warlords. Little debate surrounded the decision to intervene, and given its unexceptional goal, Bush's appeal for international cooperation received wide support. More than thirty nations enthusiastically signed up for what seemed to be an uncontroversial bit of charity work, which unfortunately failed to control the local warlords. In this case, there was room for the German government to participate and Chancellor Kohl pledged a German contingent of 1,600 troops to aid the UN relief effort. After all, who could quarrel with a mission of handing out food and blankets? (As it turned out, the German Social Democrats could, arguing again that Kohl was acting in violation of German law.) In Somalia, as in other missions that would gradually bring Germany to accept a more active international involvement, absolutely no national self-interest was involved.

But it was the German role in the Balkan crisis that brought all the old European suspicions about the return of the Ugly German to the fore. The Balkans had long been a European worry. Yugoslavia itself had been established after World War I, a union of Balkan ethnic groups previously part of the Turkish Ottoman Empire—Serbs, Croats, Muslims, Albanians, Hungarians, and others. After the collapse of the German and Austro-Hungarian Empires, Yugoslavia was designed to block the expansion of Germany and Austria into southeastern Europe. In 1941 Nazi Germany attacked Yugoslavia, and among the war's most odious regimes was the Chetnik government in Croatia, which was allied with Hitler's forces.

Throughout most of the Cold War, Yugoslavia had been held together by the will of one man, Josef Broz Tito, whose death in 1980 allowed a new generation of leaders to rise, some of whom were hell-bent on exploiting ethnic divisions and resentments for their own purposes.

By the spring of 1991 the country was clearly headed for a breakup, because the Serbian leadership in Belgrade was trying to extend its influence over the other republics where ethnic Serbs constituted a minority. The European and American impulse was to urge caution and respect for the integrity of a democratically united Yugoslavia, which they continued to do as late as the spring of 1991.

By summer, however, vicious ethnic fighting had erupted in Croatia, where Croats were being expelled in droves from majority Serbian areas. Further, Serbian leader Slobodan Milosevic had refused to turn over the leadership of the Yugoslavian collective presidency to the next in line, a Croat. And in Slovenia, the national guard had refused to give up weapons belonging to the Yugoslavian army and was readying for a fight.

In a move that caused criticism of high-handed German behavior, Bonn took a leading diplomatic role early on. Germany's old alliances in the area did not go unmentioned, and the Kohl government was accused of trying to revive Germany's traditional sphere of influence. In the Kohl government's view, Yugoslavia was already breaking up, and by recognizing realities and internationalizing the problem through diplomatic recognition of the breakaway republics, the Germans might cause fighting to subside.

At the time, Germany held the leadership in the Council for Security and Cooperation in Europe and pushed for the principle of self-determination. In a speech on November 27 to the German parliament, Kohl forcefully threw his weight behind the idea. After heavy German prodding, the European Union on December 16 voted in favor of recognition of any Yugoslavian successor state that desired it, and for the recognition of Slovenia and Croatia on January 15, 1992.

The hostilities ceased soon after, in part because the Croats and the Slovenes now had the international community behind them. It should also be recognized, though, that Serbia at that point occupied one-third of Croat territory, which was close to what it had wanted anyway. A stalemate had been reached.

Though forced to go along with the German policy, many did not agree with it. The British wanted to stay as far away from the problem as possible, and France and the United States hesitated to recognize what had by then become realities. Germany was accused of precipitating the breakup of the country, rather than helping it. The UN envoy to Yugoslavia, former U.S. Secretary of State Cyrus Vance, and the European Union envoy, former British Foreign Secretary David Owen, pronounced the German step "a grave error."

Many Europeans also saw Kohl's initiative as provoking the Serbs to fight for a greater Serbia, giving them the pretext of protecting ethnic minorities in the breakaway republics, an argument that ignored the fact that Serbian leader Slobodan Milosevic needed no encouragement whatsoever for his nationalistic rampage.

Predictably, the accusations against Germany for reverting to great power behavior left the Kohl government highly exasperated. After all, in the case of Iraq, the Germans had been called wimps for not sending troops to participate in the Persian Gulf War. The charge then had been that Germany was a "checkbook power," in the words of *New York Times* columnist William Safire, footing the bill and leaving it to others to do the dying. One year later, the Germans had suddenly become the Horrible Hun again, the bully of Europe, ready to shove their views down the throats of fellow Europeans.

The Kohl government argued that what was driving German policy was the right to national independence and self-determination, principles that were enshrined in the Yugoslav constitution itself. At the time, Kohl noted, talking about preserving Yugoslavia intact was wishful thinking on the part of Germany's European allies. Milosevic had started the war with his dream of a greater Serbia. Cyrus Vance and David Owen, with their fancy maps for the minute ethnic subdivision of the former Yugoslavia, were not living in the real world.

But the crisis was not over. When war broke out again, it was in Bosnia-Herzegovina, a small state as ethnically mixed as Yugoslavia itself. The majority Muslim government of Bosnia also wanted independence. At this point the German government gave way to the Americans, who by March 1992 were pressing for unified diplomatic action by the West, on much the same principles that had motivated the Germans earlier.

The United States declared diplomatic recognition of Bosnia on April 6, but it turned out not to have a calming effect at all—quite the reverse. Bosnia soon became a bloody battle-field for competing ethnic groups and grandiose Serbian ambi-tions, in a war that was to last for three years and claim hundreds of thousands of casualties.

The new American Clinton administration was reluctant to become involved in what was widely seen in the United States as an ugly, purely European problem. Accordingly, the Europeans were forced to attempt action on their own, a course that would illustrate beyond doubt the difficulty in fashioning a common European foreign policy.

The British and the French took the lead in operations to keep supplies flowing to besieged Bosnian cities, which meant that Germany's position as a merely diplomatic participant was untenable. It was not enough for Germany to stick to high-minded diplomatic pronouncements while its allies were sad-dled with the increasingly hazardous peacekeeping duties, daily putting the lives of their soldiers on the line. Kohl's Defense Minister Volker Ruehe, supported by Kohl, took the lead in pushing for German deployment. As he put it, "You cannot build Europe with conference papers alone."

For Kohl, the rule-of-thumb had been to keep the modern Bundeswehr firmly out of any area previously occupied by Hitler's Wehrmacht. That obviously applied to the former Yugoslavia, and going beyond that position was not easy. By the winter of 1993 fewer than half the people in western Germany, and only one in five in the former East Germany, were in favor of international missions.

By 1994 the constitutional issue had become pressing. Although scholars believed that deployment outside the NATO area by the Bundeswehr was indeed constitutionally possible, the politicians were hesitant to expose themselves too far on such a touchy issue. First having accused Germany of strong-arm tactics, Germany's allies now accused Germany, the country with the largest army in Europe, of hiding behind its constitution—not a terribly logical way of looking at things.

By then the Kohl government had deployed military units to Cambodia and Somalia. And, in fact, Germans were at the time helping to man AWACS surveillance planes and were participating in the blockade of the Balkans in the Adriatic Sea. But none of these troops were anywhere close to where the fighting was taking place. Nevertheless, the Social Democrats contended that even in these out-of-area missions the Kohl government was acting illegally. Kohl, for his part, was frustrated because he was unable to muster the two-thirds parliamentary majority necessary for a constitutional amendment that explicitly allowed military deployment.

To clear the air and resolve the issue, the Free Democrats, led by Foreign Minister Klaus Kinkel, brought suit against their own government. In a landmark decision, on July 13, 1994, Germany's constitutional court ruled that there were no legal barriers to German participation in peacekeeping missions outside NATO territory. The court further decided that military participation in peacekeeping missions could be approved by a simple majority in parliament. (The justices did chastise Kohl for not seeking parliamentary approval of previous missions.)

"Peace forces and their task of securing peace are part of the United Nations' system of collective security as it has developed through the practical application of the UN charter, which the Federal Republic of Germany joined in 1973," ruled the eight-member panel of judges in Karlsruhe.

This was a major victory for Kohl. "What I have always wanted became clear in this ruling. We are members of the UN and if we make use of our UN rights, we must also carry out our duties," Kohl stated.[4]

Following the ruling of the German Supreme Court, the major break with the German taboo on military force in the Balkans came in the summer of 1995. The four-hour debate in the German Bundestag on June 30, 1995, was acrimonious. Rudolf Scharping, leader of the Social Democrats at the time, opposed sending as much as a single plane. The Greens, predictably overwrought, warned that the decision was "a blank check for the entry of Germany as a warring party." But in the end, Kohl got the support he was looking for by a vote of 386 to 258. "It isn't an easy decision for us," Kohl stated during the televised debate. "But we cannot say no to all our friends and allies who expect us to take part in this mission for peace in the center of Europe."

Accordingly, on September 2, 1995, fourteen German Luftwaffe Tornado jets were deployed in Piacenza, Italy, and from there they flew their first combat missions over Bosnia since World War II. The aircraft were to support a British, French, and Dutch rapid reaction force whose purpose was to destroy heavy Serbian artillery. A German field hospital was set up in Split, Croatia, and German military transport planes were placed at the disposal of the other allies. By 1996 Germany had deployed three thousand ground troops as part of the NATO Implementation Force.

By this time, the popular mood had changed. According to a study by the Defense Ministry, which was constantly monitoring the public pulse on these questions, 85 percent of Germans supported their military, and 69 percent wanted their army to be part of UN peacekeeping operations.

In Kohl's view, what the situation in Bosnia demonstrated was that Germany could no longer avoid responsibility on the international scene, especially in cases of aggression and genocide. On this point, he received crucial support from notables like Nobel Prize winner and concentration camp survivor Elie Wiesel, who backed German military intervention to stop the Serbian ethnic cleansing campaign. While the thought of German troops outside its borders might be painful to many Jews, Wiesel argued that the Holocaust made participation where ethnic cleansing was concerned all the more important.

"Every person we leave behind without help, every life we give up, will pursue us like an eternal reproach," Wiesel stated.

The leader of Germany's small Jewish community, Ignatz Bubis, also threw his support behind the chancellor. "Many people hide behind the argument that Germany committed sins in [the] former Yugoslavia, and we cannot intervene there militarily. I disagree. Because Germany sinned back then, it has all the more duty to rush to help people there."

The humanitarian argument was one that resonated among Germans. Already Germany had made room for 300,000 Balkan refugees, and the scenes from Croatian and Serbian concentration camps with skeletal figures and piles of bodies on the evening television news looked only too hauntingly familiar. Standing by while this was happening was no longer morally acceptable.

Furthermore, says Bitterlich, the proximity of Bosnia to Germany made a difference. "Bosnia is nearer than the Gulf," he adds. "Therefore, I think when you are going step by step toward a normal role for Germany... it is easier to sell something that the public understands as the national interest because it is so close to Germany."

ACCORDING TO ONE HISTORIAN, rather than a classic case of *Drang nach Osten*—the urge toward the east—the Kohl government's preoccupation with the Balkans and Central and Eastern Europe can be better described as *Zwang nach Osten*—Germany being pulled eastward out of necessity.[5] From the German perspective, the potential for escalating chaos looms just beyond its eastern borders, and its allies have failed to appreciate fully the seriousness of the danger this represents to Germany.

Germany's efforts to build relations in the east under Kohl have focused on Poland, the largest nation in the region with forty million people, Germany's neighbor, and one with whom the Germans share a great deal of mostly unhappy history. Here Kohl sought to build a relationship of trust like the one

Germany had established with France, no easy task given the sheer lopsidedness between Europe's richest nation and one of its poorest.[6]

Germany thus has been supportive of Polish, Czech, and Hungarian efforts to enter both the European Union and NATO. But exactly how far and how fast NATO should expand was the subject of some finessing on the part of the Kohl government, mainly out of consideration for the Russian reaction. This exercise in extremely touchy diplomacy at times placed Germany slightly out of sync with its NATO allies.

Clearly, it was in Germany's interest to push the NATO border eastward, away from the newly designated capital of Berlin, which otherwise would lie highly exposed. Furthermore, a major cause of war in Europe has traditionally been the power vacuum in Central and Eastern Europe, where nations have been incapable of defending themselves from either Russia or Germany, or both. NATO enlargement will once and for all shore up the gains of the Cold War and eliminate the imperial option for Russia in Europe.

The fact that NATO expansion would permanently shift the balance of power in Europe was not lost on the Russians, who expressed their displeasure loudly and repeatedly. Kohl's 1995 speech to the Polish parliament in 1995 illustrated this dilemma. The chancellor, in a flourish, promised the Poles entry into NATO by the year 2000, rather to the discomfort of his own aides who preferred a little more vagueness on the subject. "No state can stop another from joining or not joining an alliance," Mr. Kohl told the wildly applauding Poles.

After that bold statement, however, Kohl had to backtrack because of Russia's displeasure. Just one year later, Kohl told the Russian president that inclusion of former Warsaw Pact countries into NATO "needs to be postponed for a long time." Needless to say, this time he delighted the Russians—but caused consternation among the East Europeans. In July 1997 the Kohl government finally cast its support behind the first round of NATO expansion along with NATO's other fifteen members.

NATO expansion proved to be remarkably uncontroversial, particularly given the virulent antagonism against NATO displayed by the peace movement in the old days. The entrance of the new members enjoyed the support of 90 percent of the Bundestag, which reflected the mood in the media and the public as well.[7]

At the same time, Kohl's relationship with Russian leader Boris Yeltsin remained a German priority. Initially, relations between the two leaders had been strained. The bone of contention was former East German leader Erich Honecker, who sought to evade justice in 1991 by escaping to Russia. Yeltsin at first refused to hand him over to the Germans so he could stand trial in a German court. But Kohl prevailed. From then on, relations improved rapidly because of substantial German aid to Russia and because Kohl went out of his way to support Yeltsin through his numerous political crises. For his part, Yeltsin considered Kohl his "true friend" and insisted on dragging Kohl off to a sauna every time he paid a visit.

One good reason why Kohl sought to avoid any move that could upset the Russians following unification was that a sizable contingency, some 350,000, were still on German territory after Unification Day. Kohl wanted nothing to interfere with their departure. When Yeltsin visited Germany to witness the withdrawal of the last Russian troops in 1994, he grabbed the baton of a military band leader and started conducting the band with great and drunken vigor. On occasion Kohl pleaded for "psychological understanding" of Yeltsin, which indeed he may well have needed.

The intense interest taken by the Germans in Yeltsin's survival was revealed when they sent a heart expert to help treat Yeltsin's heart condition. While this was certainly done to help the Russian leader obtain the very best medical care, it seems likely that a bit of intelligence work went on to get an accurate assessment of his chances for survival. And Kohl was the first Western leader to meet with Yeltsin after his extensive open heart surgery, in January 1997.

Some analysts have argued that Kohl placed too much hope in one man, and a man in an unstable physical condition at that. Germany is now stuck with all the loans to Russia it has guaranteed, and hopes of Russia's transformation into a democracy have long receded.

THE MOST IMPORTANT PUSH of the post-unification German foreign policy under Kohl—and the one closest to his heart— was the intensified effort of integrating Germany in Europe. Kohl never tired of quoting Adenauer, who said that "there are two sides of the same coin, German Unity, European Unity." Chief here was the push for a common currency. Adopting the Euro symbolizes Germany's commitment to the European ideal. For Kohl it constituted the crowning achievement of his political life's work—of anchoring Germany solidly in Europe and in the West.

In the late 1980s the Kohl government had been reluctant to set a date for the European Monetary Union. This was partly because of the obvious difficulties involved in stitching together European economies, widely disparate in standards of living, size of public sector, and national debt.

The price exacted by French President Francois Mitterrand when he gave his reluctant support for a united Germany was Kohl's agreement to a framework and a timetable for a European currency union. Accepting the Euro for Kohl was the economic and political equivalent of keeping a united Germany in NATO. It meant a sacrifice of sovereign power by the Continent's most powerful country in the name of peace in Europe.

Up until this point, no timetable had been fixed, but at a 1990 meeting in Dublin, Kohl committed himself to a firm date for its introduction, January 1, 1999, as well as to cooperation in foreign and security matters. These commitments were enshrined in the Maastricht Treaty of December 1991, which laid down the steps for European integration.[8]

A common currency, if held strong, would be a major advantage to Europe, saving billions in transaction costs and removing the uncertainty of changing from one currency to another. Competition would be strengthened by making prices immediately apparent. Furthermore, a common currency unit would force fiscal discipline on European nations that might not have the backbone to adopt it on their own. No longer would governments be able to manipulate monetary policy, interest rates, and so on, to deal with local unemployment and social spending. Instead, they could just point to the Central European Bank and say, "We had no other choice." This argument is something Americans should understand; President Bill Clinton owes much of his "success" to the fact that the U.S. economy during his two terms in office has been run by Federal Reserve Chairman Alan Greenspan.

Nonetheless, the heated debate surrounding the Maastricht Treaty proved to European politicians, including Helmut Kohl, that the European idea was less popular than they had thought, that they had been further out than their populations.

For years, the definition of "Europe" had been left mostly to the French (or to the British, when it came to looking at its downsides). Germany, meanwhile, had quietly been paying the bills.

The primary voice in the definition of "Europe" for years belonged to Jacques Delors, who served for ten years as president of the European Commission. Kohl and Delors had a close personal and working relationship; Delors was one of the few European statesmen to give his full support to unification, and he made sure that the new states could join the European Union immediately upon unification. However, as one of his biographers has pointed out, while Delors did more than anyone to foster the European idea, he has also done more than anyone to discredit it by going too far.[9]

Although from a humble background himself, starting out as a bank clerk in Paris and putting himself through college with evening classes, Delors shared all the worst instincts of France's elite political colleges—a penchant for centralization or dirigisme in the administrative tradition dating back to the time of Colbert, Louis XIV's finance minister.

Initiatives like the Social Charter under the Maastricht Treaty came from Delors, a charter that would make labor legislation uniform for all of Europe and sharply increase union power. The British government under John Major took one look at it and chose to opt out immediately, having just managed under Margaret Thatcher to break the stranglehold of the British unions. Delors also favored outmoded ideas like social contracts and industrial policy on a European level. In 1992 he did his level protectionist best (which was fortunately not good enough) to derail the GATT free trade agreement. In short, Delors's vision was to turn all of Europe into one gigantic France, not exactly an ideal way of running a continent.

Just how unpopular this drive toward centralization was could be measured by Denmark's rejection of the Maastricht Treaty in 1992, even though politicians in all the major Danish parties urged the Danes to vote yes. The general view was that Maastricht deprived member countries of too much of their sovereignty. Even more embarrassing, the true extent of unpopularity of the Delorsian vision of Europe was on display when the Maastricht Treaty was approved by only the narrowest margin in France itself.

Most of the concerted opposition to the idea of a "United States of Europe" came from the British, especially the idea of a "Europe" with Germany at the center. This was expressed most bluntly by one of Prime Minister Thatcher's closest associates, Environment Minister Nicholas Ridley, who memorably stated that the European Community had turned into "a German racket for taking over Europe." Ridley was forced to resign, but many thought that Mrs. Thatcher herself felt the same way.

As British commentator Robert Harris pointed out bitterly, a democratic Germany, which seemed stronger than at any time since 1941, was close to achieving the war aims that a totalitarian dictatorship could not. Communism was finished, and trading areas dominated by the Mark had materialized. Germans wanted to call the tune in Europe, and they wanted to send manufactured goods east in exchange for raw materials. "Isn't that what is about to happen?" asked Harris. Predictably, these accusations were driving the Germans to distraction; they saw their own willingness to give up the Mark as a voluntary sacrifice, not as an attempt to dominate Europe.

French dirigisme was also a ripe topic for British satire, which, even fervent supporters of Europe Union would have to admit, was often wickedly funny and effective. The British tabloids developed a whole cottage industry reporting Euro-follies like the classification of carrots as "fruit," strict regulations on the size and curvature of Euro-cucumbers, and the exile of the banger, a small sausage with a large place in the proud British heart.

The debate about mad dictates from Brussels would invariably degenerate into a discussion of the alleged planning of a Euro-condom, which Italian men insisted was too small for their tremendous sexual equipment. Eventually, the stories got so bad that the European Union had to set up an office in Brussels to separate truth from fiction and jump into action every time the British tabloids discovered another indignity.

Consequently, the German government realized that it had left too much of the definition of "Europe" to others and needed to present its own image of a united Europe, one that was less open to ridicule and misrepresentation. One of National Security Adviser Joachim Bitterlich's first acts in office was to remove any reference in Kohl's speeches to "the United States of Europe," which seemed to convey the idea of a centralized Europe, where the sovereignty of the individual states had been wiped out. In retrospect, Bitterlich would also have preferred that the Europeans adhere to the old terminology of a "European partnership" rather than the more heavy-handed word "union."[10]

Meanwhile, some of the enthusiasm waned even in Germany itself, which had consistently been the country most favorably disposed toward Europe. Many Germans were fed up with being "Europe's cash cow." They were tired of being subject to all the criticism and, at the same time, expected to foot all the bills. In 1996 Germany contributed some $10.6 billion to the European Union, while Britain, for instance, paid $6 billion. Much of this went to finance the union's Common Agricultural Policy, an exorbitantly expensive enterprise subsidizing unprofitable farmers, and to regional development of poorer countries such as Ireland, Portugal, and Greece. At the same time, Germany paid two-thirds of all Western aid to Russia.

Before unification, West Germany tied with Denmark for the number one spot on the list of wealth indicators. After unification, Germany slid to number six, though it still pays more than 60 percent of the net transfer to the European Union. Whenever the Germans have pointed to these inequalities, the conversation is abruptly steered elsewhere by the other European Union countries.

As the time for the common currency drew closer, there was widespread concern among Germans that their cherished monetary stability would be undermined and their purchasing power diluted by substituting an uncertain Euro for the Mighty Mark.

Thus public pressure in Germany forced the chancellor to sharpen his demands. Accordingly, on the eve of the European Union conference in December 1995, Kohl's government toughened its stand on the political and economic union, asserting that other member nations must respect the rigorous economic criteria laid down in the Maastricht Treaty for adopting a single European currency. Among them: A country's budget deficit must not be more than 3 percent of its GDP, and the national debts must not exceed 60 percent of GDP. Strict limits on inflation and interest rates were also imposed.

Alluding to the rampant inflation that helped bring down the Weimar Republic and paved the way for the Nazi regime, Kohl stated that "stable money is just not another topic for us Germans. Neither is it German hysteria when we, with regard to European economic and monetary union, keep on emphasizing that we must adhere to the stability criteria of the Maastricht Treaty and that under no circumstances are they to be dismissed."

When Kohl speaks about Europe in private conversation, he reveals what has kept him going throughout the years. He speaks with an emotional conviction and an urgency that come from personal experience. Momentarily, it makes the jokes and Eurospeak about unpronounceable terms like "subsidiarity" appear insignificant.

To Kohl, the European Union is not a matter of the shape of gherkins, but a matter of war and peace.[11] At a time when most politicians are concerned with next the day's headlines, Kohl thinks in centuries. He ticks off the futile attempts that were made in our century to ensure peace in Europe: Before World War I, the French and German students united to preserve peace, but to no avail—the War to End All Wars ensued; in 1925 another attempt was made, the Treaty of Locarno between Weimar Prime Minister Gustav Stresemann, French Prime Minister Aristide Briand, and the leaders of Britain, Belgium, and Italy, whose purpose was to normalize relations between Germany and its former enemies; in 1935 thousands of World War I veterans from France and Germany attended a meeting at Verdun under the banner "Never War Again," but four years later they had to don their uniforms and go to war— as did Kohl's own father. Ironically, it was Josef Stalin who finally concentrated the minds of the West Europeans and made them come together.

More recent events point to the continuing fragility of European stability. Few would have believed that after more than forty years of peace, Europe would see ethnic cleansing, concentrations camps, and mass graves in the Balkans, an hour's flight from Germany.

Kohl's ultimate goal was—and still is—to break the pattern and make sure that peace prevails. "We are determined to make this process irreversible," he says. In his view, the means to do so is the common currency, which will create a strong bond between the European economies.

In the house of Europe that Kohl envisages, quarrels must be settled inside, not in the street. "The streets mean war," he says. Kohl's Europe is a Europe where young people from all over the continent can assemble peacefully on the Charles Bridge in Prague or on the Spanish Steps in Rome or in Piccadilly Circus in London or on the Eiffel Tower in Paris or in Heidelberg in Germany, united by a common culture and shared values.

Thus it was not a question of "a European superstate," but "a European community," he says. The Kohl government sought to "build a European house in which people could feel comfortable and remain different in many ways." The aim was not "a grey uniformity," but a community in which Europeans would "remain Germans, British, Italians, and French."

The free democracies, notes Kohl, depend on the engagement and the personal responsibility of the citizens. Their participation in the political process presupposes that decisions whenever possible are made on the level closest to them. It is a matter of reaching a sensible balance between the local community and the regional, between the nation-state and the European Union.

The way Europe should work, according to Kohl, is that only decisions that affect the whole should be taken on the European level, and what can be better dealt with on the regional or local level should be decided there. This also means of course that the national governments must take up their responsibilities where it is necessary and not push all unpleasant matters onto the European Union.

Finally, there is the question of free trade. As for the fear, often expressed in the United States, that the European Union will develop into a Fortress Europe, Kohl contends, "Precisely as an export nation, we know that the fresh wind of competition keeps a national economy healthy.... Ludwig Erhard once told us as young people in this connection: 'Open the windows and the doors! If you close everything, it gets warm, but also sticky and you fall asleep.' That also goes for today. Germany emphasizes free commerce. The European house will not be a fortress. The border posts that we have pulled up in Europe will not be used as building material for new commercial barriers against the outside world."

Kohl demonstrated his beliefs in negotiations with Poland, the Czech Republic, and Hungary about their association with the European Union. Some of Germany's European partners were loudly objecting to having imports from these countries of steel, food, and textiles—which happened to be what these countries had to offer. Kohl supported them on the grounds that you cannot call for viable democracies and then deny them the ability to sell their products.

THROUGHOUT, KOHL HAS INSISTED that "no one really needs to be afraid of the Germans. No one is running around with jack boots wanting to mug someone. I don't believe we've earned the mistrust. No one can agree more than the Germans with the words of Thomas Mann—that we are German Europeans and not European Germans."

Nor did Kohl's own drive for German unification have much in common with that of Otto von Bismarck; the circumstances this time were entirely different. Bismarck stated that the future of Germany would "be decided not by speeches and majority votes... but by iron and blood." But as Kohl has pointed out, "This time unification was achieved peacefully, through the ballot box." Though Kohl took charge and provided leadership, the impulses came from outside Germany. It is to the Poles, the Hungarians, and the Czechs that the East Germans owe their freedom.

There is one clear and simple difference between the Germany of the past and of today. In 1900 the average age of the population was twenty-five, and the vast majority of the country was poor. By the end of this century, the population will have an average age of fifty (Germany has one of the lowest birthrates in Europe), and most will be well off. Aggressive nationalism does not thrive in such an environment. With a wealthy, aging population, chances are that it will be risk averse, careful not to endanger what has been achieved.

The opinion polls support this view by showing that there is no strong national consensus about Germany's role in the world. They show that an overwhelming majority of Germans reject a major new role for the country abroad. Many would prefer to be like the Swiss—fat and happy.

It seems clear that Germany is not about to become a Fourth Reich. But it is equally clear it cannot be an outsized Switzerland, a fat introverted hedgehog, in the words of *The Economist*. Many of the challenges to Europe now lie on the perimeter of the Continent. If Germany were not to take full part in meeting these challenges, the NATO alliance would be weakened, and defense policies would be renationalized. In other words, Germany must take its place as a leading nation in Europe in accordance with its size and economic power.

8

KOHL'S NEW GERMANY: REBUILDING THE EAST

WHEN WINSTON CHURCHILL TOLD the British people during World War II that all he could promise
them was "blood, sweat, and tears," it was essentially
all he had to offer. The British responded and rallied, proud of
their national grit. When Franklin Delano Roosevelt tried to
pull the American people out of the depths of the Great
Depression, he chose a tactic suited to the American national
character. Exuding optimism and confidence at his first inau-
gural address in 1933, he told the Americans that all they "have
to fear is fear itself." And then he started pondering how to
tackle the country's overwhelming economic problems.

In 1990 Helmut Kohl faced a huge challenge of his own:
One part of Germany was prosperous and free (if somewhat
given to complaining), while the other was impoverished,
repressed, and ravaged by more than four decades of communist

rule. Kohl had to find a way to weld the two German states into a national whole.

Throughout the summer and fall of 1990, Kohl chose the path taken by Roosevelt. He promised the East Germans "that blooming landscapes are on their way" and would be there within five years. And he insisted that this could be done without raising taxes.

It soon become clear that Kohl's timeframe was on the optimistic side, as was his no-tax promise. Kohl's original idea had been that private business would change East Germany. But West German industry was reluctant to move east in the beginning, among other things because of unsettled property rights, and thus the federal government was forced to play a major part in the reconstruction.[1]

In the fall of 1992 Kohl proposed the so-called Solidarity Pact, which prioritized rebuilding the East over expanding the economy in the West. The purpose of the Solidarity Pact was to redistribute wealth from West to East, and it passed in the Bundestag with support from the major parties. In terms of tax incentives, low interest loans, and subsidies, between 1990 and 1997 public net capital transfers from West to East averaged 195 billion Marks annually—$130 billion, targeted at a region of 17 million people. Bonn has pumped more money into East Germany annually than the entire Marshall Plan gave to *all* of Europe.

The money had to come from somewhere, specifically the pocketbooks of the West Germans. The vast expenditure meant imposing a 7.5 percent unification tax in 1991. Although it was supposed to last for only one year, it continued through 1997 and caused much unhappiness among the Westerners. (It was reduced to 5 percent in 1998.) Many older West Germans remembered their own hardships in post–World War II days when the currency reform of 1948 took away everything they owned. Back then, they had received one new Deutsche Mark for fifteen old Reichsmarks. They did not think the Easterners deserved such largesse without having to lift a finger.[2]

Most economists now believe it will take decades for the Eastern part of Germany to catch up to Western standards. A recent study published by the German government and produced by the Rhineland Westphalian Institute for Economic Research estimated that, with an annual average growth rate of 4 percent in the East (an optimistic estimate) and 2.5 percent in the West, it will take until the year 2038 for the East to fully attain Western standards.

Helmut Kohl was roundly criticized for promising too much and even accused by the opposition of deceiving the German people to win the first unity election. Was Kohl deliberately breaking his own first rule of leadership to "tell it like it is"?

Two answers can be given to this question. From a psychological angle, it would have been counterproductive to tell a population that had already endured decades of socialist rule that they must patiently endure years of further hardship. They needed someone to hold out the promise that better times were ahead, as indeed they were, although they would arrive more slowly than had been hoped.

Says Birgit Breuel, the third and last director of the Treuhandanstalt, the giant privatization agency that was entrusted with the task of turning East German state-owned property over to private hands, "I think it was important at the time to give people hope and give them a feeling it was worthwhile to strive for it. Kohl defined the goal." In her opinion, the Churchill approach would have been a terrible idea. "Blooming landscapes" was not meant as a detailed plan, but more as a vision.

The second explanation is that Kohl and his government simply did not know the state of the country they had taken over. With some exaggeration, it has been suggested that East Germany in 1989 looked much as Germany had after World War II.[3]

More accurate perhaps were the comments of a British observer who compared the New Laender after unification to Liverpool twenty years after it ceased to be an important port city—with a touch of North Korea thrown in for color. The housing stock was a mess with 40 percent of the multifamily dwellings needing repair and 11 percent uninhabitable by West German standards. Only 25 percent of East German households had a telephone (compared to 98 percent in West Germany). Roads and railways were in disrepair; most of the trains crawled along at a few miles an hour. Every power station had to be shut down after unification because by Western standards they were too dangerous to operate. Strip mines were found to have devastated large swaths of the landscape. Moreover, the country was massively polluted; whole towns were unsuited for human habitation. Everywhere the effects of eye-stinging chemicals could be felt, mingled with the ever-present stale odor and dust of coal-burning. As readers of spy thrillers know, and as every foreign correspondent's wife can testify, a visitor returning from East Germany could always be recognized from the smell of his clothes.

Ironically, the East German economy had for a long time been regarded as the tenth largest in the world by organizations such as the United Nations. This must rank among the grossest economic misjudgments ever made, but it gave rise to the myth that the Germans were the only people on earth who could make communism work. The truth was that *not even* the Germans could accomplish this. After unification, members of the old Communist leadership, like Eric Honecker's successor, Egon Krenz, and East Berlin Party boss Guenther Schabowski, confessed that the country had been broke since the mid-1980s and that only West German assistance had prevented it from going bankrupt.

It is one thing for UN economists to make mistakes in their estimates (it would not be the first time), but it is quite another for the main West German economic institutes to be equally deluded. How could the economic intelligence out of East Germany have been so bad? After all, West German industrialists traveled regularly to East Germany on business trips. Did they not have eyes? Did they not report what they saw to West German economists?

Much of the answer could be found in the East German regime's knack for carefully stage-managing reality. West German visitors were allowed only to see a series of elaborately staged Potemkin villages. Recalls Birgit Breuel, "I was there rather often. You would only meet people who were allowed to meet you, and you were only allowed to see things you were allowed to see. You did not get a real inside view. There was no chance."

If West German businessmen went to meet with the management of a factory, they did not get an opportunity to inspect the factory itself. Meetings were held in carefully chosen ground, such as the posh Grand Hotel in East Berlin, where Western visitors lived in splendid isolation—their rooms were bugged, of course, as were the dining-room tables.

Looking back, says then–National Security Adviser Horst Teltschik, one of the Kohl government's mistakes when it took power in 1982 was not to get a clear view of what was going on in the East German economy. "We were not courageous enough in 1982 to reestablish the research group, the so-called Wissenschaftlicher Beirat within the Ministry of Inner German Relations, which did the economic research on the GDR." Teltschik explains: "This group had been abolished by the Social Democrats and the Free Democrats back in the early 1970s as a relic of the Cold War. We did not reestablish it because we ourselves were a little bit afraid of being accused of being Cold Warriors." The East Germans, of course, would have raised holy hell.

During the 1970s the Ministry of Inner German Relations was itself cut way back in personnel, reduced to some three hundred people including drivers and messengers (compared to the Foreign Ministry's five thousand). Many of the key analysts were former East German political prisoners, which paradoxically meant that their advice and opinions were not particularly welcomed or respected. Typical of many Soviet and East European refugees in the West in those days, they were suspected of harboring a "grudge" against their former countrymen. Therefore, it was felt, they were incapable of being "objective."

One of the few people who got it right in the Ministry of Inner German Relations was Armin Volze. In the autumn of 1990 he estimated the East German production level at only 30 percent of West Germany's. But he was careful to say that this was an estimate, not an analysis, since he did not have all the relevant data to support it. The West German Ministry of Economy set the figure at 60 percent. (As of today, the New Laender has reached only 62 percent, even after a huge infusion of qualified personnel and money.)

The last minister for Inner German Relations before the fall of the Berlin Wall, Dorothee Wilms, did in fact begin to worry about the absence of reliable data in 1988. Accordingly, she invited Horst Teltschik to join a working group in the ministry. At the group's first meeting, the minister was very careful not to admit publicly that such a group even existed. "But by then," says Teltschik, "it was too late for us to form a clear picture."

Some had even optimistically expected a surplus from the privatization and sale of assets and advocated that they should be distributed among the former East German population. That, of course, was not to be. It soon became evident that whatever economic output the East Germans could boast of had been achieved only by running machinery into the ground, exploiting the work force, and ignoring the environment.

Just after the fall of the Berlin Wall, Prime Minister Hans Modrow estimated the country's total wealth at around 1.5 trillion Deutsche Marks, roughly $1 trillion. His successor following the elections in March 1990, Lothar de Maizière, corrected that estimate downwards to 800 billion Deutsche Marks. By Unification Day, October 3, 1990, Treuhand Director Detlev Rohwedder issued yet another correction, stating that he believed some nine thousand state-owned enterprises in East Germany with forty thousand production sites were worth all of 500 billion Deutsche Marks. By the next spring, Rohwedder was driven to declare that East German assets and liabilities would probably cancel each other out.

Eventually, Birgit Breuel concluded that there would be a

final net loss in the East German account of 420 billion Deutsche Marks. Two hundred fifty billion of that came from losses incurred during privatization of state-owned industries, 28 billion from the East German national debt, about 110 billion from the cost of the currency union, and 30 billion from the still unpaid costs of housing construction.[4]

This was what Kohl inherited.

Kohl made his most important decision in February 1990, when he decided to give the East Germans an exchange rate of one Ost Mark to one Deutsche Mark. This move, designed to protect East German pensions and savings, amounted to largesse on a colossal scale.

In doing so, Kohl had overruled Karl-Otto Poehl, the president of the Bundesbank, the German equivalent of the Federal Reserve. Just before Kohl unveiled his economic plans, Poehl called the money union premature, "a fantasy." He argued that a 1:1 rate was far too generous, and pointed out that before reunification the exchange rate had been about 5:1. Even at a 5:1 rate, Poehl said, the East Germans were uncompetitive. Poehl predicted a 1:1 rate would mean mass unemployment in the East, plus tax increases in the West to underwrite unification. Poehl resigned in 1991.

On the political level, Kohl was clearly right, and in this case, the political level was the more important. The decision on the Mark exchange rate was an essential part of Kohl's aggressive strategy on unification—to prevent the Easterners from moving West.

But as Poehl had predicted, this decision did not come without profound implications for the competitiveness of the East German worker. The problems soon became apparent, and the initial euphoria that attended the fall of the Berlin Wall was replaced by a sense of disappointment in both parts of Germany. The prosperous Westerners grumbled about having to foot the bill for unification, and the Easterners found that their expectations for instant paradise had been unrealistic.

What happened in the New Laender was comparable to

industrial changes that had taken place elsewhere in Germany—for instance, in the painful restructuring of the coal, steel, chemical, and heavy industries of North Rhine Westphalia. The difference was that in North Rhine Westphalia the process took twenty-five years; in the New Laender the same process lasted just four.

Says Helmut Kohl, "We need to have a particular under-standing for the people of the New Laender. To a certain degree, they have to go through in quick-motion the change of structure that the people in the old Laender had decades to do."

The privatization process was especially painful. In 1990 the Kohl government had set up a government agency, the Treuhandanstalt, whose task was to privatize the state-owned East German industry over a period of four years, transforming the country into a modern economy. Accordingly, the Treuhandanstalt privatized 14,000 businesses, shut down 190 huge government enterprises, and liquidated 3,500.[5] The phi-losophy of Treuhand Director Detlev Rohwedder was that keeping these firms going with artificial life-support might be a relief in the short run, but in the long run they would bleed the economy in the East. Only what was economically sound should survive.

The result was massive layoffs, a profound shock for the for-mer East Germans. East Germany had kept 92 percent of its working-age population "employed" in some job, no matter how stupefying, wasteful, or useless. Full employment levels were the be-all and end-all of the Communist regime. The West German economy, even for all its social aspects, viewed labor as a resource to be used as productively as possible, like any other market economy. (Even at what would be considered full employment, only 66 percent of the working-age population has been part of the West German work force.) Altogether, in the first four years almost 40 percent of all jobs that had existed in 1989 in the East were lost, much of that due to the sudden disappearance of the Soviet market.

The attitude of the German unions only made matters

worse. A key question in the success of the economic transformation of the New Laender was whether people in the East would accept lower wage increases in order to protect jobs and curb inflation.

Kohl and his economists argued that it was essential that the rise in wages be gradual, that the goal was not instant Western wages, but maintaining a strong rate of growth and reincorporating as many people as possible into productive jobs. After all, in other European regions, such as Scotland or the south of Italy, wages are lower than the national average. Yet people stay, unwilling to trade the satisfaction of local life for the higher wages they might earn elsewhere.

The German unions would have none of it, arguing that a society with two different sets of wages would produce two different sets of workers, first and second class. Their demands prevailed. Eastern wages went up sharply and the Easterners got the same social benefits as their Western colleagues. Productivity remained at only 62 percent, while unit labor costs were 30 percent above that of Western Germany. Inevitably a price had to be paid, and that price was unemployment. Instead of having two classes of workers, Germany now has the employed and the unemployed.

By 1994 only 6.4 million of East Germany's 1989 workforce of 9.8 million had work. While progress has been made, the figures have remained stubbornly high, with the unemployed totaling some four million people for the country as a whole. The figure would be even higher were it not for a vast array of government-sponsored workfare and training programs.

The transition to Western employment principles meant severe upheaval for the entire social structure. Housing complexes in the old East Germany, for instance, were built on the assumption that they would not be used during the day—both parents would be out working, while the children were being brought up by the state to be little model Prussians. It is almost impossible to convey the sheer joyless bleakness of the housing projects the East Germans built everywhere, concrete high-rise boxes separated by vast asphalt expanses. The buildings make no concessions for the need of children to play, or the need of adults to interact with their neighbors. Today, the great majority of the unemployed are women, stuck with their children in the East German barracks, far from shops, playgrounds, and civilization. Some politicians have publicly voiced their fears of urban ghettoization of the unemployed.

The economic blow was cushioned by Germany's generous welfare system, and the situation never got out of hand as in Germany after World War II, when painful economic reforms, currency exchange, and the freeing of prices brought Germans into the streets crying, "Erhard to the gallows!" Still, the anger and frustration in the East found expression in street demonstrations and occasional acts of terrorism. In 1991 the revived left-wing terrorist group Red Army Faction assassinated Treuhand's director, Detlev Rohwedder. In a distasteful display of mockery, young East Germans took to wearing buttons that read, "It wasn't me."

Before Birgit Breuel took over as head of Treuhand after Rohwedder's death, she made some searching personal deliberations: "I was a close friend of Detlev Rohwedder. It was a terrible time when he was murdered. I talked to my family for a long time wondering whether I should take the job or not. I myself was quite sure I should take it." Asked how the murder of Rohwedder affected the way she saw her job, Birgit Breuel answers, "I was the most hated person in Germany, for sure, but it did not affect my work because I was convinced the work had to be done, and that was all."

But some observers believe that the murder led to a softening of the initial free-market philosophy of the Treuhand. Instead of automatically selling off enterprises to the highest bidder, the prize often went to the bidder who promised to keep on the most employees or who promised to take over a less attractive property in addition to a profitable one.

As popular as he was before unification, Kohl was personally exposed to expressions of public hostility during some of his trips to the former East Germany. On one occasion, in the city of

Halle in 1991, he was pelted with eggs and tomatoes by leftist protesters. Kohl became so furious that he charged into the crowd and managed to grab hold of one of the hecklers, who had to be rescued by police from the wrath of the chancellor. It later turned out that warnings of impending trouble for this event from West German security personnel had been disregarded by the state interior minister, who turned out to be an old Stasi informer and had to resign. From that time on, concerns for Kohl's security when he was traveling in the East increased, and his security detail was expanded.[6]

STILL, IF WEST GERMANY could bounce back so quickly from the total devastation of World War II, why has it taken so long for the New Laender to revive? A crucial difference between the situation in Germany in 1990 and Germany after World War II is that, after the war, the Germans were all in the same boat and had to start all over again under the careful supervision of the Western Allied powers. Says Birgit Breuel, "At the time of Ludwig Erhard, everybody in Germany had the same goals: they needed food, they needed homes, they needed jobs, they needed everything."

Remembers Helmut Kohl, "As a first-semester student, I walked from the Frankfurt railway station to the university campus, which took me past a heap of ruins. If anybody had asked me then how Frankfurt would look within a few decades, I would never have predicted what has become reality."

After unification, however, Germany remained divided economically and socially. The Westerners had an interest in defending their accumulated privileges. The Easterners, for their part, were dependent on the kindness not of strangers, as was the case with West Germany after World War II, but of their own German cousins. Taking hand-outs from family may well be more difficult than taking it from strangers, and it certainly causes more resentment and squabbling. At the same time, the Easterners had options and alternatives not available to the World War II generation. People could move from one part of Germany to the other in search of economic opportunity, which gave them less of a stake in the rebuilding of their own communities.

Various psychological conditions arose in Eastern Germany, such as inferiority complexes and bitterness over being second-class citizens in their own country. In the beginning, the Easterners tended to look on Westerners who took up the challenge to settle in the East with deep suspicion, not as pioneers who wanted to take a chance and build something new, but as carpetbaggers and colonizers, people who could not quite cut it in the West and so came to lord it over the Easterners.

And of course there will always be those who live up to their bad reputation. In the beginning, there were unfortunate examples of Westerners who took advantage of the Easterners' naiveté in business matters, thereby confirming all the old communist propaganda about rapacious capitalists.

Young German men in the immediate postwar years had to grow up fast because the war had wiped out an entire generation. They had to take responsibility at an early age; sons became the heads of families. After unification, there was not quite the same motivation. A sentiment often expressed by the Easterners was that, although *all* of Germany had lost the war, the West was rewarded while the East was punished. They felt they were owed something, which is never conducive to accomplishment.

While the Poles, Czechs, and Hungarians initially complained that they had no rich relative like the West Germans to bail them out, at least they had the satisfaction of knowing that whatever results they achieved were due to their own efforts and hard work.

As a consequence of the trauma of uncertainty experienced by many former East Germans, polls in 1992 revealed declining faith in the market economy even as living standards were improving. While more than half the population confirmed that they could afford to buy more, approval of the capitalist system was dropping, from 77 percent in 1990 to 44 percent in 1992.

Thus, since unification, opinion polls reflect a move away from the emphasis on freedom and toward egalitarian values and social justice, which hampers economic progress. To speak of "unfettered capitalism" and an "elbow society" as the East Germans do when they speak of conditions in their new country clearly shows a profound lack of knowledge of how the rest of the world works.

In opinion polls conducted by the Allensbach Institute, when East Germans are asked if prices should be fixed by the state or kept free in order to have a greater choice of goods and better quality, 55 percent of the East Germans came out in favor of fixed prices.

According to Allensbach founder Elizabeth Noelle-Neumann, in similar polls taken in the mid-1950s among West Germans, a majority also supported fixed prices, to which they had been accustomed under the Nazis. The difference between then and now is that, in the case of postwar West Germany, public acceptance of free prices and a market economy grew steadily and gradually, with no regressive nostalgia for the past.[7]

The situation has not been improved by the fact that the German media often portray the collapse of East Germany not as a result of the communist system's inner failure, but as a casualty of the capitalist economy. In this scenario, the people of the East become victims rather than free individuals who have been given the chance of a new beginning. Indeed, the whole notion of freedom seems long forgotten.[8]

In fact, capitalism is not particularly popular in the western part of Germany either. Back in 1988 some of Germany's bishops publicly castigated Kohl for creating "an egotistical society" at the CDU Party Congress in Wiesbaden, for being insensitive to the plight of the poor, and for being a proponent of heartless capitalism—this, even though Germany is one of the most generous welfare states in the world.

While acknowledging the plight of the East Germans, Kohl has continuously stressed that there is no substitute for hard work. After World War II, says Kohl, "The whole nation pulled

up its sleeves to help the Bundesrepublik to blossom and pros-
per. No one asked in those days what the state could do for you.
We need precisely the same readiness to assume personal
responsibility, the same 'yes' to hard work if we want the inner
unification of our country."

Finally, Lothar Spaeth, the former prime minister of
Baden-Wuerttemberg and today the chairman of Jenoptik, has
pointed out a crucial reason for Eastern Germany's slow recovery. After unification, the pioneer businessman had to play
according to the much more complicated rules of the 1990s,
whereas things were much simpler back in the 1950s and 1960s.

The expensive government-sponsored training and employment programs themselves have become part of the problem.
After all, a job-training program is not the same as a job. After
watching East Germany's economic recovery slow down in
1995, the German Economics Ministry stated that the programs
were not workable in the long term, for they were too expensive
and restricted the scope of action for private companies.

STILL, 5 PERCENT OF A NATION'S wealth does not transfer eastward, as has been the case in Germany, without showing some
results. All these troubles aside, the physical transformation of
the East has been progressing steadily, and perhaps the
Germans with their cultural pessimism are not always the best
judges of their own progress. Often they resemble the patient
who is taking his temperature every half-hour and wondering
why he is not getting better.

The fact is that already more than 700,000 entrepreneurs
have started up in the East since 1990, and construction is taking place all over East Germany. Since unification, 11,000 kilo-
meters of autobahn have been repaired or built; in a reversal
of the old days, it is not uncommon to find that the roads get
better, rather than worse, as you travel east. In a few years, the
eastern part of Germany will have a more sophisticated infra-
structure than western Germany, jumping a generation of
technology. The railway system has also been completely over-

hauled. And while most of the old West Germany still has copper wire for its phone cables, the five eastern states have the newest fiber optic cables, and five million new telephones have been connected. New power stations have been built, resulting in a dramatic drop in pollution. The same goes for sewage filtration plants.

A couple of crucial political decisions have contributed to speeding up integration and boosting eastern Germany. One was to reconstitute the New Laender as federal states the way they had existed prior to the Nazi takeover in 1933. Back then, Hitler did away not just with all political parties, except of course his own, but also with the federal structure that had existed since 1871.

Restoring the old federal framework was meant to help the East Germans reestablish some idea of local identity. Economically, perhaps it did not make much difference, since the areas involved are not that big. Politically, however, it had significant benefits. If the former East Germany had been accepted as one federal state, like, say, North Rhine Westphalia, the East German population would have formed one big sullen mass. Divided into different Laender, these people got a chance to develop separate local identities as well as separate representation in the Bundesrat, the upper house of the German parliament.

Another central decision by the Kohl government was to relocate Germany's capital from Bonn to Berlin by the year 2000. Leading Social Democrats like Walter Momper, the mayor of Berlin, argued against the idea because of the Nazi past, when Berlin's cityscape was overwhelmed by Hitler and Speer's grandiose creations meant to last throughout the Thousand Year Reich. In Momper's view, the capital should remain in Bonn, a city characterized by its unobtrusive sleepiness. Meanwhile, Berlin should become the German "capital of imagination, of creativity, and of self-development"—fancy words, but not likely to inspire the economic confidence that the East desperately needed.

Others emphasized the significant costs of moving the German capital east, including ministries, embassies, and the rest. Estimates ranged from ten billion Marks to several hundred billion. (The latter estimate, not surprisingly, came from the mayor's office in Bonn, where the political establishment saw its real estate values plummet.)

For Kohl, the political concerns outweighed the costs. In his view, the move was crucial to promote the economic upswing of the eastern part of Germany. Moving the Bundestag there would mean a huge boost for the city and its surrounding areas. Also, it showed a commitment to the revitalization of eastern Germany and forced politicians from the West to view local problems up close. They would simply not have the luxury of armchair solutions arrived at while sipping white wine on the Rhine. For supporters of the move, Berlin remained the central symbol of a unified Germany.

On June 20, 1991, the German parliament voted in favor of Berlin. Kohl had known for a long time that this was the only correct decision. As he told his colleagues after the vote, "In June 1987, I stood with Ronald Reagan in front of the Brandenburg Gate when he cried, 'Mr. Gorbachev, open this gate!' If someone had asked me at that time—but no one did—what the German capital was, I would have said 'Berlin.'"[9]

Similarly, great efforts have been made to restore cities like Erfurt and Weimar; the latter historic city has been meticulously restored. Efforts have also been made to revive the traditional Leipzig fair, which has taken place since the Middle Ages. The communists had tried to keep the tradition alive, but, needless to say, the products proudly on display by the East German state did not cut much of a technological edge. Today, an impressive exhibition center reminiscent of Victorian London's famed Crystal Palace has gone up, which could put Leipzig back on the map as a key industrial and banking center in the East.

A great symbolic piece of reconstruction is the rebuilding of the Frauenkirche in Dresden. The structure was practically pulverized during the Allied firebombing in 1945, which in one night flattened the old baroque city on the Elbe river. The church had been left in ruins by the East German government (which was not big on churches). Initially, after unification, the city fathers thought of leaving it as a permanent monument to the horrors of war, like the Gedaechtniskirche in Berlin, but the idea was rejected on the grounds that one such ruin was enough. Germany now needed more hopeful symbols. The reconstruction is funded by donations from the people of Dresden and reflects a determination to rebuild the country.

Still, while cities like Leipzig, Dresden, and Berlin are catching up to the West, other areas remain stubbornly hard to bring along, particularly rural areas like Mecklenburg-West Pomerania or those dominated by the drab communist landscape of concrete tower blocks like Brandenburg.

But for all the mumbling and grumbling, the complaining about costs, and the talk about inner walls still separating the two German states, an opinion poll conducted by the Allensbach Institute in 1996 drew a revealing picture. The question was asked: "Sometimes people wish they could turn the wheel of history back. How do you feel? Have you ever thought that it would be better if the two German states had not reunited, that it would be better if there had been an independent German Democratic Republic?" And the follow up question: "If it were possible, for instance, in a referendum, would you support a retreat on unification or not?" In Western Germany, only 15 percent said that they would go back, and in the former East Germany, even fewer people, 10 percent, thought a return to the German Democratic Republic was an appealing idea. In both West and East, 70 percent declared that they would prefer things the way they are today. When it comes to the bottom line, the Germans know their minds.[10]

JUSTICE VERSUS RECONCILIATION IN THE EAST

BACK IN THE EIGHTEENTH CENTURY, Frederick Wilhelm of Prussia, father of Frederick the Great, had a most peculiar hobby. He collected giants. The pride and joy of his life, they were put to service in his Potsdamer Grenadiers. He acquired as many as two thousand of these oddities, six to seven feet tall, which was tall indeed in those days. He would go to extraordinary lengths to add to his collection; some he paid vast sums for, others he had kidnapped from neighboring countries. When the supply dried up, he even tried breeding them. Many of them were not particularly bright, to say the least. At Frederick Wilhelm's death in 1740, the Grenadiers were reorganized and the most moronic dismissed. Before long, the European landscape was filled with disoriented giants, trying to find their way home.[1]

Some 250 years later, in 1990, the dreaded East German state security service, the Stasi, was dismantled. Visitors to Germany half expected to see a similar sight: unemployed goons slouching home to their local villages with the collars of their trademark leather jackets turned up over their ears. That didn't happen of course. And in contrast to Frederick Wilhelm's slow-witted giants, Erich Honecker's security force was not for show, but rather it was a highly trained elite force whose tentacles reached into every aspect of East German life.[2]

What the Kohl government faced when it took over East Germany was not just economic reconstruction. Brought up in the spirit of Margot Honecker, the education minister and wife of Erich Honecker, whole generations had been raised to be obedient servants of the state, to rat on neighbors, to suppress any feelings, and, above all, to stop playing with their genitals. British historian Alistair Horne has compared the freeing of the East Germans to the freeing of the prisoners in the last act of Beethoven's opera *Fidelio*, when the oppressed emerge blinking into the radiant sunlight of freedom. It takes a while to adapt to personal freedom, and for some it has come too late.

In an echo of his "grace of a late birth" comment about World War II, Helmut Kohl warned the West Germans not to judge too harshly those who had the misfortune to live in the former East Germany. "I do not know what would have happened to me if I had been in Leipzig in 1950 where my wife comes from. Would I have crossed over to the West? Would I have stayed and accommodated? Or would I have landed in the infamous Bautzen prison because of resistance to the regime? I cannot answer this question. When we are honest, we must admit that none of us can answer that kind of question," says Kohl.

"We in the West—as opposed to the people in East Germany—have for years been living on the sunny side of German history. That is not something we have deserved, we were just lucky," Kohl adds.

The scale and brutality of the East German system was staggering. The all-pervasive influence of the state and the

Party during the Communist period was stronger even than that of the Nazis, and, of course, it went on for much longer. The security service included some 100,000 full-time spies and some 300,000 part-time informers.

The files in the former Stasi headquarters in Norman-nenstrasse, which was occupied in December 1989 by demonstrators, are immense and take up 125 miles of shelf space. Altogether they contain six million dossiers, covering about one-third of the East German population. A typical file contains at least forty names of informers, which gives an idea of how many people were involved. The victims are described in the most intimate detail. There was even a so-called "smells library" on dissidents. Socks and used underwear were stolen from the dissidents' laundry baskets and preserved in neatly labeled glass jars, to enable police dogs to pick up their scent if and when needed.[3]

"Internment" camps were planned to receive 200,000 troublemakers, just in case things ever got out of hand. Heinz Eggert, who became justice minister of Saxony after unification, once joked to a former Stasi officer that he would not have had to travel very far to reach the camp since it was located right next to his home. To which the Stasi officer gave a rather chilling response, "You, Mr. Eggert, would not have reached it alive."[4]

In the former East Germany, the scars of betrayal are everywhere: scientists betrayed fellow scientists, sportsmen betrayed fellow sportsmen, artists and clergymen betrayed their own. Brother was turned against brother, sons against their parents. There are even examples of husbands and wives spying on each other—the ultimate betrayal.

The informing extended all the way up to the Politburo, where Honecker did his best to prevent the formation of cliques by encouraging members to inform on each other, creating an atmosphere of fear and suspicion.

When Defense Minister Heinz Kessler heard spy chief Markus Wolf talk about the need for reform in the spirit of Gorbachev (Wolf was always more loyal to the Soviets than to his own regime), Kessler made a beeline for Honecker to tell him that his espionage chief was up to no good.[5]

The object, as far as the state was concerned, was to isolate and destroy the individual. German psychologists talk of mass psychosis manifesting itself in apathy and aggression, and political scientists fear the impact the communist legacy will have on the long-term political culture of the country. Some even talk of a specific dysfunctional East German identity, characterized by emotional stuntedness, a tendency toward subordination, and psychological repression.

Perhaps the essence of the East German system and what it demanded of its citizens was best caught by the novelist Heinrich Mann in his characterization of East German leader Walter Ulbricht: "I cannot sit down at a table with a man who will suddenly maintain that the table we are sitting round is not a table but a duckpond, and then tries to force me to agree with him."[6]

ONE OF THE FIRST QUESTIONS that faced the Kohl government in 1990 was what to do with the Stasi archives. The initial impulse among some judicial experts was to destroy the files or seal them forever, to put a lid over the past, which could poison the atmosphere for decades. But this was ruled out by the East German opposition figures. Chief among them was Joachim Gauck, a prominent Protestant minister who today is federal commissioner for the Stasi files in Berlin. Gauck argues that the East Germans must acknowledge their history, no matter how painful the experience. "Only through facing up to the past can one build a better future," he says. "In Germany, we know who betrayed whom, and who resisted. Elsewhere, say in Poland, which did not go through a similar process, you have constant rumors, which is even more poisoning to the atmosphere."

The information contained in the Stasi files is no longer the property of the state, Gauck and his staff argue. If it belongs to anybody, it belongs to the victims. The files are necessary for rehabilitation, for people to get their sentences annulled, and to compensate the victims. In any event, to have kept the files secret would have been politically impossible. Says Johann Legner from the Federal Commission for Stasi Files, "The East Germans considered the files the booty of their revolution. They occupied the building, they stopped the officials when they wanted to destroy them. They considered it their legal heritage."

After an intense debate over access and control, it was agreed in the internal unification treaty between the two German states that the files be centrally deposited in Berlin and that in principle everybody should have access to his own file, provided that the interest of a third party was not endangered. No intelligence service was to have access to the files, but prosecutors would still be able to mine them for the wealth of information on terrorist operations.

The issue, morally and politically, is how to bring reconciliation and justice to the New Laender. The difference between the situation after World War II and after unification is that, back then, there were the Allies to conduct the Nuremberg process, which created its own special legal foundation. But today, officially, there are no victors and no losers. The Federal Republic did not conduct a war against East Germany and did not want to act as the victor after unification. Moreover, West Germans were not comfortable with sitting in judgment over their fellow countrymen, who, after all, paid the price of losing World War II for forty-five years longer than the West Germans.

According to Helmut Kohl, who admits to having entertained doubts about the consequences of making the files accessible but ended up supporting it, it is clear that a society cannot forever tear itself apart over the past. It is equally clear that people want to see justice done and the guilty punished. "In this we have to do with the age-old tension to do justice and mercy," says Kohl. He continues:

> Both are important values, both should characterize a society with a human face. The victims want justice, the guilty demand leniency. In looking at the GDR we must take into

account that the communist dictatorship lasted over four decades, and hardly anyone believed—least of all those who ride a high moral horse today—that it would disappear so quickly from the picture.

It is my opinion that every representative of the communist system who is guilty of breaking the law, should be held responsible before the court.

But one should not treat with moral superiority those who in a seemingly hopeless situation did not behave like heroes. One must always keep before one's eyes what it means to live forty years with a communist dictatorship. For instance, there were people who from a very young age were forced to work for the Stasi. What youngster has not at some point committed an act of foolishness, for instance, in school? In this way, a sophisticated, criminal system caught many people in its net and blackmailed them for years. And they almost inevitably compromised themselves.

The argument for reconciliation, according to Kohl, is that the overwhelming majority of East Germans were not hardcore communists. They were people who tried to survive in a totalitarian world, a mixture of opportunists and pragmatists, like most people, deserving a chance because they have never had one.

OBVIOUSLY, THE INFORMATION CONTAINED in the files has to be handled with great caution. For one thing, there is the question of what constitutes an informer. Stasi informers would often line their own pockets by submitting the names of friends and relatives as sources who needed to be paid. No information may have been forthcoming, but who is to know, five or ten years later, whether someone did or did not receive money for information. All that is left is the incriminating entry in the files. In this way, the victims of the old system could become victims of the new system as well. There is also the possibility that Stasi operatives, particularly during the last days of the Modrow regime, contaminated the files by inserting false information about their enemies and by removing other material.

Then there is the problem of distinguishing between different types of information, warns historian Manfred Goertemaker, editor of the autobiography of East German leader Egon Krenz, who has examined thousands of files. "If you wanted to travel abroad as a historian, you had to cooperate with the Ministry for State Security. But there are different ways of doing this. Some cases are straightforward; people spy on their colleagues and offer advice on how to destroy their careers. Many, however, are vague and general in nature, and do not contain much except a general assessment of the political climate in whatever institution was involved. In short, the informer was not really interested in telling the security service anything; he just fulfilled an obligation."

Werner Kraetchel, a leading member of the Lutheran protest movement in East Germany, has stated that everybody who lived in East Germany was to some degree guilty. At some point, everyone made a compromise or chose silence or sought an advantage for their children. The whole point of the Communist regime was to coopt its citizens. To hold any kind of serious job above that of common worker or street sweeper, one had to be a member of the Communist Party. If parents deviated from the Party line, their children would be denied educational possibilities. That meant compromises had to be made.

But to say that no one is without guilt is both a very harsh judgment and a very forgiving one. And it is a moral judgment, not a legal one. The danger is also that everybody suddenly becomes a victim, both the Stasi and its targets. There is such a thing as too much understanding.

Here fundamental questions of justice and fairness present themselves: How does a political dissident like Horst Erdmann get justice? Erdmann spent a decade in Bautzen prison for the "crime" of distributing pamphlets calling for free elections in Germany during the 1953 Berlin uprising. At the time he was a young medical student. He suffered badly in prison, and was smuggled out of East Berlin in 1964 in the trunk of a car. But he was never able to complete his studies because of chronic health problems. Today, his heart is so frail he cannot even go on an airplane. Somehow, a disability pension does not quite seem enough for a ruined life like this. Erdmann knows who his tormentors are.

Or take the case of the church warden who turned in a six-teen-year-old boy for telling a bad Erich Honecker joke, which earned the boy a two-year jail sentence. Or how about the woman who wanted to emigrate and placed a cardboard "A" for *Ausreise* (an application for one of the exceedingly rare permis-sions to leave the country) in the window of her flat? She, too, was given a two-year prison sentence.

In terms of justice being served, the German record has been less than impressive. Says Juergen Aretz, Kohl's chief of the New Laender section in the Chancellery, "Unfortunately, I don't think we are handling it very well. I'm not content with what our courts have obtained up till now, and I do not think Chancellor Kohl is very happy with it." The Chancellery, how-ever, was powerless to influence the decisions. "Our justice sys-tem is absolutely independent, even more so than in the United States."

The primary obstacle here has been the agreement struck between the two sides during the unification negotiations—that criminals could be prosecuted only according to East German law, as it applied at the time, not according to West German law or international law on crimes against humanity, as in the case at Nuremberg. Here the German past played a role again. Because the Nazis had a habit of introducing retroactive laws to punish their political and "racial" enemies, Germany today has an iron-clad rule against retroactivity. Only acts contrary to East German law can therefore be prosecuted.

The problem here, of course, is that the East German lead-ers themselves created the laws (though some *pro forma* con-cessions to civilized norms were made that were subsequently ignored). In short, they are judged by their own rules. East

German law gave the security services and the border guards practically unlimited power. Though physical assault, murder, and kidnapping were criminal offenses under East German law, just as under the Western system, the legal code contained a series of justifications and exceptions to these laws, which the German courts have been obliged to take into consideration.[7]

At the top of the list of East German criminals was Erich Honecker, who gave border guards the infamous order to shoot to kill anyone trying to escape. Though no written order was found, Honecker made a public statement in 1974 that it was a public duty to shoot people who were trying to flee the Worker's Paradise. He demanded that "weapons be ruthlessly used" and "that every comrade who successfully uses a gun should be praised." Altogether, some nine hundred people were killed trying to escape the East German State, eighty of them at the Berlin Wall. This should certainly have been enough for a conviction. What made things a bit awkward was that West German leaders, first Helmut Schmidt and then Kohl himself, had had to deal with Honecker, thereby conferring *de facto* recognition on him.

In 1992 Honecker was brought back from Moscow, where he had sought refuge in the Chilean Embassy, in order to face trial for the shoot-to-kill order. But to the public's dismay, Honecker was deemed too ill with liver cancer to stand trial. He was allowed to travel to join his family in Chile—his wife Margot, the education minister who was responsible for so many children being taken away from their parents, and their daughter Sonja. There he could be seen puttering about in a straw hat, contemplating the triumphs of the East German regime. And there he died in 1994.

Equally unsatisfactory was the trial of four-star General Erich Mielke, the hated minister of state security, who when facing a hostile crowd back in 1989 made the immortal statement, "But I love you all!" Despite his long service in the East German regime, Mielke was prosecuted for two 1931 killings of policemen during a communist riot in the Weimar Republic.

Many found the proceedings slightly surreal, given the things Mielke was guilty of between 1949 and 1989. But it would have taken years to collect the evidence from his time as minister of state security. Thus, since the 1931 murder cases were never closed, it was decided to go ahead with the prosecution. The files on the murders, which had disappeared in 1945 and remained lost for decades, were found in a suitcase in a safe behind Mielke's own desk in the Security Ministry in Normannenstrasse. He had apparently kept an eye on them for all those years.

Suddenly, however, Mielke seemed to have been struck with senility. Again, health considerations won out, and the prosecution was dropped, though some doctors deemed him perfectly capable of standing trial. This was seen as another gross miscarriage of justice. After all, Nazi leader Rudolf Hess had been held in Spandau prison until the day in 1987 he committed suicide, at the age of ninety-three.

Health concerns also prevailed in the case of Guenter Mittag, the economic "genius" behind the East German economy and hardline Communist Party ideologue, as well as in the case of former Prime Minister Willy Stoph, who suffered a nervous breakdown.

As for Markus Wolf, chief of the East German spy agency, he was at first given a six-year jail term in 1991 on treason and bribery charges. Wolf's lawyers, however, successfully argued that the East German espionage service was like any other intelligence service, the West German Bundesnachrichtendienst or the CIA, for instance. Therefore, Wolf was only serving his country; accordingly, he was acquitted on appeal by Germany's constitutional court in 1995. That the state he served was a criminal state that sponsored state terrorism was somehow overlooked.

The urbane Wolf, with his carefully cultivated John le Carré mystique, is today a best-selling author and a frequent guest on TV talk shows. Juergen Aretz recalls one occasion on which he was promoting a book he coauthored, *The Forgotten Victims of the GDR*. On his way to a radio interview, Aretz passed a publishing house where Markus Wolf was happily signing books. "The scandal is that this fellow was sitting there signing books instead of sitting in jail making baskets."[8]

In a Dusseldorf court in 1997, Wolf finally received a two-year suspended sentence after being convicted of kidnapping, coercion, and bodily harm, something normally considered serious offenses, but apparently not in Wolf's case.

Many of the East German leaders were mediocrities, but Wolf was the exception. Just as in the case of Albert Speer, Hitler's brilliant architect and armaments minister whose efforts helped prolong the war for months, there has been a little too much awe surrounding Wolf. Wolf, like Speer, was the kind of man who made totalitarian systems function. Also like Speer, he ought to have realized that he was serving an evil system. Hence, they should have been judged more severely than others, not more leniently.

In August 1997 Egon Krenz, who for years had been Honecker's right-hand man, was sentenced to six years and six months in prison for manslaughter in the killing of four East Germans along the Berlin Wall. Krenz immediately appealed his sentence. By comparison, Aretz notes, in the former East Germany a young chemist, Gisela Mauritz, was sentenced to six years and eight months for *Republikflucht* (trying to leave East Germany) and for searching for her son, who had been forcibly removed from her because of her political convictions. In the final round of high-level prosecutions, along with Krenz, East Berlin Communist Party leader Guenther Schabowski and Communist Party economic "expert" Guenther Kleiber were given sentences of three years.

The initial fear that the main culprits were literally getting away with murder while the small players had to pay for their crimes turned out to be false. It seemed that everybody got away with murder.

Understandably, there is frustration among the prosecutors, says Berlin Attorney General Christoph Schaefgen. Though

Schaefgen vigorously defends the principle of nonretroactive justice as a precondition for the rule of law, he is clearly not entire pleased with the results. "As a private person, I would say our present system does not go far enough."

"The problem is the judges," says Aretz. "This is my private opinion. The trouble is that in American terms we have very liberal courts. I do not mean to be sarcastic, but if you have had a difficult childhood, or you are coming from difficult social circumstances, you really must put a lot of effort into being found guilty. Many of our judges are transferring this approach to the field of political crime." In short, the impression is that they do not know the difference between a totalitarian system and a democratic one.

And, in fact, had the German justice system really wanted to get these people, it could have. As a member of the United Nations, East Germany had among its laws paragraph 95 of the criminal codex, which stated, "Nobody who acts contrary to fundamental human rights can appeal to laws, orders, or guidelines: that person is responsible before the law." Of course, human rights were not taken too seriously in East Germany. But the courts "do have a tool if they wanted to use it," says Aretz. "They never tried."

Again, there is little the politicians can do. If Kohl had criticized the judges, notes Aretz, for instance, the ones who let Wolf get off with a suspended sentence, the opposition would immediately have accused Kohl of interfering with the justice system.

Some also find it troubling that in all the talk of the need for reconciliation and people needing a second chance, the real victims of the East German system will be forgotten. They might even be regarded as disturbers of the peace, nut cases who remain permanently fixated on the past, embarrassments who are a barrier to reconciliation, so-called "inner unification," and progress. That means they have lost a second time.

Says Kohl, "Under no circumstance should we accept—and unfortunately that happens all too often—that the victims are branded as disturbers of the peace, as troublemakers, while the guilty claim the right to disregard injustice. What we now need is the spirit of inner forgiveness, reconciliation. But we should not force the victims to forgive those who have harmed them. They must take this step out of their own conviction. This would be easier for them if their earlier tormentors were to confess their guilt and ask for forgiveness."

Reconciliation has several preconditions. Kohl is a Catholic, and, according to Catholic doctrine, forgiveness and reconciliation need several steps. Admission of guilt has to be followed by contrition, then the promise to change, and finally an effort to make up for the damage.

Unfortunately, remorse or even expressions of regret have been in fairly short supply from the former East German leadership. Erich Honecker's only regret was that his society had been a bit behind in luxury consumer goods. "Yes, we had no bananas," he once put it in an isolated flash of humor.[9] Egon Krenz certainly never expressed any contrition either. He kept complaining that he was a victim of "victor's justice" and had only been following Soviet orders anyway. One of the few top leaders to express remorse was Guenther Schabowski, who stated at his trial that "those who died at the Wall are part of the burden we inherit from our misguided attempt to free humanity from its plagues. Our search for utopia led us to lay everyone on a Procrustean bed in which the individual was cut to what was thought to be the ideal size."

Much more common, unfortunately, has been the case of the former Stasi members who have set up organizations and networks, so-called *Seilschaften*—a term used by Alpine climbers who are connected by the same rope and thus depend on each other for survival. They show a certain chutzpah in the names of their organizations, portraying themselves as people hunted because of their political convictions.

One such organization styles itself the "Society for the Protection of Human Rights and Values," another the "Society for Legal and Humanitarian Support," a third the "Solidarity Committee for the Victims of Political Prosecution." There are a host of others that take up the cases of old Party comrades under prosecution in the media. (This is in contrast to the 1950s and 1960s, when it would have been unthinkable to put an ex-Nazi on TV except as a photograph in connection with a court case. Today, former East German officials pop up all over the place, complaining about alleged injustice.) Kohl is said to be angered by the gall of the successors of the old Communist Party, with their outrageous political demands.

Making matters worse, some members of the former Stasi are actually flourishing, making a mockery of justice. Just after unification a Stasi joke went like this: "What do you do about Stasi members who have trouble finding a job? Make them taxi drivers. All you have to do is say your name, and they will instantly know where you live."

But many have done better than that. Stasi people, it should be remembered, were disciplined and well educated—more than 50 percent possessed a university degree. Some have found a place in the private economy and are getting ahead. Many ordinary East Germans who have trouble finding jobs are angry when they see their former jailers doing better than themselves.[10] This is especially true of those who suffered disadvantages in their education and professional careers because of their political convictions, and now lack the qualifications to compete in the new system.

"It is difficult for people to understand that capitalism is not a question of character, of morality, but of success, that in a Western society you have to accept that a Stasi officer can be successful," says Johann Legner from the Federal Commission for Stasi Files.

"Let us not forget that when the people of East Germany in 1989 and the beginning of 1990 were yelling 'Put the Stasi to Work,'" says Attorney General Schaefgen, "they did not mean at the management level, but at the floor level, physical labor. That is not a bad idea." What Schaefgen finds particularly offensive is that some former Stasi members have resurfaced in the legal profession:

*Personally, I am still angry at the fact that during the
Modrow period, after the collapse of the Communist regime,
many high state security members who were legal experts
and lawyers simply left the security service and registered
as lawyers.*

*With unification in 1990, they just stepped into the new
Federal Republic as lawyers, and that is unacceptable. They
can only be removed if you can prove they have done harm
to somebody else. There is only one case in Berlin where we
managed to prove this, and where the individual was then
expelled from the legal profession.*

One former East German opposition activist, Baerbel
Bohley, summed up the situation by saying, "We wanted justice,
and instead we got the rule of law."

Was any of this foreseeable to the men who negotiated the
unification treaty with the East Germans?

As minister for the interior, Wolfgang Schaeuble handled
the negotiations on behalf of Kohl. "Sure, we foresaw it," he
says. "In a way, it would have been easier if Gorbachev had said
that he would make a deal under the condition that the East
German leadership be given amnesty. If the Soviet Union had
made the precondition, the Germans would probably have
accepted it. The Germans might not have liked it much, but
they would have understood it as the price for unification. But
the Soviets made no such demand."

Indeed, recalls Schaeuble, the prosecution of Honecker and
a few others had already started under Hans Modrow's
Communist government, which wanted to find a couple of scape-
goats on whom to pin the blame for malfeasance in the GDR.
They wanted to sell the East Germans on the idea that not everything in East Germany was bad, only Erich Honecker. In the
negotiations with Lothar de Maizière's transition government
nobody on the East German side made demands for amnesty,
probably because there would have been a huge public outcry.[11]

The traditional way to draw a *Schlussstrich*, to put a final end to a revolution, argues Schaeuble, is for a country to go through a short period of terror. This is what happened in Romania with the execution of dictator Nicolae Ceausescu and his wife. This was obviously not the case in East Germany, which had a peaceful and nonviolent revolution. Since the German state is based on the rule of law, the Germans have no choice but to go the cumbersome legal way, which does not leave anybody fully satisfied.

What has been achieved in Germany after unification and what is unique in the former East bloc is that the Stasi files have been left open. The whole inner workings of dictatorship is laid out, and you can look at it to the last detail. It has been said about denazification that it did not go nearly far enough, but the Nuremberg records made it impossible to deny what had taken place. The same now goes for the Stasi archives.

To have the whole story told is the basic right of the victims, Kohl insists. "Those who did not bend to the dictatorship, those who have spent their best years in Bautzen prison, they have a special claim to our regard. Above all, they have a claim that the injustice committed by the communist system should be carefully documented for future generations. This is also in accordance with the principles of a strong democracy. We will not permit the enemies of freedom—and that means extremists on the Right as well as on the Left—to have the opportunity to hide the terrible consequences of a totalitarian ideology."

The other main achievement of the process, says Schaefgen, is that former Stasi members are by law prevented from being employed in the civil service, which keeps their pernicious influence out of the German state system. The problem after World War II and the fall of Nazi Germany was that the Americans realized they would be stuck with running Germany forever if they excluded everybody with ties to the Nazi Party. However distasteful the idea may have been, their expertise was needed to rebuild the country they had helped destroy, which meant that the thorough cleansing that denazification was meant to be did not go anywhere near as far as had first been intended. Add to that the beginning of the Cold War, which soon gave the Allies other things to worry about, other priorities.

In Germany, this time around, the civil service cleansing was thorough. For instance, only one diplomat was retained from the Foreign Service of the former East Germany. Officials could simply move from West Germany to the East to fill the vacant positions. The necessary personnel was available to do this.

The cleaning out process has set Germany apart from most of the former communist states in Eastern Europe, where the functions of the state are still hampered by former members of the communist regimes. Only the Czechs cleaned out properly. In the words of a Polish foreign minister, Poland never had a West Poland to draw on. This meant that the Polish state had to continue functioning with many bureaucrats from the communist regime left in place.

One interesting question remains: In a situation in which it is possible for victims to look into the files and identify the people who did them so much harm, in a situation in which the legal system seems less than reliable for obtaining justice, might not some be expected to take matters into their own hands? After all, if you and your family have suffered a lifetime of injustice, legal principles like the perniciousness of retroactive justice may be less than convincing. But there have been surprisingly few examples of violent settling of scores in the former East Germany by individuals—though Egon Krenz did get punched in the nose in a restaurant once by an irate former subject.

Why have there been so few East Germans trying to get back at their tormentors? Several answers have been offered. Dr. Hans-Joachim Maaz at the Hospital for Psychotherapy and Psychosomatics in Halle wrote *Behind the Wall: The Inner Life of East Germany*, the first investigation of the psychological damage done to the East German population. According to Maaz:

They are so inhibited by their own insecurity and lack of self-worth that they cannot even conceive of taking matters into their own hands. They expect justice from above, rather than think of doing something about it themselves.... In their subconscious, many believe they somehow did something wrong, and therefore deserve to be victims. They do not have the courage to protest.

Revenge also takes a certain amount of energy and initiative. Many who have been ground down by a totalitarian state simply do not have either one. If you have lost everything, revenge becomes pointless. The same phenomenon has been observed among Holocaust survivors.

The pent-up anger and frustration of the former East Germans has been directed not at their former oppressors in the Stasi and the Communist government, but as xenophobia against guest workers and refugees from Eastern Europe, who are seen as a particular threat to their jobs. In both East and West Germany there have been ugly instances of attacks on foreigners and of their homes being set on fire.

Pointing to the stability of the German electorate, Kohl initially tended to brush off neo-Nazism and violent extremism as a mental problem, not a political one. True to form, the German courts tended to look for excuses rather than ways to punish the perpetrators. It was thought that the skinheads needed counseling more than anything else, that these misguided young people could surely be persuaded to see the error of their ways. In many cases, skinhead thugs were given suspended sentences for attacks on foreigners. In one case, in the town of Frankfurt-on-Oder on the Polish border, five neo-Nazis who killed an Angolan with a baseball bat were given only three- to five-and-one-half-year sentences for "causing bodily harm," rather than being convicted of murder.

But as the attacks grew in number and viciousness, increasingly taking on the character of coordinated efforts, the German government realized it had a more serious problem on its hands. Some of the most vicious attacks were in the West. In

1992 in Moelln near Luebeck, three Turkish women were burned in their house, and, six months later, in 1993 in Solingen near Dusseldorf, five Turks were killed in a firebombing.[12]

The attacks on foreigners invariably prompted comparisons to the ill-fated Weimar Republic, both in Germany itself and abroad. International concern was rising, and foreign firms were reluctant to invest in the New Laender.

The German left-wing press predictably laid all the trouble at Kohl's door. "This republic is not Weimar," Kohl responded firmly at the time. One major difference was that the neo-Nazi attacks led to mass demonstrations in Berlin and other major cities across Germany denouncing the perpetrators of the violence against foreigners. In Berlin alone, some 350,000 people participated in one protest in March 1992. To see only xenophobia in Germany, the Germans argue, is like judging the United States solely on the Los Angeles riots.

The Kohl government responded by banning three neo-Nazi organizations, all signs resembling Nazi symbols (the real ones had been outlawed since 1945), and any gestures and forms of greeting reminiscent of the Nazi salute. Police enforcement was strengthened, and the courts for their part started handing down heavier sentences on the perpetrators of violence.

At the same time, in 1993, Germany tightened its extremely liberal asylum laws, which were written into the German constitution as an act of contrition for Germany's crimes in World War II. Until recently, foreigners, often economic refugees, only had to show up on the German border and utter the magic word "asylum" to gain admittance. By law, they could not be turned down.

What the Kohl government did was impose border control closer to the standards of other Western countries. Thus the number of asylum-seekers dropped from a high of 438,191 in 1992, to 116,367 in 1996. There was a 50 percent decrease in attacks on foreigners, and the extreme right-wing parties, the Republicans and the German People's Union, were thus deprived of one of their strongest issues. In 1996 only 7.4 percent of applicants were granted asylum.

It should also be noted that during the Balkan war Germany took in some 250,000 refugees, which was four or five times as many as did France, Austria, and Sweden.

UNIFICATION AND ITS AFTERMATH brought renewed attacks on Kohl by Germany's left-wing intelligentsia. Some left-wingers even suggested that, for historical reasons, Germany should not be allowed to celebrate its day of unification. The writer Guenter Grass used the term "skinheads with neck ties" to characterize Kohl's conservative government and accused it of "renewed barbarism against asylum seekers." Alternatively, Grass described Kohl as a nasty new Bismarck. Apocalyptic is too cheerful a word when applied to Grass and his vision of Germany's future.

In opposing unification, Grass fretted about the emergence of a new *Grossdeutschland* launching a business blitzkrieg against its neighbors. Then he warned that the East Germans would experience "the dictates of profit-owned colonial masters who are only prepared to invest when the bankrupt estate of the GDR has fallen to a giveaway price." Grass is among those who mourn what they see as a missed opportunity for creating that ever-elusive phenomenon, the truly just socialist state.

In 1995 Grass published the first major literary work to deal with unification, *A Wide Field*. In the book, Grass portrays unification as a colonial takeover, explicitly using the word *Anschluss*, which was the word used in 1938 to describe Hitler's annexation of Austria. The chief "villain" is the Treuhand Anstalt, the agency charged with privatizing East Germany's run-down, state-owned industries—ominously situated in Hermann Goering's old Luftwaffe headquarters, notes Grass. He sees the closing-down of uncompetitive industries and subsequent mass layoffs as the key instrument of the destruction of East German civilization and way of life.

Grass's treatment of the 1991 terrorist murder of Detlev Rohwedder, the head of the Treuhand, sounded to some as if he actually condoned it. This prompted sharp criticism and forced

Grass to state that he was only trying to explain why this could have happened, not to applaud the deed.

Equally offensive were his attempts to idealize life in the defunct German Democratic Republic, comparing it favorably to the "empty materialism of the Bundesrepublik." In his book, a Jewish woman, formerly a citizen of East Germany, contemplates emigrating to Israel since she cannot abide the thought of living in the new Germany. Grass seems ignorant of how Jews were treated in communist countries.

Officially, Grass's revulsion to unification comes from the Holocaust. According to Grass, because of Auschwitz, Germans are forever damned, they cannot "even have the right to self-determination granted to other peoples without hesitation," he once wrote. As in his earlier books, *The Tin Drum*, *The Flounder*, and *The Rat*, Grass is obsessed with the German soul, which he sees as permanently beset by a sickness, infecting every aspect of German society. He longs for Germany just after the war. As he writes in the novel *Dog Days*, about the immediate postwar period and its rationing: "Never has Germany been so beautiful. Never has Germany been so healthy. Never have there been more expressive faces in Germany than in the days of 1,032 calories."

The weaknesses of Grass's position are obvious. Though some Europeans might secretly have preferred to see Europe permanently divided for fear of a resurgent Germany, this would have condemned not only the East Germans, but also the Poles, the Czechs, and the Hungarians to perpetual enslavement, which clearly they were not prepared to accept.

The continued existence of two German states living in a kind of federation—the idea espoused by Grass and his old party, the Social Democrats—one technologically advanced and prosperous, the other poor and backward, was equally unrealistic. The former East Germany was an artificial political construct, whose *raison d'etre* collapsed along with the Berlin Wall.

To talk of a special East German civilization is nonsense—unless the inevitable by-products of communist totalitarianism, such as poverty, envy, and stuntedness, can be called a civilization. Nostalgia for the "closeness" of a society where one half of the population snitches on the other is lunacy. In short, there was nothing worth preserving of the German Democratic Republic. As to Grass's charge that the East Germans were not properly consulted, he seems to have forgotten that the East Germans overwhelmingly supported Kohl's unification plans.

On the topic of the sick German soul, while it is true that denazification after the war never reached its intended extent because of the imperatives of the Cold War, the vast majority of Germans living today have come of age after World War II and thus cannot be assigned any individual guilt for the war—unless of course one believes in hereditary evil, the gene of Nazism passed on from father to son, which Grass seems to imply. What today's Germans do have is a responsibility to see that the past is not forgotten, and there are no signs that they are shirking this responsibility.

To see German unification as a hostile takeover, and Kohl, the ultimate centrist, as some kind of closet radical right-winger really takes a fevered imagination, not to mention a rather large closet.

10

THE LAST CAMPAIGN

IN WHAT HAS BECOME KNOWN as the "refrigerator inter-view," French journalist Jean-Paul Picaper asked Helmut Kohl about his thoughts when he awoke in the middle of the night. Did he contemplate the famous "mantle of history"? "That is a question I don't ask myself," the chancellor said. "When I get up at night, I'm not thinking about history, but about plundering the refrigerator. When I go to the refrigera-tor, history is not all-important to me." Perhaps. More cynical souls might suspect that it is perfectly possible to hit the refrig-erator and think about your place in history at the same time.

Much has been written about Helmut Kohl's alleged obses-sion with records and his place in the history books. And only a fool would deny the attractions of power. History is replete with leaders who did not know when it was time to bow out, but stayed beyond their usefulness.

But if his personal vanity had been Kohl's main concern, he should probably have retired right after unification, when his popularity and esteem had reached their zenith. This was what Foreign Minister Hans-Dietrich Genscher chose to do, when he called it quits in 1992 with a suddenness that surprised everyone. It reminded Henry Kissinger of a diplomat at the Congress of Vienna in 1814, who commented at the death of a colleague, "I wonder what his motive could have been."

For Kohl, the option of stepping down after unification might have looked attractive. Things were bound to become more complicated in terms of rebuilding the New Laender. Furthermore, throughout his career, Kohl had absorbed more punishment than most politicians; bowing out while the going was good might have been tempting.

Some have indeed speculated that Helmut Kohl was planning to hand over the reins of power to Wolfgang Schaeuble, but Kohl's timetable was upset when Schaeuble was crippled by an assailant's bullet. Kohl spent hours at Schaeuble's sickbed, crying.[1]

But according to former Kohl aide Stephan Eisel, that scenario is unlikely: "German unification, European integration, and the Euro were much too fresh a challenge at this point for him to have resigned in 1992 or 1993," says Eisel.

A more likely scenario had Kohl handing over the reins halfway through his fourth term. A week before his 1994 election victory he had announced that this was going to be his last election campaign. The assumption was that he would hand over the chancellorship to Schaeuble sometime in 1996. But this plan was scuttled by the slender CDU/CSU majority in parliament, where some Free Democrats might have used the chancellor shift to desert the coalition. Furthermore, in 1997 opinion polls suggested that Kohl was the most viable candidate.

When Kohl announced during his 1997 Easter vacation in Austria that he would run for a fifth term in 1998, there was still the sense that he was a man with a mission. What was equally important, he thought he could win. After all, the classic pattern in Kohl's career as chancellor was being low in the polls for months only to surge ahead in the final stretch before election day.

Admittedly, the last few years had not been easy ones. German economic growth was sluggish. In dealing with the situation, Kohl was repeatedly accused of passivity, of indifference to the economy. The argument that Germany needed new leadership and fresh blood resurfaced. "That was not entirely fair," says Michael Rutz, editor-in-chief of the weekly newspaper *Rheinischer Merkur*. The government had come up with proposals for addressing the situation. The problem was that Kohl's hands were tied; he was unable to move on these issues because the Social Democrats controlled the upper chamber of parliament, the Bundesrat, and thus were able to block vital legislation.

Thus Kohl's cuts in social programs ran into immediate opposition in 1996—the German unions went on strike and succeeded in making the government retreat on the most significant part of the plan, the cutback in sick pay, which was considerably watered down.

Moreover, Kohl's plan for tax reform, which was touted by the administration as the "plan of the century" and presented in January 1997, died a victim of the opposition in the Bundesrat, where the Social Democrats were positioning themselves for the upcoming election in the fall of 1998.

Then, too, it hardly helped Kohl when former President Richard von Weizsaecker, in a widely publicized interview in the autumn of 1997 with *Der Spiegel*, resurrected some of his old grudges against Kohl and stated that Germany had a petrified government that suffered from a lack of ideas and leadership and was clinging to power for its own sake.[2]

Kohl was reportedly furious, and, though von Weizsaecker is regarded as one of Germany's holy cows, Kohl and his men had had enough of the former president's sanctimoniousness. They made it public that von Weizsaecker had not become a member of the CDU again after he left office. Von Weizsaecker claimed he had intended his membership to be "passive" following his retirement from politics in 1994.[3]

Blocked on the domestic front, Kohl instead concentrated all his efforts where he could make a difference: the introduction of the common European currency, which in the greater scheme of things was the more important. But because of the Germans' reluctance to part with their Mark, this position would not win any popularity contests for Kohl.

There were some bumps along the way. An unpleasant surprise was the French election results in 1997. Though French President Jacques Chirac and his conservative coalition government enjoyed a solid majority in the French parliament, Chirac chose to call elections ten months early. The idea was to have a secure majority when all the crucial and unpopular decisions on budget cuts had to be taken to meet the Euro criteria. Chirac's move turned out to be a major miscalculation.

Instead of the conservative victory Chirac needed, France's Socialists under Lionel Jospin won, forcing the conservative Chirac into a power-sharing arrangement with a Socialist prime minister who had argued that France should resist American economic dominance and defend its welfare state against the Anglo-Saxon model. Jospin's leftist coalition includes the Communists, who emphatically do not favor the European Monetary Union, as well as the French Greens, who are, well, Greens.

Jospin, a humorless Protestant whose sanctimoniousness has been compared to that of "a Swedish pastor," which is not a compliment, ran on a lavish platform. The Socialists advocated extensive government job creation programs, adding some 350,000 jobs to the public sector, shortening the work week by four hours, increasing wages by 4 percent, ending privatization, and giving France more political control over European monetary policy. In 1997 France ran a budget deficit of 4.6 percent, too high to meet the Maastricht standard.

For a while, Jospin's election created severe doubts about the political will of the French to meet the demands of Maastricht. But in the end, Jospin did not want to go down in history as the man who blocked Europe.

Ironically, because of the costs of unification, for a while Germany itself, with its 3.2 percent deficit in 1997, seemed to have difficulty meeting the strict criteria. To qualify for the criteria in the Maastricht Treaty for the European Monetary Union, the government had to undertake austerity measures.

One major embarrassment on the part of the Kohl government was the attempt by Finance Minister Theo Waigel to cover the deficit by revaluating the country's gold supply upwards, taking care of part of the deficit problem with a stroke of a pen by adding some $7 billion on the plus side of Germany's accounts without raising taxes or implementing painful budget cuts. This idea was immediately vetoed by Bundesbank Chairman Hans Tietmeyer, who argued that resorting to this kind of manipulation was not acceptable and would undermine Germany's credibility as the defender of a strong currency. As one paper noted, these were the kinds of tricks one would expect from some of Germany's less responsible southern neighbors, not from Germany. Waigel had to beat a humiliating retreat.

Urged on by Kohl and his argument that if the leaders did not stick with the timetable laid down in the Maastricht Treaty, the treaty would lose its binding force, European politicians bit the bullet. Political will, a round of tax increases, cuts in public spending, and better-than-expected economic growth—not to mention some creative accounting maneuvers—assured that by the spring of 1998 eleven nations that wanted to be part of the European Monetary Union would get in. Even Italy squeezed in with an alleged budget deficit of 2.7 percent. Only Greece did not make it, while Britain, Sweden, and Denmark chose a wait-and-see attitude, perhaps joining at a later date.

The European currencies were permanently fixed in relation to each other on May 1, 1998, and Euro bills and coins were to be phased in over a six-month period in 2002, replacing the lire, the Mark, the franc, the peseta, and all the rest. In retrospect, May 1 may in some ways be seen as a more important date than the election date. The question of course is whether the European governments will be able to sustain that kind of fiscal discipline beyond the critical year of 1998, particularly given that much needed structural economic changes are nowhere in evidence.

The problem with Kohl's success on this issue was that to many Germans it was still a somewhat theoretical subject. Says Michael Rutz, "Foreign policy is undoubtedly king among German politicians, but the German people are like other people—they concentrate on domestic policy."

Where Kohl gravely miscalculated in his election plans was his belief that his opponent would be the Social Democratic Chairman Oskar Lafontaine, the man he had already beaten in the unification election. Kohl could not conceive that Lafontaine would be willing to give up his personal ambitions to become chancellor.

Instead, the Social Democrats chose Gerhard Schroeder, the popular fifty-four-year-old prime minister of Lower Saxony, whose strong showing in local elections in March 1998 convinced the desperate Social Democrats that here was the man who could bring them back to power after sixteen years in the political wilderness. Opinion polls showed that Schroeder was the only man who could beat Kohl in the election.

Not deterred by this, Kohl hit the campaign trail like the seasoned fighter he is, challenging journalists to keep up with him. He sounded his traditional themes of stability and his own record of achievements. He reminded the voters that Schroeder had been on the wrong side of every major issue confronting Germany over the past decades—the medium-range missile issue, unification, and deployment of German troops outside Germany. Schroeder had also suggested that the expansion of the European Union into central Europe should be slower, since an influx of Polish workers could hurt the German worker. Kohl further pointed out that Lower Saxony together with Lafontaine's Saarland rank among the poorest of the old federal states.[4]

Kohl's election machine further hammered away at the dire consequences of a Red-Green coalition, both on the domestic and on the international front. It pointed to the states where this idea had been put into practice—in Hesse a decade earlier, in Schroeder's own Lower Saxony until four years earlier, and in North Rhine Westphalia, where it was still ongoing. The Social Democrats' entry into this latter alliance was specifically cited as an example of the Social Democratic–Green cooperation with national implications. Ever since, the Social Democrats and Greens have quarreled over everything from the expansion of the airports in Dusseldorf and Bonn, to coal-mining, to the expansion of the highway net. Environmentalism in this extreme form poses just as much a threat to the economy as socialism ever did.

The element of internal security was also hit hard by Kohl's campaign, especially the "Days of Chaos" in Hannover under Schroeder, when punks, anarchists, and other assorted riffraff descended on the city for a weekend of havoc three years in a row, terrorizing the citizens, smashing shop windows, and urinating in the streets. At the time, the Greens were hard against police interference, supporting instead a strategy of "deescalation" that aimed at not "provoking" the punks; in the meantime, Schroeder made strong speeches without doing much to stop the mayhem.

But what Kohl was up against was a Bill Clinton–style stealth campaign. Schroeder showed himself to be intensely media conscious and assiduously emulated Clinton and Britain's Tony Blair in projecting a moderate and forward-looking image. His craggy good looks helped Schroeder, too, as did a fondness for huge Cuban cigars—a symbol of success he used to polish a pro-business image.

Schroeder's campaign stressed personality and was long on talk about the future, about the need for a new middle—neither left, nor right—but was extremely vague on the issues. Kohl was being portrayed as a spent force who had achieved great things for Germany but who was now hopelessly out of touch. The constant theme was the need for change. One TV spot showed a starship taking off for earth after the crew had been teleported aboard, with one person left in the blastoff—a disoriented-looking Helmut Kohl.

A dedicated Socialist in his youth, the much-married Schroeder (four times at last count, allegedly a new wife for every political phase he has been through) has changed with the times, projecting a more business-friendly image—among other things, he sits on the board of Volkswagen. Schroeder is clearly an ambitious man; he comes from a working-class background and is a lawyer by training. Legend has it that in the late 1980s a slightly inebriated Schroeder was grasping the iron gates of the Chancellery in the middle of the night, shouting, "Let me in! I want to be in here!"[5]

Schroeder cast himself as a pragmatist, seeking what works. When confronted with his own shifting positions, he would dismiss the question off-handedly. "When reality collides with your political program, you have to consider that your political program could be wrong." Kohl hit back that Schroeder was a mere front figure, window dressing on a still-unreconstructed Social Democratic Party.

The main election issue was jobs. Kohl had promised fewer than four million jobless by the end of 1998. By election time, the numbers were indeed headed in the right direction, but he was far short of the goal to halve unemployment, as agreed upon by his government, the labor unions, and the employers' associations in early 1996.

Kohl received what looked like a political opening when the Greens, who had worked hard to convey the impression that they were politically housebroken and responsible, published their election manifesto in March, calling for a threefold increase in gasoline taxes—to more than $10 per gallon—an end to German NATO membership, and the legalization of marijuana.

Though they recanted these positions, the declaration scared the hell out of German car manufacturers, and many Social Democrats as well.

Among other amusing suggestions emerging from individual Green members was that a curfew should be imposed on all men, forbidding them to be on the street after 10 PM, so women could feel safe. Another would allow Germans to travel by plane only once every five years.[6]

Still, despite these embarrassments for the Social Democrats, a final electoral surge in Kohl's favor did not occur. On election day, September 27, 1998, Kohl and his CDU/CSU union got 35 percent of the vote, the Social Democrats 41 percent, the Greens 6.7 percent, the Free Democrats 6.2 percent, and the Party of Democratic Socialism (the successor party to the East German communists) 5.1 percent. The defeat was the first for a sitting chancellor, and Kohl was defeated both in the East and the West, though the losses were heaviest in the East. Kohl's CDU dropped from 42.1 percent to 37 percent in the old states and from 38.5 percent to 27.3 percent in the new states. As has been the case so often, the Allensbach Institute was the one that got it right.

Ultimately, what Kohl was up against in the election was a general it-is-time-for-a-change mood in the population, which Schroeder exploited for all its worth. The political postmortem has been going on ever since. Despite all the talk of a new start and the desire for new faces, on a deeper level, the election result was in essence a vote *against* reform, a vote for keeping the status quo, a refusal on the part of the German voter to face facts.

Despite Kohl's efforts to cut back on public spending in the 1980s, severe flaws in the German economy had already become discernible, signs that the country was losing some of its competitive edge. The German economy had become over-regulated; labor costs were high; taxes were soaring; the welfare system was bloated. All these were negatives for a nation whose exports account for one-third of its GDP. Yet the Kohl government had avoided radical surgery, since minor adjustments were still able to produce positive results. Besides, Germany's main European competitors were laboring under the same or worse conditions.

But with the fall of the Berlin Wall, the structural flaws of the German economy were fully exposed. If in retrospect the

Wall can be said to have had a beneficial side to it—surely the only one—it was that it shielded the West German economy from competition from the East. "Germans must realize that it was a comfortable thing to sit behind the Wall in a niche of history," Kohl once noted.

Again and again, Kohl told German workers that if they wanted to retain their competitiveness, they needed to work harder, retire at a later age, and give up some of their innumerable perks and holidays. (Germans take six weeks of holidays a year, the most in Europe.) "We need a young generation that does not talk first about retirement pensions but about the adventure of life," Kohl stated at an election rally in Dresden.

In today's marketplace, Germany has to compete not only with countries of the former Eastern bloc, but with the rest of the world. For a country that has some of the highest labor costs anywhere, this is a problem. The figures speak for themselves: In Germany in 1997, the average wage was $17.50 per hour. Income taxes were between 33 and 50 percent; consumer taxes were 15 percent; and companies paid up to 65 percent of their profits in taxes. Benefits like pensions, health, and unemployment insurance added an extra $14 to labor costs, whereas the cost in the United States was only $6.[7]

When confronted with figures like this, it is no wonder that major corporations like Mercedes Benz and BMW have increasingly exercised the one option left to them—namely, to move their production abroad. BMW has opened a plant in Spartanburg, South Carolina, thereby reducing its labor costs by one-third, and is producing minivans and engines in southern China. Mercedes has opened a plant near Birmingham, Alabama. Other firms have moved to Poland and the Czech Republic. Why use a German worker if you can get the same result from a skilled Czech worker at a quarter of the cost?

Among the few positive signs have been instances of workers bucking their own hard-line unions in order to keep jobs in Germany. BMW workers, for instance, agreed to work on Saturdays, which would have been unimaginable before unification—but in exchange for a four-day work week. And when Mercedes Benz declared in 1996 that it would stop contributing to the communion clothes of the children of its employees, nobody went on strike.

But it will take more than giving up communion clothes. Unless the unions truly reconsider their positions, more jobs will leave Germany. Fortunately, in the spring of 1997, Dieter Schulte, the chairman of the Deutsche Gewerkshaftsbund (the German Federation of Labor) recommended, over the protest of some of his own people, more restraint in wage demands and more decentralization in wage negotiations, limiting the general wage contracts to a very few points and allowing more flexibility by the companies themselves.[8]

Add to this the burden of public spending. What Kohl stated in his first statement as chancellor to the Bundestag in 1982 holds equally true today: "For too long, too many have been living at the expense of others: the state at the expense of the citizens, the citizens at the expense of their fellow citizens, and all of us at the expense of future generations." Today, the public sector again takes up about 50 percent of the GNP, and taxes and social contributions are higher than in 1982. The comparable figure for Germany's main competitors, the United States and Japan, are 35 percent and 32 percent, respectively. Like all advanced European welfare states, Germany has simply become too expensive.

The health-care sector gives particular cause for concern. As people live longer, the need for more medical care increases. More than 20 percent of the German population is over sixty, and with the nation's low birthrate that percentage is rising. This means that the growing demand for senior care must be paid for by a shrinking pool of younger workers. Currently, three workers carry the costs of one senior citizen. In twenty years, the ratio will be more like 1:1. Unless this development is brought under control, the system will collapse.[9]

IN THE END, WHAT HELMUT KOHL was up against was deeply ingrained attitudes—about unemployment, business, work, the role of the state—that have evolved over decades. Some of them differ markedly from those of the United States. In order to regain its competitiveness, Germany needs to change its consensus on these matters, but this will be a slow and laborious process.

By contrast, according to the American work ethic, unemployment is morally degrading, and hence there is a certain pressure on the individual to get back to work. This is considered in the long run better for a person's health and dignity than being dependent on the handouts of the state.

In Germany, the American approach to welfare is considered harsh and lacking in compassion; there, no stigma is attached to unemployment. Most Americans would take a great number of jobs in order to get off the dole that Germans would not dream of touching, but leave to foreign guest workers, something which again is reflected in lower U.S. unemployment statistics.

As a result, like other European welfare states, Germany faces a new phenomenon: the permanently unemployable—children who have grown up in the welfare environment, often in single parent homes, for whom welfare is a way of life. The work ethic is no longer passed on. In past days, when people went on the dole, it was because they were temporarily out of work. These new people, however, cannot be called the working class; they come from an unemployable underclass. What employer in his right mind is going to hire a punk with green hair, multiple body piercings, and a dog named Himmler?

A telling example of how hard it is to change attitudes in Germany is that it was regarded as almost a cultural revolution when the country's extremely tight regulations for shopping hours were relaxed in 1996. For as long as anyone can remember, Germans have had to rush home from work to do their shopping because the shops would close at 6:30 PM on the dot on weekdays and at 2 PM on Saturdays. Sundays, of course, there was no shopping at all.

According to the trade unions, the family life of their members would suffer beyond repair if they were required to work different or longer hours. Changing the rules would amount to abuse of almost Dickensian proportions on the employer's part. Besides, they argued, this would have no impact on sales. Now shops are open until 8 PM on weekdays and 4 PM on Saturdays, and, unsurprisingly, it has had a positive impact on sales, and the German family has not disintegrated.

The interesting point here is not so much that not even the East Germans could make communism work, but rather that the West Germans have been able to make social democracy work for so long—with Germany's lack of flexibility in the labor market, its ambivalence towards business, and its huge tax burden that would send any full-blooded American into the street in a state of revolutionary uproar. Germany has been compared to Britain before Mrs. Thatcher came to power; no matter who nominally held power, the country was really run by the Labour Party.

A basic tenet of Ludwig Erhard's philosophy was that only a strong economy could provide good social conditions. First, you needed a policy that favored a strong private sector and a policy that encouraged personal responsibility. Then you could afford a social safety net. Over time, however, the emphasis in Germany changed from market economics to social programs. Getting the proper balance back became the major challenge.

Originally, West Germany was based on a social contract between employers' organizations and trade unions, with the government acting as mediator and referee. The employers would offer generous packages and job security and in return the unions would restrain their demands, giving Germany one of the most stable economies in the world.

Some are now wondering whether the German consensus model, which worked well for forty years, is still working. To some economists, Germany no longer looks like a free-market economy, but like one that has ossified into a cartel. Before a new consensus is reached, a lot of German firms might move abroad—taking their jobs with them.

Says one former government minister, "Sometimes one cannot help having the feeling that the mess is not deep enough yet."

So, QUESTIONS REMAIN: What does Kohl's defeat bode for Germany? Is there life after Kohl?

The strange thing is how quietly this election result has been accepted in Germany. This was not a routine election; some commentators talk about a seismic shift. With the addition from unification of seventeen million people, the old balances of power—the balance between Catholics in the south, who tend to vote conservative, and Protestants in the north, who tend to vote Social Democratic; between the individual and the state; between freedom and equality—have been upset.

What is more, it is a shift that occurs at a time when Germany needs to go in the exact opposite direction. A third way between capitalism and socialism is not what Germany needs. This is what it has already got, and it is not working. It is unlikely that the Social Democrats will be able to provide the economic reforms that the country needs, given that their constituency is precisely the entrenched interests. They are already committed to reversing some of Kohl's modest reforms in the social sector.

On foreign policy, as John Vinocur of the *International Herald Tribune* has pointed out, with Russia heading towards economic meltdown, and America preoccupied by scandals, it is as if the Germans had gotten so used to Kohl's steady hand on foreign policy, that they have come to take this kind of leadership for granted. And indeed, Schroeder has stressed the need for continuity, on NATO and on the Euro. As he has put it, the work "at the strategic heights" has been accomplished by Kohl, it is now up to him "to toil on the plains."

Schroeder may feel that way. The real question is how Finance Minister Oskar Lafontaine feels. Lafontaine envisages a centralized Europe with coordinated social and wage policies, a common minimum wage so that the element of competition among the member states is eliminated, and government-directed economic growth. He has already called on the Bundesbank to lower interest rates.

This is precisely the opposite of the course that Germany followed under Helmut Kohl, which stressed a strong common currency, the element of healthy competition, a transatlantic link, and the traditional independence of the Bundesbank from government directives.

As noted, in Europe there is a split between the free traders—the Germans, the British, the Dutch, and the Scandinavians—and the more protectionist-inclined countries—the French, the Italians, and other southern countries. If Germany were to join the latter group, the specter of a protectionist Fortress Europe suddenly looms on the horizon.[10]

Add to this Schroeder's Green coalition partner, and radical policy shifts are possible. Foreign Minister Joshka Fisher is considered the most articulate and pragmatic of the Greens in parliament. But the pressure exerted on Fisher from rank-and-file members in an unhierarchical and chaotic party, in which every member is an activist, is bound to be considerable. As one commentator noted, it might be difficult to be foreign minister when elements of your party want to restrict your flying to once every five years.[11]

In short, the Germans may come to rue the day they threw Helmut Kohl out of office. Helmut Kohl's personality, his down-to-earth perspective, and his ability to make the right decisions were crucial to good government. Given traditional German pessimism, that national tendency to see the sky perpetually falling, Kohl's calm reassurance of "Patience, the future is brighter than you think," will undoubtedly be missed.

POSTSCRIPT

A VIEW OF GERMANY'S FUTURE ultimately boils down to personal perspective, judgment, and experience. Before emigrating to America, I was born and grew up in Denmark, which fought the Germans several times in the nineteenth century and was invaded by the Germans in World War II; living in a small country, you develop a certain sensitivity toward large neighbors.

My father, a young cadet, was stationed on the Danish–German border when the Germans invaded in 1940. He fled to Sweden on a fishing boat, and joined the Danish Brigade there. For years, my mother, travelling by train to the French Riviera in a compartment full of hat boxes, would pull down the blinds as the train passed through Germany. As children, we would take special pride in getting bad marks in German and excelling in English. In short, there are many good historical reasons for us to follow developments in Germany closely.

On the other hand, as a foreign correspondent, I have covered Germany for more than a decade and have found it to be one of the most responsible and humane, if somewhat uptight, democracies in Western Europe. German law guarantees the rights of the individual. And while World War II will never be forgotten, fifty years of democracy, much of it American-inspired, must count for something.

NOTES

NOTES ON CHAPTER 1

The best works on the peace movement in Germany are: David R. Gress, *Peace and Survival: West Germany, the Peace Movement, and European Security*; Dennis L. Bark and David R. Gress, *A History of West Germany, Vol. 2: Democracy and Its Discontents, 1963–1991*, second edition; and Alex Alexiev's papers for the RAND corporation, to whose research this account is indebted.

1. Jonathan Carr, *Helmut Schmidt: Helmsman of Germany* (New York: St. Martin's Press, 1985).

2. A low moment in Schmidt's career came in December 1981, when he was in East Germany visiting Erich Honecker. While asleep, news came of the military crackdown on the Polish trade union Solidarity and the imposition of martial law. The next morning a highly distressed Schmidt announced to journalists that his East German host was just as "shocked" as he by the crackdown, leaving many with the impression that both Germanies shared an interest in seeing the unrest in Poland tamed in the name of stability and business as usual.

The visit was best summed up by a photograph taken at Schmidt's departure, showing him accepting a cough drop from Honecker, the ultimate illustration of appeasement. See Jonathan Carr, *Helmut Schmidt*, pp. 174–176.

3. Jonathan Carr, *Helmut Schmidt*, pp. 166–167.

4. Kohl won the March 1983 election with ease, in part because German industry favored him heavily. Major firms had made their new orders conditional on a Kohl victory, and many skilled workers gave him their votes in the belief that his policies would better protect their jobs.

By 1985–1986 Kohl's policies—moderate cuts in all sectors of the federal government—had restored economic growth in Germany. Kohl brought the public sector deficit down to 2 percent, and granted tax relief to entrepreneurs. A period of steady growth began, 2 percent in 1983, rising to 3 percent in the following years. These fiscal efforts allowed the German Bundesbank to lower interest rates; high interest rates had been caused by inflation and had been a major hindrance to investors.

By the end of 1989 the Federal Republic had the highest number of jobs ever, 2.5 million more than in 1982, lowering the public sector's share of the economy by nearly 6 percent, from 51.7 percent to 45.8 percent, an almost balanced federal budget, low interest rates, and a low inflation rate. It was financially prepared for unification. That unification turned out to be much more expensive than anyone could have anticipated, and that Germany today faces serious problems comparable to those of 1982 is another matter.

5. Oskar Lafontaine, *Angst vor den Freunden* (Reinbek: Rowohlt, 1983). Cited in Dennis L. Bark and David R. Grass, *A History of West Germany, Vol. 2: Democracy and Its Discontents 1963–1991*, second edition (Oxford: Blackwell, 1993).

6. Luigi Barzini, *The Europeans* (London: Penguin Books, 1983), p. 112.

7. In what can be termed a nationalism of the Left, Kelly repeatedly used the phrase *"Wille des Volkes,"* the will of the people, a phrase with unfortunate Nazi overtones. The Greens also had an unpleasant tendency to break out into song in the Bundestag as a protest, bringing back memories of Nazi behavior in the old Reichstag.

Everywhere she went, Kelly was followed by Gert Bastian, a former general and commander of a West German tank division, a rather pathetic figure who carried her posters and pacifist declarations, and a walking illustration of the folly of old age. As a member of "Generals for Peace and Disarmament," a Soviet-front group, his chief function was to convince people that the arsenal of the Warsaw Pact was vastly inferior to that of the West.

The Petra Kelly saga reached its bizarre conclusion when the bodies of Kelly and Bastian were found in her apartment in October 1992. Apparently the general had shot Kelly in her sleep and then killed himself.

8. Even the Greens themselves occasionally felt compelled to complain about the heavy-handed Communist methods. Thus after a planning session for the upcoming Reagan 1985 visit, one participant vented his frustration: "The Communists dominated the meeting completely. It took place under seemingly democratic rules, but it was a joke. We could barely get a word in."

The Soviets applied extra pressure by simultaneously pulling out of the long-range negotiations, a smart move on their part. Only 3 to 5 percent of the three million West Germans participating in the peace demonstrations were extreme leftist or Communists. Yet these elements made up 40 percent of the demonstration coordinators and more than 50 percent of the demonstration organizers. Like all Marxist strategists, they would maneuver themselves into key positions and make sure that the people who controlled the flow of the demonstrations were their own. And if they could not find enough supporters locally, they would send in busloads from other areas. See Alex Alexiev, RAND paper 1985.

9. Figures on Soviet manipulation of peace demonstrations from Alex Alexiev, RAND paper, 1985.

10. Philip Zelikow and Condoleezza Rice, *Germany Unified and Europe Transformed: A Study in Statecraft* (Cambridge: Harvard University Press, 1995), p. 29.

11. Bark and Gress, p. 403.

12. Christian Mueller, *Helmut Kohl: A Man on the Crest of His Time* (Bergisch Gladbach: Gustav Lubbe Verlag, 1996), p. 19.

NOTES ON CHAPTER 2

Countless biographies have been written in German about Kohl. By far the best of the preunification period is Werner Filmer and Heribert Schwan, *Helmut Kohl*, a collection of eyewitness accounts that provide some of the most vivid details about the chancellor.

1. Christian Mueller, *Helmut Kohl: A Man on the Crest of His Time* (Bergisch Gladbach, Germany: Luebbe Verlag, 1996).

2. Coming from the Rhine region, Kohl is also of course a wine connoisseur. At a wine-tasting test soon after becoming chancellor, he was reported to have immediately spotted an English wine, which was

noted with great respect in the British papers at a time when every-body was scrambling to find out who this new German leader was. Perhaps, if one reflects for a moment on the quality of English wine, this may be less of a compliment than first assumed.

3. The play is *Des Teufels General* (*The Devil's General*), quoted in Christian Mueller, p. 7.

4. Quoted in Guenter Muechler and Klaus Hofmann, *Helmut Kohl: Chancellor of German Unity* (Bonn: Press and Information Office of the Federal Government, 1992), p. 15.

5. Interview by Michael Rutz with Eduard Ackermann for a one-hour TV documentary on Helmut Kohl, *"Rekord im Kanzleramt."*

6. Werner Filmer and Heribert Schwan, *Helmut Kohl* (Dussel-dorf: ECON Verlag, 1990).

7. Kohl is a man who sets great store on being the master of his own time. While in office, he had only contempt for politicians who run themselves ragged, going from appointment to appointment try-ing to catch up with an unending list of twenty-minute assignments that others have made for them. Accordingly, Kohl and his trusty pocket diary were inseparable. Every year, the chemical firm BASF in Ludwigshafen, where he got his first job as a young man, sends him a pocket diary. It comes with a pencil and eraser.

Following daily consultation with Juliane Weber regarding all who seek an audience, Kohl would decide who the fortunate select few would be. He then meticulously entered all his appointments in his diary himself. Needless to say, Kohl's little book became a valuable commodity; on the road, an assistant would guard the briefcase con-taining it with almost the same diligence as do American officers in charge of the U.S. president's "football" that contains the nuclear launch codes.

8. Kohl's reflections on power are taken from a joint Helmut Kohl/Helmut Schmidt interview in *Die Zeit*, May 3, 1998.

9. Martin Luther quote cited in Filmer/Schwan, *Helmut Kohl*.

10. Bismarck's eating habits cited in Filmer/Schwan, *Helmut Kohl*.

11. Juergen Leinemann, *Helmut Kohl: Die Inszenierung einer Karriere* (Berlin: Aufbau Taschenbuch Verlag, 1998), p. 43.

12. Hans Klein, *The German Chancellors* (Chicago: edition q, 1996), p. 339.

13. The pond incident appears in Filmer/Schwan.

14. Juergen Leinemann, *Helmut Kohl*, p. 43.

15. Kohl was also not above occasionally humiliating his own min-isters in public. One minister, obviously a bitter man, once com-plained about being treated like "snot on the sleeve" by the chancellor.

16. For Kohl and polls, see, "*Rede von Bundeskanzler Dr. Helmut Kohl beim 50, Jahre-Jubileum des Institutes fur Demoskopie Allenbach in Haus der Geschichte am 24*, September 1997 in Bonn."

17. Christian Mueller, *Helmut Kohl: A Man on the Crest of His Time* (Bergisch Gladbach, Germany: Luebbe Verlag, 1996).

18. Brandt and Bahr quoted in Ernst Freidrich Jung, "Kalte Krieger und Falsche Profeten," in *Die Politische Meinung*.

19. Quoted in Dennis L. Bark and David R. Gress, *A History of West Germany, Vol. 2: Democracy and Its Discontents, 1963–1991*, second edition (Oxford: Blackwell, 1993), p. 325.

20. Richard Burt was once asked to address the CDU members of the Bundestag together with Soviet arms negotiator Yuli Kvitsinzki. Burt thought the idea a bad one, objecting to the format which would set an American and a Soviet on the same level, conveying a kind of moral equivalence. But since it could not be changed he tried to think of something to say that the Soviet could not answer and thereby put some pressure on him. Burt stated that he had noticed that reunification was falling out of the political lexicon and that it was very important that the Germans not give up the dream of unification. This of course forced the Soviet to say that the whole notion was absurd, a provocation, and should not even be mentioned.

About a week later at an all-night political ball, Kohl, who had read about the incident, came up to Burt and complimented him on his speech, adding, "It saddens me, though, that we need to hear this from an American diplomat."

21. The discreet trade in human beings continued: East Germany would sell political troublemakers and other people who somehow failed to appreciate the blessings of East Germany. The Kohl government was able to buy the freedom of growing numbers of people who wished to emigrate to West Germany. In the first three months of 1984, more people were sold than during all of 1983.

NOTES ON CHAPTER 3

1. The otherwise tiresome 1967 film *Taetowierung* (or *Tattooing*) captured this destructive generational relationship with uncanny foresight. In the movie, Benno, an orphan, is in deep trouble at reform school. He has stolen a gun, and when he refuses to reveal its whereabouts to his classmates, they apply an electric drill to his chest—hence the name of the movie. Benno, as it may be gathered, is hardly likely to become a pillar of society. Nonetheless, he is taken in by the Lohmans, a liberal idealistic family, owners of a small factory,

who believe that Benno can be saved and turned into a productive citizen through love and understanding. Every attempt is made to accommodate Benno's wishes. Predictably, nothing works, and Benno drifts from job to job and into petty crime. Finally, in a fit of momentous boredom, Benno blows away his benefactor Mr. Lohman.

The movie proved prescient when, on July 30, 1977, Susanne Albrecht, the goddaughter of Juergen Ponto, head of the Dresdner Bank, let her friends into his house, knowing that they were planning to kill him. In a further blurring of the lines between art and reality, the star of *Taetowierung*, Christoph Wackermann, joined the Red Army Faction and was captured in 1977 in Holland. See Walter Laqueur, *Germany Today: A Personal Report* (Boston: Little, Brown & Co., 1985), p. 56.

2. Soelle quoted in Walter Laqueur, *Germany Today*.

3. Frank Schirrmacher, "Das imperative Ich: Verabredung mit einer Kunstfigur: Gunther Grass und die Lehre von unangewendeten Erwachsensein," *Frankfurter Allgemeine*, Ocober 11, 1997.

4. Marion Graefin Doenhoff, *Kindheit in Ostpreussen* (Berling: Seidler Verlag, 1988).

5. Jan Bo Hansen, *Weekendsavisen*, August 8, 1996, and Alice Schwarzer, "Marion Doenhoff: *Ein Wiederstaendiges Leben*," Kiepenheuer und Witsch, 1996.

6. See *Blindheit durch Annaeherung: Dokumentation einer Zeit-Reise in die DDR: Die politische Meinung*, Ausgabe Nr 281, April 1993.

7. Werner Filmer/Heribert Schwan, *Helmut Kohl* (Dusseldorf: ECON Verlage, 1990).

8. Still, he drew the line in 1976, when at a CSU party congress in Kreuth, Strauss threatened to dissolve the traditional union between the two sister parties and go national, widening his base beyond Bavaria. Kohl immediately warned that if he did, the CDU would invade Bavarian territory. After three days, Strauss backed down.

9. Peter Boenish, "Kohl und Strauss," in *Helmut Kohl: in Spiegel seiner Macht*, edited by Reinhard Appel. (Bonn: Bouvier Verlag, 1990).

10. Settling in Hamburg at the time, Genscher competed to become one of the first Fulbright scholars, but came in second. The scholarship went to a career diplomat who later went to work for Genscher. Once he asked an American diplomat, "Wouldn't history have looked a bit different if I had won that scholarship?"

11. *Newsweek*, December 12, 1988.

12. Ibid.

13. Filmer/Schwann, *Hans Dietrich Genscher* (Dusseldorf: ECON Verlag, 1988).

14. Genscher had already earned Washington's displeasure by favoring aid to Nicaragua and opposing aid to El Salvador. He also tried to get a common European response to prevent Ronald Reagan from a military retaliation against Libya's Muammar Gadhafi in 1986, ten days after it had been established that Libya was behind the Berlin disco bombing in which two American servicemen and one Turkish woman had been killed and 230 people wounded. The attack turned out to have been masterminded by the Libyan People's Bureau in East Berlin. Genscher was on his way to Washington with all these proposals when informed that the strikes on Tripoli and Benghazi were taking place.

15. Actually, by German standards, where aristocracy traces its roots back to somewhere in the mists of the thirteenth century, the von Weizsaecker family is a relative newcomer. They were on the staff of the king of Wuertenberg, and von Weizsaecker's grandfather was ennobled only in 1917, which makes them nouveau aristocrats, who perhaps are a little more likely to take themselves seriously.

16. Reinhard Appel, *Helmut Kohl im Spiegel seiner Macht* (Bonn: Bouvier Verlag, 1990).

NOTES ON CHAPTER 4

1. See Robert S. Wistrich, "Helping Hitler," *Commentary*, July 1996.

2. As noted by Marc Fisher, in *After the Wall* (New York: Simon and Schuster, 1995).

3. Anyone who believes that the Germans have tried to avoid confronting their past need only watch German TV for a week. Here Germany is in sharp contrast to, say, the Japanese, who to this very day find it hard to say they are sorry.

4. The *Green Calendar* is quoted in Dennis L. Bark and David R. Gress, *A History of West Germany, Vol. II: Democracy and Its Discontents, 1963–1991*, second edition (Oxford: Blackwell, 1993).

5. John Ardagh, *Germany and the Germans* (London: Penguin, 1996), p. 348.

6. Luigi Barzini, *The Europeans* (London: Penguin, 1983), p. 74.

7. Richard Burt.

8. See Charles S. Maier, *The Unmasterable Past: History, Holocaust and German National Identity*, p. 66.

9. Ibid., p. 85.

NOTES ON CHAPTER 5

The main sources for German unification are Helmut Kohl, *Ich wollte Deutschlands Einheit*; Philip Zelikow and Condoleezza Rice, *Germany United and Europe Transformed*; Horst Teltschik, *329 Tage*; and Wolfgang Schaeuble, *Der Vertrag*.

1. Jeffrey Gedmin, *The Hidden Hand: Gorbachev and the Collapse of East Germany* (Washington, D.C.: AEI Press, 1992), p. 90.

2. Kohl, *Ich Wolte Deutschlands Einheit*, p. 89.

3. See description *Los Angeles Times*, December 17, 1989.

4. Kohl, *Ich wollte Deutschlands Einheit*.

5. See Alan Watson, "Thatcher and Kohl: Old Rivalries Revisited," in *Eminent Europeans*, edited by Martyn Bond, Julie Smith, and William Wallace (London: Greycoat Press, 1996).

6. Scowcroft continues: "Suppose Gorbachev went to the chancellor and said, 'Look, you can have a choice. You can have a separated Germany the way it is now, or you can have a unified, but neutral Germany.' What would he do? Kohl told us over and over again that Europe and the unity of Atlantic Alliance were the most important things. But when he did something like not telling us before his Ten Point announcement, it left some nagging worries."

7. Kohl, p. 262.

8. Only the first four thousand Ost Marks were exchanged at 1:1 (six thousand for persons over sixty). Beyond that the rate was 2:1. Bark and Gress, p. 787.

9. Klaus Dreher, *Helmut Kohl: "Leben mit Macht."* (Stuttgart: Deutsche Verlags-Anstalt, 1998).

10. Guenter Muechler and Klaus Hofmann, *Helmut Kohl: Chancellor of German Unity* (Bonn: Press and Information Office of the Federal Government, 1992), p. 191.

11. Karl Hugo Pruys, *Kohl: Genius of the Present* (Chicago: edition q, 1996), p. 302.

12. Typically, when asked what kept him going during the grueling pace of the unification, Kohl answered, "A good meal in a pub now and then and taking the odd nap in the car."

13. When Willy Brandt was dying, Kohl was also supportive. Among the portraits in the Chancellery was a ghoulish portrait of Brandt by Georg Meistermann, which upset Brandt because it looked disconcertingly like a death mask. When he learned this, Kohl had it removed and replaced with a more conventional portrait by Oswald Peterson.

14. Helmut Schmidt, quoted in Bark and Gress, p. 744.

NOTES ON CHAPTER 6

1. Zelikow and Rice, *Germany Unified and Europe Transformed: A Study in Statecraft*, p. 192.

2. Ibid., p. 735.

3. Today, both Kohl's and Gorbachev's sweaters are on exhibition in the Haus der Geschichte in Bonn.

4. Genscher's comments in the Soviet Union quoted in Udo Bergdoll's essay, "Kohl und Genschers FDP Portrait einer Zerruettung," from *Helmut Kohl Im Spiegel seiner Macht*, edited by Reinhard Appel (Bonn: Bouvier Verlag, 1990).

5. Horst Teltschik, *329 Tage: Innenansichten der Einigung* (Berlin: Siedler, 1991), p. 226.

6. Jeffrey Gedmin, *The Hidden Hand: Gorbachev and the Collapse of East Germany* (Washington, D.C.: AEI Press, 1992), p. 121.

7. Indeed, Gorbachev was so popular in Germany that the German population had stopped considering the Soviet Union a threat long before the situation on the ground warranted such relaxation. In 1989, for instance, Kohl had great difficulty holding the line on defense. On top of Foreign Minister Genscher's veto on the renewal of short-range missiles, the general population was becoming impatient with NATO maneuvers, with what became labelled as "NATO noise."

Farmers complained that their roads and wheat fields were being churned up by NATO tanks, and their livestock frightened. Newspaper photos from the time show an irate farmer pointing to his cow that had just miscarried or to his pigs that had fretted themselves silly because of a tank engine roar. A question often asked was how Americans would feel if one million soldiers were milling around in Oregon, which was roughly the size of western Germany, holding constant maneuvers.

The low-altitude flights of fighter jets that would go as low as 250 feet over farms and villages, setting grandpa's false teeth chattering, had become a particularly sensitive issue. This increased concern among Germany's allies, who saw such flights as necessary to retain critical combat skills, one of which was knowing in details the terrain you had to fight over.

8. The story appeared in the London *Sunday Times*, January 31, 1988.

9. Kohl, p. 341

10. Martyn Bond, Julie Smith, and William Wallace, *Eminent Europeans: Personalities Who Shaped Contemporary Europe* (London: Greycoat Press, 1996), p. 269.

11. Germans also found Mrs. Thatcher's suspicions of the European Community problematic, particularly after her "full and frank" speech on the subject in Bruges, Belgium, in 1988, which thoroughly denounced any attempts to interfere in Britain's domestic affairs. It was felt in Bonn that the British could not be trusted to be "Europeans" along with everybody else.

12. Bond, Smith, and Wallace, *Eminent Europeans*, p. 279.

13. *The Independent,* July 16, 1990.

14. Winston Churchill, speech at Albert Hall, May 14, 1947, and speech in Zurich, 1946.

15. See the analysis by Michael Gurfinkiel in *Valeurs Actualles,* October 14, 1995.

16. To this day, the expellees and their descendants are a significant nationalistic voter bloc, particularly in Bavaria. After the war, some thirteen million Germans were expelled from Poland and Czechoslovakia; today, an estimated 2.2 million belong to expellee organizations.

It is interesting to compare Kohl's handling of the Polish Solidarity movement in 1989 with that of the Social Democrats in 1981, when the Social Democrat opposition was worried about the Poles rocking the boat. Kohl actually helped Solidarity gain power by refusing to extend credits to the Rakowski government that might have helped it retain control longer.

17. Quoted in Rice Zelikow.

18. Horst Teltschik, *329 Tage,* p. 226.

19. Udo Bergdoll's essay, "Kohl und Genschers FDP," in *Helmut Kohl im Spiegel seiner Macht,* edited by Reinhard Appel (Bonn: Bouvier Verlag, 1990), p. 205.

20. At an early stage, the Foreign Ministry had shown that it did not have the intellectual capacity and firepower, the political feel, to handle a situation that was decisive for German and European history. For thirty-one years, the Foreign Ministry had been in the hands first of the Social Democrats and then the Free Democrats, who had made all personnel decisions. They were still thinking in conventional detente terms. Genscher embodied the German foreign policy of the 1970s; he did not have the stature to meet the challenge of 1989.

21. When Reagan was briefed on foreign policy as president-elect, he asked what could be done to roll back Soviet expansionism. Nuclear war was ruled out. So was conventional war, since the Soviets were superior in all categories of arms, tanks, planes, missiles, and manpower. Eventually, Reagan rather wistfully asked if there wasn't some area where the Americans had more than the Soviets. The answer came back from his advisers: "Money." One participant in the

meeting afterward reported that a wolfish smile appeared on Reagan's normally friendly face. He said, "Then, that's what we're going to fight with!"

Over the next eight years, $350 billion was pumped into U.S. defense annually, about the size of the West German budget at the time. When Gorbachev, after having been rebuffed by Reagan at the Reykjavik summit in his attempt to get the Americans to scrap SDI, asked his advisers what it would take to stay in the race, he was told, "We can't stay in this race." At the time, the Soviets were spending an estimated 37 percent of their Gross National Product on defense. America spent 6 percent over eight years.

22. Karl Hugo Pruys, *Kohl: Chancellor of German Unity* (Chicago: edition q, 1996), p. 187.

NOTES ON CHAPTER 7

1. In the end, Germany did make a military contribution of sorts, which again provoked denunciations at home, minuscule though they were. After the suspension of hostilities, German minesweepers were dispatched to the Gulf at the request of the American government in March 1991. Deployment inside the NATO area became the question in December 1990, when Turkey requested the deployment of the Allied Mobile Force (AMF) to deter an Iraqi attack on Turkish bases. The AMF included German air and land units, which meant that Germans could not entirely remain on the sidelines. For days, Germany equivocated about whether it could guarantee the requested military support. Initially, Germany sent eighteen ancient Alpha jets to strengthen Turkish defenses. Only when under heavy prodding from the Turks, who cited the possibility of Iraqi gas attacks on Turkey, using technology supplied illegally by German firms, did Germany do a little more, sending anti-aircraft systems and six hundred troops to man them.

2. Vernon Walters, *When the Wall Falls*, p. 153.

3. The Kohl government suffered further embarrassment when it was revealed that private German firms, together with French and Italian ones, had added to Saddam Hussein's chemical, biological, and nuclear capabilities as well as his program for upgrading his Scud missiles to increase their range. In doing so, they had broken the international arms embargo and circumvented Germany's rather lax export regulations. They had also contributed to the construction of Saddam's underground bunker.

The U.S. government had approached the Germans over the issue throughout the 1980s, but without success. The problem was

exports not only to Iraq, but to Libya, Syria, and Iran as well. One of
the problems was that the German constitution forbade wiretapping
and similar surveillance methods, without which it was hard to fight
these illegal technology transfers. Only state prosecutors were allowed
to undertake such measures and only in cases involving terrorism.

When Kohl introduced legislation to stop illegal weapons exports,
civil rights activists and opposition Social Democrats, citing the abuse
of state power in the Nazi past, vigorously opposed any such measures
on the grounds that they could strengthen the state's power over the
individual. The Social Democrats blocked legislation in the Bundestag
that would have allowed customs agents to bug suspected arms deal-
ers, open their mail, and confiscate material not only made in
Germany, but also shipped through Germany.

4. Privately, though, German officials were relieved that the ruling came after the French push to get peacekeeping troops into
Rwanda, a venture no one had much stomach for. And when it came
to Haiti, they were less than eager to exercise their new powers. The
call for help with Haiti came from the Clinton administration in the
fall of 1994, as it worked to assemble an international force to give UN
legitimacy to an invasion. The purpose was to restore ousted president
Jean-Bertrand Aristide, who had been marooned in the United States
since military honchos ousted him in a coup. The coup and the international embargo against Haiti that ensued caused a flow of rickety
boats carrying tens of thousands of refugees to the coast of Florida. By
1994 this had become a major political problem for the United States.
But the Kohl government had to turn down the request for peacekeeping troops. As Bitterlich pointed out, he had to tell the U.S.
administration that it would simply be impossible to persuade the
German people to commit troops so far from home at this point.

"At the time the Americans were a bit puzzled by the answer they
got," says Bitterlich. "I remember some people saying to me, please
formulate a diplomatic answer to Clinton. But this was nonsense. I
had to tell the truth, that we were not ready with anything military, but
we wanted to support the American action with development aid."

5. Gregory F. Treverton, *America, Germany, and the Future of
Europe* (Princeton: Princeton University Press, 1992), p. 199.

6. Often, it is a case of being damned if you do, and damned if you
don't. The Poles desperately need German investment in their country but at the same time complain that Germans exploit cheap Polish
labor. Currently, it is estimated that 500,000 Poles are employed by
German capital. But Poland by law prevents Germans from buying
land there, fearing that huge chunks of Silesia and the former East

Prussia would end up in German hands. Often as a schoolyard taunt, the children of members of the German ethnic minority in Silesia, which numbers about one million, are called "Helmuts."

7. Even so, Kohl's vision of a Germany integrated in European institutions like NATO and the European Union was not entirely without its critics, from both sides of the aisle. Some new voices from the New Laender picked up where the historians' debate in 1986 had left off. They attacked Kohl's policies as too centered on the European Union, as surrendering German sovereignty, and as too pro-American. Again, there were echoes of the early attacks on Adenauer when he was denounced as the chancellor of the Allies.

Kohl's new critics saw the postwar Bonn republic as an American imposition. In their opinion, America forced its own multiculturalism on Germany and deprived it of German identity. They regarded the United States as a country that does not work, torn by racial divisions, with a justice system that has been undermined by multiculturalism (*vide* the O. J. Simpson case), that has ruined its education system, and that has exploded in violence. They argued that political correctness means that issues can no longer be debated openly and honestly, while the middle class tries to forget it all in wild consumerism based on credit. Americans may have to live with its racial conflicts, but why should others be forced to emulate it, they asked. See Jacob Heilbruin, "German's New Right," *Foreign Affairs*, December 1996.

8. Even selecting a design and a name for the common currency turned out to be hard. The French, of course, were pushing for the "ecu," the name of an old French coin, as well as the abbreviation of the European Currency Unit. But Kohl protested, on the grounds that the name sounded too much like "kuh," German for cow. Eurofranken and euro-franc were vetoed by the British, who took to calling the currency the "Frankenstein." Eventually, the currency became simply the Euro, combined with the smaller unit, the cent.

9. See Charles Grant, "The Theory and Practice of Delorism," *Eminent Europeans* (London: Greycoat Press, 1996).

10. Much of the misunderstanding centers on the word "federal." "Federalist" in the German sense refers to a state where the power of the central government is checked by sixteen financially and politically independent states. This arrangement was heavily inspired by the Allies, especially the United States, after World War II, which made them a powerful counterweight to the central government in Bonn. This after all was the American model, an element in the system of checks and balances designed to prevent too much power from being accumulated at the center.

Accordingly, all legislation that has been passed by the Bundestag must also be passed by the Bundesrat, which, as mentioned, is composed of representatives of the states. The individual states have their own prime ministers and their own legislatures. In German, "federalist" is synonymous with decentralized.

Most people who know anything about Germany know this. Still, opponents of the European Union have succeeded in making "federalist" a dirty word, a word meaning centralization.

11. In a widely quoted speech at the University of Louvain, Brussels, February 2, 1996, Kohl stated, "The policy of European integration is in reality a question of war and peace in the twenty-first century. My deceased friend Francois Mitterrand shared this view. He stated before the European Parliament in Strasbourg on January 17, 1995, that nationalism is war.

"I know some people do not like to hear this. My warnings may contain an unpleasant truth. However, it is no use burying one's head in the sand. If there is no momentum for continued integration, this will not only lead to a standstill, but to retrogression....

"During the next five years we will prove that a viable Europe can be built with fifteen and more states. At the same time, however, the slowest ship in the convoy should not be allowed to determine its speed. If individual partners are not prepared or able to participate in certain steps towards integration, the others should not be denied the opportunity to move forward and develop increased cooperation in which all partners are welcome to take part."

The speech was a clear dig at British foot-dragging within the European Union and occasioned a furious response, again demonstrating the continued emotional power of the World War II vocabulary. In London's *Sunday Telegraph* on February 4, 1996, Dominic Lawson accused the chancellor of being hysterical with his "Unity or Fight" speech, of having been "driven deranged by the collapse of his pan-European dream," and pointed out the poor taste of using the maritime metaphor, given Germany's U-boat record during World War II.

NOTES ON CHAPTER 8

1. People were given until the end of 1992 to make claims to repossess property nationalized by the East German communists. This was one reason for the slow privatization process—private business hesitated to move in because of the unresolved question of property ownership, a major legal tangle to unravel. Since 1933 the Eastern part of Germany had undergone three waves of confiscations.

First, there was property that had belonged to Jews and had been confiscated by the Nazis. This, of course, would have to be returned to the descendants of the original owners. Then, there was the property confiscated by the Soviets after 1945, immediately upon the communist takeover—this was not returned after unification. And last, there was the property that had been confiscated by the East German government—more than one million people filed such claims. No businessman in his right mind would want to invest in land and buildings until all ownership issues had been sorted out.

Commercial and property rights were given to the descendants of the original owners. The 1990 unification treaty stated that people with claims to business property or land in which business had been located were to be given monetary compensation. The properties themselves, however, would not be given back. As for private property, according to the treaty, the original owners or their descendants would be entitled to reclaim the houses.

The housing situation in the East has been exacerbated by this provision. In some small villages three-quarters of the inhabitants, many of whom had lived there all their lives, suddenly faced eviction. Many of the new owners have never lived in their property and have no intention of doing so now, but simply want to sell it. As a consequence, property prices, especially in the suburbs of Berlin, have skyrocketed, again giving rise to grumblings about greedy Westerners. There have even been cases of people committing suicide at the prospect of eviction.

It has been suggested that the law should have been written the other way around, that it might have been better if business properties be returned to the original owners and compensation provided in the case of private property. Allowing occupants to stay in their homes would have caused less social disruption. (See Bark and Gress, pp. 748–749.)

2. Figures are from Stephan Eisel, "Political Dynamics in Germany," in *In Search of Germany*, edited by Michael Mertes, Steve Muller, p. 178.

3. Even the bullet holes from World War II remained intact. Before long, movie directors discovered that it was an ideal spot to shoot World War II films.

4. Eisel, p. 176.

5. *The German Chancellors*, edited by Hans Klein (Chicago: edition q, 1993), p. 317.

6. Karl Hugo Pruys, *Kohl: Genius of the Present* (Chicago: edition q, 1996), p. 306.

7. "Die Einheit braucht mehr Kommunikation. Niemand erklaert den Ostdeutschen die Marktwirtschaft," Elizabeth Noelle-Neumann, "Eine Dokumentation des Beitrags in der Frankfurter Allgemeinen Zeitung," December 18, 1996.

8. On the media portrayal of East Germany, see Hans Mathias Kepplinger, "Falsch dargestellt," in *Die Politische Meinung*, no. 261, August 1991. Though the East Germans, even those who are unemployed, are better off on almost every measurable indicator, there is an increasingly romantic longing for a feeling of community spirit. The only things that East Germans agree has improved is the quality of the roads.

Thus in the former East Germany today, there is the strange phenomenon of *Ostalgia*, nostalgia for what is now regarded as the good old days of the German Democratic Republic. The word socialism, which at the time of unification was a dirty word, has regained much of its former attractiveness and is again associated with social justice, security, and wealth for everybody.

Nevertheless, if you ask if they would want to go back, most would answer no.

9. Ibid., p. 308.

10. Elizabeth Noelle-Neumann: Speech at the Fiftieth Anniversary of the Allansbach Institute in the Haus der Geschichte in Bonn on September 24, 1997.

NOTES ON CHAPTER 9

1. Nancy Mitford, *Frederick the Great* (New York: Dutton, 1970), p. 17.

2. For the Stasi, "nothing was too dirty," according to Peter Michael Diestel, the East German interior minister. They had contacts with all known terrorist groups in Europe and the Middle East. Officially, the Communist government of Erich Honecker disapproved of terrorist acts on humanitarian grounds. But as late as 1986, discreet inquiries from the West German authorities were met with silence.

Among the disclosures after the fall of the Berlin Wall were documents showing that Honecker and his security chief, Erich Mielke, were fully aware of the plans laid at the Libyan People's Bureau in East Berlin to attack U.S. targets in West Germany. They did nothing to intervene. The result was the 1986 bombing of La Belle discotheque in West Berlin, a favorite hangout of American troops stationed in the city. Two soldiers and a Turkish woman were killed, and more than two hundred people were wounded. After U.S. intercepts of communications between the Libyan Embassy in East Berlin and the Libyan capital, President Reagan ordered the bombing of the headquarters of Libyan leader Muammar Gadhafi in Tripoli.

Equally interesting from the German viewpoint were the revelations about terrorists of a more local variety. Honecker's regime gave sanctuary to members of the Marxist guerrilla group, the Red Army Faction, in its campaign of terror and murder against West German democracy, capitalism, and NATO in the 1970s and 1980s in the hope of forcing the West German government into draconian countermeasures, giving grounds to the argument that they were a fascist police state. Their favorite targets were prominent members of the establishment—bankers, judges, and industrialists.

When the ground became a little too hot in West Germany, the Red Army Faction members were given shelter and new identities in East Germany, where they lived like respectable citizens. According to Dienstek, Honecker and Mielke saw it as their special "hobby" and responsibility to look after these people who were creating such delightful mayhem next door.

Immediately after reunification, ten Red Army Faction members were apprehended in the East. Among them was Susanne Albrecht, who on June 6 was detained in her East Berlin apartment. Authorities suspected her of being complicit in the murder of Juergen Ponto— chairman of the Dresdner Bank AG, the chairman of the West German employers' association, and a family friend—as well as in the killing of Hans Martin Schleyer. Ironically, Albrecht was caught when she returned to East Germany from the Soviet Union, where her husband was working on a scientific project, in order to be home for the July 1 conversion of the East German Mark. Alas, the power of the Mighty Mark.

3. "East Germany, Crime and Punishment," *New York Review of Books*, May 14, 1992.

4. Zelikow and Rice, *Germany Unified and Europe Transformed: A Study in Statecraft*, p. 393.

5. Jeffrey Gedmin, *The Hidden Hand: Gorbachev and the Collapse of East Germany* (Washington D.C.: AEI Press, 1992), p. 83.

6. Heinrich Mann's statement is found in Corola Stern, *Ulbricht* (Cologne, 1964).

7. Everybody who served in the East German justice system knew that it had nothing to do with justice. These were not independent courts, but socialist courts whose function it was to squash the opponents of the regime. But if the oppressors were taken to court today, they would say they were only following orders. Up until now there

has not been a single case of an East German judge who declined to sentence because of his conscience or his personal beliefs.

8. See Juergen Aretz and Wolfgang Stock, *Die vergessenen Opfer der DDR; 13 erschutternde Berichte mit Original-Stasi-Akten* (Bastei: Lubbe, 1997).

9. Melvyn Lasky, "The Trial of Erich Honecker," *National Review*, March 29, 1993.

10. One valid point, however, was made by Ekhardt Werthebach, the head of West Germany's domestic intelligence service, who pointed out at an early stage of unification that there would be a danger of shutting 90,000 highly trained officers completely out of society. This would create a dangerous core of potential enemies of the state, with the education and skills to inflict great damage.

For instance, it is believed that former members of the Stasi have been involved in the illegal smuggling of enriched plutonium from the former Soviet Union, some of which has been intercepted by German police. They have also been suspected of links to neo-Nazi skinheads. See, Christian Caryl, "The Undead," *The New Republic*, December 16, 1996.

11. At an early stage, Schaeuble himself had argued for a partial amnesty for middle-level criminals. He was also sympathetic to the idea of not going after Egon Krenz, on the grounds that he had made a full capitulation possible, and who could have, but didn't, use violent means. Others within the Kohl administration, however, fiercely dispute this point, citing Krenz's public support for the Tiananmen Square massacre, and arguing that Krenz would have had no compunction about using force in suppressing the revolution if this had been realistic. Anyway, Schaeuble's argument for a partial amnesty was seized upon immediately by the Social Democratic opposition and taken to mean a general amnesty for the Stasi, and thereafter immediately dropped.

What was later proposed was an amnesty for so-called *Mittelschwere Krimininalitet*, that is, crimes that would result in jail sentences of one to five years. In the West, this might sound like white-collar crime, but in East Germany a whole different set of much more serious offenses was involved. Such a sentence might be incurred by a former East German judge who had sentenced somebody solely for political reasons, or by police who had deprived someone of his freedom without trial, forced people to give false testimony under threat, used physical violence against prisoners, or falsified records. Or it might apply to a physician who was on duty while the Stasi people beat a prisoner to death, but did nothing.

"This is not peanuts," says Aretz. "An amnesty would have meant that after December 1997, somebody who ruined your health, who beat you until you were crippled, but did not kill you, would be able to walk away a free man. When you are a victim you see this very differently from the way a German law professor at a university sees it." Ultimately, the idea of the amnesty was rejected by the German parliament, and the statute of limitations was prolonged until October 2000.

Every day, new material crops up. Recently at the Stasi archives, 580 films were found, corresponding to some 1.4 million pages of files that included the fates of 38,000 political prisoners, most of whom had been sentenced to long jail terms or even death. Investigators also have the sacks of files that have been shredded and that are being laboriously reconstructed. "As long as we know there are thousands of files we can still trace," says Aretz, "we do not have the right to close the possibility of following up the cases."

12. Again, New Right historian Ernst Nolte could be counted on to say all the wrong things: "When someone throws burning material into a house, they do not necessarily mean to kill a human being, but could have completely other intentions," he stated in an interview with Jacob Heilbrun, quoted in *Foreign Affairs*, November/December 1996.

NOTES ON CHAPTER 10

1. See Klaus Dreher, *Helmut Kohl: "Leben mit Macht."* (Stuttgart: Deutsche Verlags-Anstalt, 1998).

2. The von Weizsaecker interview is in *Der Spiegel*, no. 3, 1997.

3. "Von Weizsaecker owes Kohl everything. Kohl owes von Weizsaecker nothing," fumes one of Kohl's closest advisers. As for von Weizsaecker's claim to great moral superiority, the adviser points out, it should be remembered that at the Nuremberg trials, the young law student Richard von Weizsaecker was part of the defense team for his father, Ernst von Weizsaecker, who had made an impressive career in the Third Reich, rising to secretary of state in the German foreign ministry under von Ribbentrop.

Defending one's father may be understandable. What is harder to understand is that Richard von Weizsaecker, after his father was found guilty at Nuremberg, kept on defending him while at the same time urging the Germans to face their history openly. "No one who did not agree with Hitler was so close to him," says the adviser of the father. So much for von Weizsaecker's claims to higher moral authority and greater ethical sensitivity.

As for Weizsaecker's political acumen, in his book, *Ich wollte Deutschlands Einheit*, Kohl made a brief exception to his rule of not criticizing the former president directly when he pointed to von Weizsaecker as one of those who chose to remain conspicuously silent when Germany's unification became a possibility.

4. See John Vinocur, "Downsizing German Politics: Gerhard Schroeder, Man from the Plains," *Foreign Affairs*, September/October 1998.

5. See Jane Kramer, "Profile of Schroeder, Letter from Europe: The Once and Future Chancellor," *The New Yorker*, September 1998.

6. Ibid.

7. When an entrepreneur learns that, on top of all the other taxes, he has to pay 50 percent of the social contributions of his prospective workers to pensions, health care, and unemployment insurance, it tends to have a dampening effect on his enthusiasm.

8. On the management side, German businessmen have become risk averse. Instead of taking chances as American businessmen routinely do with venture capital, Germans prefer to play it safe, investing in tangibles like real estate, taking advantage of government subsidies in the building industry. The result has been acres of unrented office space in the East that the region does not need. German bankers, too, are a rather timid group. Bankruptcy is viewed as an unpardonable sin, from which there is no recovery for the businessman, and no one is likely to place loans at risk with someone who has failed at one time.

That attitude, as pointed out by *The Economist*, is fundamentally different from the one prevailing in the United States, where young entrepreneurs in fast-growing fields like computers proudly display their bankruptcies like so many dueling scars. American banks almost prefer someone who has tried and failed at least once, preferably in college, on the principle that he or she has probably learned a few lessons from the experience.

9. In Germany under Kohl, there have been sporadic attempts at reform in the health-care sector and at removing some of the most glaring abuses, but much remains to be done to bring spending under control.

The 1980s were full of stories about the famous generosity of German health care. The Germans enjoyed some of the longest hospital stays in the world. Patients could spend up to ten days in the hospital for the removal of a simple appendix. And German workers could visit an attractive Kurresortat or spa at government expense once every three years, where they could loll in lukewarm water, spend the afternoon dancing, and drink herbal tea to the smarmy strains of "Love Is Blue" or "Spanish Eyes," before they hit the adjacent casino or the local *beerstube* in the evening to make up for all that clean living. This may be preventive medicine, but to the layman's eye it looks mightily like a vacation.

10. On Lafontaine's position, see Michael Rutz, "Lohnpolitik fur Europa," *Rheinischer Merkur*, no. 23. June 5, 1998.

11. See Jane Kramer.

BIBLIOGRAPHY

Appel, Reinhard. *Helmut Kohl im Spiegel seiner Macht*. Bonn: Bouvier Verlag, 1990.

Ardagh John. *Germany and the Germans*. London: Penguin, 1996.

Aretz, Juergen, and Wolfgang Stock. *Die vergessenen Opfer der DDR; 13 erschutternde Berichte mit Original-Stasi-Akten*. Bastei: Lubbe, 1997.

Bailey, George. *The Biography of an Obsession*. New York: The Free Press, 1972.

Bark, Dennis L., and David R. Gress. *A History of West Germany, Vol. 1: From Shadow to Substance, 1945–1963*. Second edition. Oxford: Blackwell, 1993.

Bark, Dennis L., and David R. Gress. *A History of West Germany, Vol. 2: Democracy and Its Discontents, 1963–1991*. Second edition. Oxford: Blackwell, 1993.

Barzini, Luigi. *The Europeans*. London: Penguin Books, 1983.

Bond, Martyn, Julie Smith, and William Wallace, eds. *Eminent Europeans: Personalities Who Shaped Contemporary Europe*. London: Greycoat Press, 1996.

Brzezinski, Zbigniew. *Power and Principle: Memoirs of the National Security Adviser, 1977–1981.* New York: Farrar, Straus, Giroux, 1983.

Carr, Jonathan. *Helmut Schmidt: Helmsman of Germany.* New York: St. Martin's Press, 1985.

Doenhoff, Marion Graefin. *Kindheit in Ostpreussen.* Berlin: Seidler Verlag.

Filmer, Werner, and Heribert Schwan. *Helmut Kohl.* Duesseldorf: ECON Verlag, 1990.

Filmer, Werner, and Heribert Schwan. *Richard von Weizsaeker: Profile eines Mannes.* Duesseldorf: ECON Verlag, 1985.

Fisher, Marc. *After the Wall: Germany, the Germans, and the Burdens of History.* New York: Simon & Schuster, 1995.

Gedmin, Jeffrey. *The Hidden Hand: Gorbachev and the Collapse of Eastern Europe.* Washington, D.C.: AEI Press, 1992.

Genscher, Hans-Dietrich. *Erinnerungen.* Berlin: Seidler Verlag, 1995.

Gress, David. *Peace and Survival: West Germany, the Peace Movement, and European Security.* Stanford: Hoover Institution Press, 1985.

Hofmann, Klaus. *Helmut Kohl: Kanzler des Vertrauens.* Bonn: Aktuel.

Klein, Hans. *The German Chancellors.* Chicago: edition q, 1996.

Kohl, Helmut. *Ich Wollte Deutschlands Einheit.* Berlin: Ullstein, 1996.

Kramer, Jane. *The Politics of Memory: Looking for Germany in the New Germany.* New York: Random House, 1996.

Krisch, Henry. *The German Democratic Republic: The Search for Identity.* Boulder, Colorado: Westview Press, 1985.

Laqueur, Walter. *Europe in Our Time: A History, 1954–1992.* New York: Viking, 1992.

Laqueur, Walter. *Germany Today: A Personal Report.* Boston: Little, Brown & Co., 1985.

Maaz, Hans-Joachim. *Behind the Wall: The Inner Life of Communist Germany.* New York: Norton, 1995.

Maier, Charles S. *The Unmasterable Past: History, Holocaust, and German National Identity.* Cambridge: Harvard University Press, 1988.

Maser, Werner. *Helmut Kohl: Der Deutsche Kanzler.* Berlin: Ullstein, 1990.

Mertes, Michael, Steven Muller, and Heinrich August Winkler, eds. *In Search of Germany.* New Brunswick, New Jersey: Transaction Publishers, 1996.

Muechler, Guenter, and Klaus Hofmann. *Helmut Kohl: Chancellor of German Unity*. Bonn: Press and Information Office of the Federal Government, 1992.

Mueller, Christian. *Helmut Kohl: A Man on the Crest of His Time*. Bergisch Gladbach, Germany: Gustav Luebbe Verlag, 1996.

Noelle-Neumann, Elizabeth. *Die verletzte Nation*. Stuttgart: DVA, 1988.

Pond, Elizabeth. *Beyond the Wall: Germany's Road to Unification*. Washington D.C.: Brookings, 1993.

Pruys, Karl Hugo. *Kohl: Genius of the Present*. Chicago: edition q, 1996.

Schaeuble, Wolfgang. *Der Vertrag: Wie ich ueber die deutsche Einheit verhandelte*. Stuttgart: Deutsche Verlags-Anstalt, 1991.

Schwarzer, Alice. *Marion Doenhoff: Ein Wiederstaendiges Leben*. Kiepenheuer und Witsch, 1996.

Teltschik, Horst. *329 Tage: Innenansichten der Einigung*. Berlin: Siedler, 1991.

Treverton, Gregory F. *America, Germany, and the Future of Europe*. Princeton: Princeton University Press, 1992.

Tusa, Ann. *The Last Division: A History of Berlin, 1945–1989*. New York: Addison-Wesley, 1997.

Ulrich, David, and Gill Schroeter. *Das Ministerium fuer Staatssicherheit: Anatomie des Mielke-Imperiums*. Reinbek, 1993.

Vogel, Bernhard. *Das Phaenomen: Helmut Kohl im Urteil der Presse*. Stuttgart: DVA, 1990.

Walters, Vernon. *The Wall Falls*.

Watson, Alan. *The Germans: Where Are They Now?* London: Methuen, 1992.

Winik, Jay. *On the Brink: The Dramatic Behind-the-Scenes Saga of the Reagan Era and the Men and Women Who Won the Cold War*. New York: Simon & Schuster, 1996.

Zelikow, Philip, and Condoleezza Rice. *Germany Unified and Europe Transformed: A Study in Statecraft*. Cambridge: Harvard University Press, 1995.

INDEX